D1560772

Diagnosis and Treatment of Sociopaths

and

Clients with Sociopathic Traits

Debra H. Beneveniste, M.S.W.

NEW HARBINGER PUBLICATIONS, INC.

Publisher's Note

Copyright © 1996 Debra H. Benveniste
New Harbinger Publications, Inc.
5674 Shattuck Avenue
Oakland, CA 94609

Cover and text design by Tracy Marie Powell.

Distributed in U.S.A. primarily by Publishers Group West; in Canada by Raincoast Books; in Great Britain by Airlift Book Company, Ltd.; in South Africa by Real Books, Ltd.; in Australia by Boobook; in New Zealand by Tandem Press.

Library of Congress Catalog Card Number: 95-72227
ISBN 1-57224-047-4

Printed in the United States of America on recycled paper.

First printing 1996, 3,000 copies

Contents

Section II
Countertransference

Section III
Treatment Strategies

Beginning Stage • Formulation of a Diagnostic/Psychosocial Asssesment • Formulation of the Initial Treatment Plan

Section IV
Special Considerations in Work with Sociopaths

Appendixes

Acknowledgments

Although I am the author of this book, in many ways I have only been a conduit for others. A great many of the people who contributed to this book will have to go unnamed. I know that many of them hope that there is something positive about themselves that they can give to others to make up for some of the damage they have caused. Others are dead and never had a chance to realize their positive potential in life. I have attempted to convey what was compelling, wise, and important about all of them, so that those qualities can live on in some way.

In order to protect confidentiality, I have changed significant amounts of identifying data. In two of the case examples presented, permission was obtained from the client before publication. For the rest, even though few secrets are successfully kept in prison, it is my intention that only the individual clients will recognize aspects of themselves in the case notes.

Others can be named. Very early in my career, Anne Rappaport dedicated significant time and effort to peer supervision with me. Harold Sock was a warm, caring supervisor who nurtured my approach with clients at a time when I was not at all sure what that approach was. And thank you to Barbara Levy for recommending the Smith College School for Social Work.

I am indebted to many people at Smith. Michael Hayes, James Sacksteder, and Jill Harper were all excellent teachers. Pam McCarthy and David Goodman were extremely knowledgeable field supervisors. Special thanks to Susan Donner, assistant dean and the former director of field work, for her commitment to establishing a correctional field placement at my job site. Having the opportunity to be a field supervisor for Smith forced me to conceptualize and articulate many of the ideas that ultimately ended up in this book.

Unfortunately, I cannot possibly list here all of the authors who have had an impact on my work as a therapist or a writer. Many are included within the text itself.

A bittersweet thank you to the Connecticut Department of Correction: I am grateful for having had the opportunity to work with their inmates. I am also grateful to them for establishing working conditions that made it impossible for me to remain. Self-employment has given me the time and space and the relief from correctional stress that I needed to be able to write this book.

Thank you to Paul Russell for his unconditional support of my desire to write (even before he knew that I had one) and for his wisdom and compassion. His recent death is a terrible loss for all of us in the professional community. A special thank you to Ruth Gordon and Cheryl Boland at Brooklyn House; they were instrumental in helping me formulate ideas for this book. I am also grateful to Peter Krestchmer for helping me track down some of the literature I needed.

I am particularly thankful to Kirk Johnson and Matt McKay at New Harbinger for their support and nurture of this work.

My mother and publishing consultant, Sheila Benveniste, guided me in how to find a publisher. Thanks, Mom. I appreciate the support and encouragement I received from my brother, Paul, and his wife, Bev. And lastly, a special thank you to my partner, Steve, for his part in making our home and life together such that I have had the peace of mind to do the work and to write this book.

Introduction

Sociopathy is not a comfortable subject to introduce. Few mental health workers do not dread the experience of realizing that the new addition to their caseload is probably a sociopath. Often, the realization happens in this way:

> Where is my pen? I just had it here.
> *I wonder if Theodore took it.*
> He did talk a lot about feeling entitled to other people's things. Patients have been complaining a lot lately that their things are missing. And we did catch him with Sandra, our new admission, the other day—and now she suddenly seems to have plenty of cigarettes.
> *Oh no.*
> I wonder if he's a sociopath. He probably is. What are we going to do with him? How are we going to keep him from victimizing everyone else?
> *He's my client.* What am *I* going to do with him?

When I told colleagues that I was working on writing something about sociopaths, most often the response was relief. One reading of this common response is that there are a lot of sociopathic clients out there. Although I do not have statistics to validate that interpretation, my sense is that many clinicians have been placed in the position of trying to do their best with a population that they do not understand and do not know how to treat.

In this book, I have attempted to address these two basic questions: How can we understand sociopaths? And how can we treat them?

From Understanding to Treatment

The first two sections of this book are concerned with understanding.

The discussion in section I, on diagnostics, grew out of my belief that no one is sure exactly what comprises sociopathy. The description of sociopathy in the DSM-IV makes it difficult to tell whether the condition is a personality disorder or a deviant subculture. Within any given diagnosis, a thorough understanding of the underlying dynamics and personality structure is an imperative; clients can then be classified accurately, and treatment strategies specific to the diagnosis can be developed. Section I attempts to provide such an understanding for sociopathy.

Yet diagnostic uncertainty is not the only problem hindering intervention. When sociopathic clients appear for treatment, negative responses like those given in the example above are virtually a universal phenomenon. This means that countertransference reactions and responses must be contained and managed before any real treatment is possible. Section II explores how to do this.

The treatment strategies presented in section III are based on this dual understanding of both the client and the therapist. As it seemed most logical to present the interventions within the context of the full course of treatment, the chapters in this section cover the therapy relationship from the day it begins to the day it ends.

Sociopaths are a difficult client population for a variety of reasons. Some of those reasons are addressed in section IV, "Special Considerations in Work with Sociopaths." Interpersonal issues of safety and cross-racial and cross-gender work are explored, and the material presented is applied to the different treatment environments where sociopaths are found: prisons, halfway houses, hospitals, and outpatient settings. Group and family therapy with sociopaths is discussed briefly.

I avoided writing about issues that I do not know well. The focus of this book is on individual treatment with adult males because that is what I have the most experience doing. My own very limited experience working with adolescents included no one whom I would consider a "sociopath-in-training." Although it might be argued that the "immaturity" of sociopaths makes working with them the equivalent of working with adolescents, I believe that teenagers with sociopathic traits have unique developmental and maturational issues that require special expertise.

Some of my work has been in treatment modalities other than individual therapy. I was fortunate to be able to do some family therapy in a prison setting (in some instances, both the father and the son were incarcerated), and I cofacilitated a long-term group in which many of the members were sociopaths. However, I think that the focus here on individual therapy is an important one. A major strength of this approach is that it illuminates the complexity of the interpersonal dynamics between client and therapist in a way that other modalities do not. In addition, once the skills presented are gained, they can easily be applied to any group or family treatment model.

Since most of my contact with sociopaths has occurred in a prison setting, many of the case examples in this book are about work with incarcerated clients. Although I have some direct experience with sociopaths (both males and females) as outpatient clients, my work in residential or inpatient settings has been limited to the indirect role of a clinical consultant providing supervision for direct care staff. I have kept these limitations in mind and done my best to apply my experience with treatment strategies in individual therapy to these other settings.

And from Theory to Practice

The theoretical orientation of this material is an unusual one for work with this client population. I am trained in psychoanalytic psychotherapy. Those are the theories that I have used in treating sociopaths, and those are the theories that I explain and apply in this book.

Most of the material on treating sociopaths that I have read comes from a cognitive or behavioral perspective. I believe that these interventions ignore the core issues underlying the sociopathic personality. Although the greatest difficulty that sociopaths have is in the area of interpersonal relationships, cognitive and behavioral therapies do not focus on the dynamics of relationships. My sense is that while sociopathic clients can gain a great deal of information from these types of treatment, these clients' parasitic interpersonal dynamics are not affected. (In fact, given the potential for manipulative and deceitful behavior in this population, in some cases providing information may actually do more harm than good.)

Most of the literature I am familiar with in this field is concerned with either theory or practice—and most of it is written as if the two were mutually exclusive. This split, coupled with the way that theoretical formulations are usually taught, can lead to the attitude that theory is no more than an academic exercise. If theory really has no relation to practice, then why should anyone learn it? At the other extreme, some schools of social work do not teach theory at all.

Some of us absorb the theory, only to end up in the position of the foreign language student who can read Dante's thirteenth century Italian, but is unable to ask a native speaker how to find the bathroom. Others skip the theory and rely on one of those "Italian in Three Days or Less" seminars; now we can find the bathroom, but our comprehension of the culture around us is limited to its traffic signs and menus.

When I begin supervision with students or beginning workers, they generally have one common area of difficulty: what they were taught in school has given them some knowledge, but they have no idea how to apply these theories or ideas when they are face to face with a real live client. They either know a lot of theory and have little understanding of how to formulate interventions from it, or they are familiar with all sorts of interventions but have no theoretical framework in which to make sense of what they are doing.

This work is an attempt to make an application of theory to actual clinical practice. My orientation relies most heavily on ego psychology and object relations theory, and I have tried to explain these sets of ideas in terms that are understandable to readers who have no academic background in these areas. I also describe the use of many cognitive and behavioral interventions; when used within a psychodynamic framework, these approaches are absolutely necessary with this population. I have tried to explain how work on thoughts and behaviors can be performed within the context of the dynamics of an interpersonal relationship.

The other unpopular stance I take in this work is that of stressing the necessity of long-term therapy. The Twelve Step programs have a belief that an addiction does not occur overnight, and neither does its resolution. Despite the current popularity of the twelve-session-or-less mode of therapy, the fact is that individuals with severe character pathology of any type, sociopathy included, are simply not going to learn to manage their symptoms, much less make major personality changes, within such a limited time frame (or within the constraints of a two-week inpatient program).

Some theorists have attempted to offer short-term models for working with this population. In my opinion, no matter what their claims, these models provide only temporary relief for the most acute of symptoms.

It is possible, however, to break up the work that needs to be done into pieces. Due to the nature of the pathology, therapy with sociopaths often takes this approach, and the chapters on terminations and on different treatment modalities focus on which aspects of the work can be accomplished within certain time limitations. Nonetheless, under no circumstance do I want the reader to conclude that I think it is acceptable or legitimate practice to do one aspect of the work in a week or two and then simply terminate with the client. Discharge planning and referrals for continued care are essential.

Finally, although I recognize that this work is complicated and difficult, I hope that these two realities do not dissuade people from attempting it. Twelve Step programs have another saying: No pain, no gain. My own experience has been that treatment with this population offers unique lessons in life and special opportunities for self-knowledge, acceptance, and growth that simply are not accessible anywhere else.

Section I

Diagnostic Considerations

1

The Syndrome

I can remember how taken aback, irritated, and frustrated I was the first time a client said to me, "Under the right circumstances, you'd become a drug addict, too. And you'd abandon your morals for the right price. Everyone does."

My first impulse was to argue with him—if I hadn't become drug addicted by then (at my terribly experienced age of 24), then it wasn't going to happen. But when I thought through the client's possible responses, I realized that arguing wasn't likely to change his mind. What it would do was to let him succeed in gaining a whole lot of personal information about me.

I earnestly replied with something akin to: "Look, not everyone operates in the same way. People are individuals, and there are lots of ways they deal with things in life."

The client looked at me with world-weary eyes, shook his head indulgently, and no doubt thought to himself, "Here comes another one of those sixties liberals."

Our exchange reminded me of something I had noticed before. Clients like him always seemed to enter into very narrow relationships with others. The world was divided into two categories: people were either drug addicts or not, and the second category included everyone who did not drink, smoke, or do drugs and who worked steadily at a full-time job. People's personality traits, hobbies, interests, or values were never mentioned; it was as though all these things were either invisible or meaningless to the client.

Later, I started thinking. I thought about what it would be like if everyone I knew had a price. Family members, lovers, best friends, acquaintances, co-workers, the couple who ran the corner grocery store—what if each of them would only do what I needed if I did what they needed first. I thought about how isolating and lonely this life would be, and how exhausting it would feel to have to be constantly assessing people to figure out which person would be most likely to meet which need.

I would also have to be very careful not to let the other person know how important the issue or item was to me, because then it would become more "expensive." I would worry a lot about others' reactions to my needs. When I wanted something, somehow I'd have to find out first if it were a "normal" need, or at least something acceptable to the other person. I couldn't bear it if I exposed a need to someone and not only had my need rejected, but also left the other person thinking that I was "weird" for having it in the first place.

With all this to worry about, eventually I would learn to make the process as unthreatening as possible. I would learn to express my needs in the easiest way possible for other people to meet them and in the easiest way for me to gauge if they were going to be met. Ultimately, I would want to distill my needs into something that other people wouldn't even realize they were meeting. That way, I would get my needs met "for free."

Yet all this meant that other people would be in control of my emotional states. Since I would have to rely on others to meet my needs, I would need to be extremely wary of people. I would be utterly dependent on them, and I would hate them for it. But I couldn't express that feeling directly, because then I would risk losing them. So I would look for more subtle ways to express it.

Letting that anger out, yet not letting others know that I felt it, would be like getting the upper hand. It would be a way to gain some control over the situation and a way for me to win, for once.

My internal world would get smaller and smaller until it would feel like there was nothing inside, just emptiness. If I were to focus on that emptiness, I would feel a gnawing tension—and with it, a drive to action, an urge to do something wild and impulsive for some excitement.

I would get so good at manipulating people that conning them would almost get boring sometimes. People would seem really stupid. I would need to get more and more things from them to make the effort worthwhile. Or sometimes I'd manipulate them just to do it. I wouldn't really need anything, but they'd just be there asking to be taken.

When I thought about it (which I would try to let happen as seldom as possible), I would think that life in general was pretty boring and pointless. Other people would seem happy, and I would hate them for that, too. I would try to get them to meet my need for happiness, but they wouldn't—and then I would do what I could to cause them some pain so they would be as miserable as I was. I would get increasingly violent and angry, and as those escalating feelings drove me further apart from other people, I would even begin to believe that I was not quite human. And feeling dehumanized would make me even angrier.

A sociopath's experience is that only a few types of relationship are possible with other people. Most often, people compete with each other. One ends up the winner, and one ends up the loser. People also scam each other. Each person tries to take advantage of the other. Here, one ends up being in control, and the other ends up being victimized.

The most positive type of relationship possible for a sociopath is that of mutual use. Each person provides a service to the other and can rely on the other to reciprocate. Both people win. And as long as no one changes the rules, no one loses.

At the heart of "using" relationships is the emptiness of the user's internal world. Sociopaths perceive others as having what they do not. And their response to this perception is jealousy, humiliation, rage, hatred, and shame. The stolen wallet or car or TV set only represents what sociopaths are attempting to steal. The actual "loot" is something much closer to inner serenity, happiness, spontaneity, or a sense of self that is enduring and based on real talents and traits. They scavenge for narcissistic supplies, for example self-esteem, in the form of material items because they are unable to provide these less tangible goods for themselves.

Stealing provides all sorts of narcissistic reinforcement. First, the stolen object itself has some kind of value. Some of that value can be measured by a price tag, but not all of it. (Ask a client "Was it worth it?" and he or she is likely to look at you a little funny. For an explanation of that look, spend an evening watching television commercials: they will tell you all you need to know about the symbolic worth of material objects.) Second, the act of taking an object from someone is a valued activity: it provides a sense of mastery at the same time as it expresses rage. The mastery involved is itself a two-tiered function. It provides a sense of competence, and because the activity is usually illegal, it also offers a feeling of excitement. Excitement in turn wards off the sociopath's chronic boredom and anxiety, if only temporarily.

All the same, it is true that not everyone operates like this. Why then do sociopaths continually end up in the same narrow set of relationships with people?

People who don't appear to compete or try to take advantage of others often simply end up in the class of victims. "Do-gooders" are particularly enticing targets for sociopaths. While altruists are often unaware of their own motivations, they make no attempt to hide their conscious agenda. They trust openly, they give things away, and they ask for nothing in return. In effect, they seem to invite manipulation. For the sociopath, it's sometimes a challenge to get a do-gooder to give something that he or she doesn't want to give (such as sex, for example). But for the most part, after these trusting souls' material items are exhausted, they have outlived their usefulness.

Sociopaths will admit that they have in fact met people who aren't simply victims, and yet do not operate in the same way that they do—people who don't seem to have anything to offer and who don't seem to know the rules of the mutual-use game. Sociopaths find these people perplexing and somewhat anxiety-provoking. They say they have no use for them and move on to others.

The reality is that these are the only dance steps that sociopaths know. In a using relationship, the rules and expectations are clear, and they know exactly what to do. In a relationship not based on mutual use, there don't seem to be any rules, and sociopaths simply don't know how to behave. They can act the part for a while, but at some point it becomes clear to them that the other person is asking them to give something that they aren't capable of giving, or do something that they aren't capable of doing. They aren't, but the other person is. Perplexity turns to disdain as the jealousy, humiliation, and rage increase. Soon enough, the stealing begins. Now the sociopaths are back in a position of control. They no longer feel unsure. They are in charge and winning again.

These issues of dependence and control are pervasive and often misinterpreted. For example, a male drug addict with sociopathic traits may make a statement commonly heard among substance abusers: "If only I could get a good job and a good woman, I'd be fine." Clinicians tend to regard this statement as an indication of the person's lack of responsibility for himself, as denial of the severity (and ownership) of the problem, and as projection. For a sociopath, it simply testifies to the need for external management of daily life issues.

It is also an offer of a contract for a mutual-use relationship. Many sociopaths do find "good women." The family and friends of the "good woman" are often perplexed by her choice of this boyfriend or spouse. What the sociopath can see is the woman's unconscious need to contain and ultimately control her own projected impulses and drives of destruction and rage. The unspoken agreement is: You control, and I'll rage.

2

Diagnostic Constructs

What makes a sociopath behave in these ways and perceive the world in such a limited and limiting manner? To answer these questions, it is best to begin where the clinician begins: with a diagnostic formulation and assessment.

Formulating a diagnosis is a basic first step in establishing an effective treatment relationship with any client. The purpose is to collect clinical impressions, symptoms, behaviors, and history and place them into an organized container. The resulting diagnosis can then provide a cognitive frame for the clinician's thoughts and reactions. The diagnosis is also a working hypothesis of what is wrong and a guide to how one might approach treatment. Information gathered from the client during the first month of meetings, the psychosocial assessment, the clinician's impressions, and the diagnostic information form the foundation of the initial treatment plan: a description of the problems, interventions, and goals that will structure the course of treatment.

In the case of sociopathy, the formal psychiatric diagnosis is currently known as antisocial personality disorder.

Personality disorders are so named because they indicate that something more than symptoms or acute reactions is at issue. In the contrasting case of neurosis, for example, a symptom forms as a means to contain an unconscious conflict; other spheres of activity remain unaffected. But personality disorders indicate a fundamental character disorder affecting the whole personality, not just one aspect of it.

Personality disorders are clusters of congruent symptoms of long duration that impact major areas of the person's functioning. Although some severe personality disorders may involve temporary, stress-induced psychoses, symptoms of major mood and thought disorders are generally absent. In other words, a personality disorder does not indicate a shattering of the personality structure, but it does indicate a consistent and significant structural weakness. Balint (1979, 16) refers to this structural weakness as "the basic fault."

The criteria listed for each personality disorder encompass how a person lives his or her life, how he or she relates with others, and how affect, thought, and conflict are organized within the character. The criteria must also indicate the rigidity and inflexibility of these ways of being and the path away from reality testing that these coping mechanisms take; without these characteristics, a personality disorder would simply be a personality style.

The two main sources of diagnoses in current use are the DSM-IV and the ICD-10. The fourth edition of the *Diagnostic and Statistical Manual of Mental Disorders*, formulated and published by the American Psychiatric Association (1994; cited hereafter as DSM-IV), is a listing of diagnoses relating to psychiatric conditions. The tenth revision of the *International Statistical Classification of Diseases and Related Health Problems*, compiled by the World Health Organization (1992; cited hereafter as ICD-10), covers all medical conditions, including psychiatric ones. The fact that the criteria for antisocial personality disorder listed in these two texts are rather different from each other makes it clear that diagnosticians have difficulty with the diagnosis.

The DSM-IV

The DSM-IV's antisocial personality disorder is a condensed version of the one in the DSM-IIIR. The diagnostic criteria listed for it are these:

   A. There is a pervasive pattern of disregard for and violation of the rights of others occurring since age 15 years, as indicated by three (or more) of the following:

      (1) failure to conform to social norms with respect to lawful behaviors as indicated by repeatedly performing acts that are grounds for arrest

      (2) deceitfulness, as indicated by repeated lying, use of aliases, or conning others for personal profit or pleasure

      (3) impulsivity or failure to plan ahead

      (4) irritability and aggressiveness, as indicated by repeated physical fights or assaults

      (5) reckless disregard for safety of self or others

(6) consistent irresponsibility, as indicated by repeated failure to sustain consistent work behavior or honor financial obligations

(7) lack of remorse, as indicated by being indifferent to or rationalizing having hurt, mistreated, or stolen from another

B. The individual is at least age 18 years.

C. There is evidence of Conduct Disorder with onset before age 15 years.

D. The occurrence of antisocial behavior is not exclusively during the course of Schizophrenia or a Manic Episode.

(DSM-IV, 649–650)

Notably, these criteria are largely limited to behavior, and the behavior described is largely criminal in nature. The traits that describe relationships indicate only victimization of others, and parts of the list sound more like moral judgments or excerpts from a criminal statute than objective descriptions of the symptoms of a mental illness. As a result of these characteristics, the DSM-IV's description of antisocial personality disorder appears more of a sociological diagnosis than a psychological one.

The ICD-10

The ICD-10 refers to antisocial personality disorder by the name "dissocial personality disorder" and describes it further as "amoral," "asocial," "psychopathic," and "sociopathic." It attempts to use more dynamic criteria than the DSM-IV:

Personality disorder characterized by disregard for social obligations, and callous unconcern for the feelings of others. There is gross disparity between behaviour and the prevailing social norms. Behaviour is not readily modifiable by adverse experience, including punishment. There is a low tolerance for frustration and a low threshold for discharge of aggression, including violence; there is a tendency to blame others, or to offer plausible rationalizations for the behavior bringing the patient into conflict with society. (ICD-10, 360)

The ICD-10 specifically notes that this diagnosis is different from the disorder they call "emotionally unstable personality disorder" (a condition also referred to as "aggressive," "borderline," and "explosive" personalities). The emotionally unstable personality is described in these terms:

Personality disorder characterized by a definite tendency to act impulsively and without consideration of the consequences; the mood is unpredictable and capricious. There is a liability to outbursts of emotion and an incapacity to control the behavioural explosions. There is a tendency to quarrelsome behaviour and to conflicts with others, especially when impulsive acts are thwarted or censored. Two types may be distinguished: the impulsive type, characterized predominantly by emotional instability and lack of impulse control, and the borderline type, characterized in addition by disturbances in self-image, aims, and internal preferences, by chronic feelings of emptiness, by intense and unstable interpersonal relationships, and by a tendency to self-destructive behaviour, including suicide gestures and attempts. (ICD-10, 360)

Overall, the diagnosis for dissocial personality disorder does sound more neutral in tone and uses psychodynamic terminology, such as "low tolerance to frustration" and "a low threshold for discharge of aggression," as opposed to the DSM-IV's reliance on more value-laden words such as "lying" and "conning." However, it seems peculiar to me that impulsivity is purposefully omitted from the criteria for the disorder, and that the emotionally unstable personality is described as "aggressive" and "explosive," while the dissocial personality is not.

Relation to Narcissistic Personality Disorder

Tyrer (1992) notes a significant lack of clarity among the diagnostic indicators of various personality disorders. He states that the antisocial, narcissistic, histrionic, and borderline categories in the erratic, flamboyant, or dramatic cluster of personality disorders were not distinguishable from each other on a consistent basis when various research methods were applied. He suggests that all four types should be collapsed into one diagnostic entity.

One specific complaint about the DSM-IV is that the narcissistic and antisocial personality disorders are not clearly distinguishable from each other. The DSM-IV lists the following criteria for narcissistic personality disorder:

(1) has a grandiose sense of importance (e.g., exaggerates achievements and talents, expects to be recognized as superior without commensurate achievements)

(2) is preoccupied with fantasies of unlimited success, power, brilliance, beauty, or ideal love

(3) believes that he or she is "special" and unique and can only be understood by, or should associate with, other special people or high-status people (or institutions)

(4) requires excessive admiration

(5) has a sense of entitlement, i.e., unreasonable expectations of especially favorable treatment or automatic compliance with his or her expectations

(6) is interpersonally exploitative, i.e., takes advantage of others to achieve his or her own ends

(7) lacks empathy: is unwilling to recognize or identify with the feelings and needs of others

(8) is often envious of others or believes that others are envious of him or her

(9) shows arrogant, haughty behaviors or attitudes

(DSM-IV, 661)

Kernberg (1975, 228) has described antisocial personality as a subgroup of pathological narcissism, and when sociopathy is viewed in terms of personal and interpersonal boundaries, it does look very similar to narcissistic personality disorder. The structure of the personality is very similar; it is the symptoms and behaviors which are slightly different.

While it's tempting to imagine that the main difference between the two disorders is the amount of criminal activity involved, this distinction simply overlooks the class-specific nature of the criminal behavior associated with each disorder: antisocials commit street crime, while narcissists commit white-collar crime.

The two disorders are similar in other ways as well. Both are very difficult to treat, and both create massive countertransference reactions in therapists.

Social Deviance

The DSM-IV lists "failure to conform to social norms" as the first symptom of antisocial personality disorder. Blackburn (1992) argues that social deviance should not be listed as a symptom of mental illness nor as a characteristic of a personality disorder:

> Not all of those who are socially deviant show the traits of personality disorder, nor do all those with personality disorder violate legal or ethical norms. While socially deviant behavior may sometimes be a *consequence* of personality disorder or even mental illness, antisocial behavior in itself cannot logically be used to define a disorder of personality. (69)

In addition to questioning the wisdom of including any type of deviant behavior as the leading symptom of a mental illness, I would also challenge the accuracy of the DSM-IV's formulation. I would instead argue that it is a case of failure to conform to some norms and hyperconformity to others.

Sociopaths view money as the major way to gain power, prestige, and control. When their money is not spent on drugs, almost all of it is used to acquire items geared to impress other people, such as expensive clothes, jewelry, and cars. In doing so, they reflect a norm that pervades American culture. Certainly, when advertisers wish to reach the broadest popular audience, they routinely suggest that the purchase of the product in question will produce sex appeal, power, and importance for people who otherwise would not feel that they have those attributes.

In this context, it is interesting to note that while the authors of the DSM-IV are careful to register their disdain for the sociopath's criminal lifestyle, they avoid any mention of where all that stolen money goes. Given its absence in the list of criteria for antisocial personality disorder, one might conclude that reliance upon money as a major source of self-esteem is one aspect of the sociopath's personality that the authors do not consider pathological.

3

Uses and Applications of the Diagnosis

Thus far, the discussion of the antisocial personality disorder has been confined to the mechanisms of the diagnosis itself. However, use of diagnoses is not limited to the researchers who compile them. They are used by everyone from direct-care staff to insurance company quality-assurance personnel. Even when a diagnosis is clearly written and consistently used to label the client population it was meant to describe, factors such as the type of education, treatment orientation, and personal philosophy of the clinician will have a great impact on the diagnosis ultimately chosen.

Although the ICD-10 definition of the antisocial personality disorder is more comprehensive and ultimately more useful, the DSM-IV is the more commonly used resource for diagnoses. Therefore, the DSM-IV diagnosis will be the focus here.

Even in a research vacuum, the antisocial personality disorder diagnosis is fraught with difficulties. Confusion is increased when common uses of the diagnosis are taken into account. Four main factors seem to have an impact on whether the diagnosis is applied to any given client: gender, race and class, the client's likability, and substance abuse.

Gender Issues

The DSM-IV states that the overall prevalence of antisocial personality disorder is 3 percent in males and 1 percent in females. Since criminality is still largely a male domain, and since the antisocial personality disorder diagnosis relies heavily on criminal behaviors, it follows that the vast majority of clients diagnosed with antisocial personality disorder are men.

In contrast, depression and borderline personality disorder are considered to be mental illnesses of women, and many more women than men are diagnosed and treated for these conditions. Several gender stereotypes reinforce this dichotomy. It is much more acceptable for a woman to suffer from painful feelings than it is for a man. When women are depressed, common symptoms are crying, feelings of hopelessness, and suicidal thoughts and gestures. Because men are raised not to express affect directly, they tend to rely on activities to dissipate painful feelings. When men are depressed, common symptoms are substance use, aggressiveness, irritability, isolation, and reckless behavior. However, these symptoms are not listed as indicators of depression in the DSM-IV. Instead, they are listed as components of antisocial personality disorder.

The only acceptable feeling for men to have, the only "manly" emotion, is anger. Men learn early on to mask their feelings of fear, sadness, loneliness, vulnerability, depression, anxiety, and confusion with feeling angry. Eventually, many men come to label every feeling they have as anger, and consequently, after a while, all they feel is anger.

Viewed from this context, the diagnostic indicators of antisocial personality disorder suddenly take on new meaning. When a client exhibits aggressiveness and persistent irritability—the only two affects listed in the DSM-IV for antisocial personality disorder—these characteristics might indicate the presence of the disorder, or they might indicate a man who was raised to believe that it is unmanly to experience an emotion other than anger. (If the only feeling I were permitted was anger, I imagine I'd have a case of persistent irritability myself.) A clinician working from this perspective might be led to suspect that an aggressive and irritable client may in fact be a very depressed, isolated, or frightened man who presents all these affects as anger.

The diagnostic feature of "reckless behavior" is another example of how gender affects diagnostic labeling. A female who uses drugs or drives recklessly is most likely to be diagnosed as borderline personality disorder, where both behaviors are given as examples of "impulsivity in at least two areas that are potentially self-damaging." For a male, a record of either behaviors is more likely to be taken as an indicator of the "reckless disregard for the safety of self or others" given as a characteristic of antisocial personality disorder.

Race and Class

Because the diagnosis of antisocial personality disorder is so strongly focused on criminal behaviors, racial and socioeconomic factors must be taken into account. Criminal behavior correlates positively with poverty and minority status in this country; it follows that antisocial personality disorder is a diagnosis that is applied more often to members of minority groups and to the poor.

Stevens (1993) found that the diagnosis of antisocial personality disorder was applied arbitrarily, and that an African American inmate was more likely to be diagnosed as such than was a white inmate. These characteristic applications of the diagnosis appear to validate the hypothesis that antisocial personality disorder is more of a sociological label than a psychiatric one. They also help to explain the pervasive alienation suggested by the DSM-IV's first criterion for antisocial personality disorder: failure to conform to social norms with respect to lawful behaviors.

The Unlikable Client

A related difficulty occurs as a result of the common perception of the diagnosis. Antisocial personality disorder is one of the most unpopular of all the mental disorders. The diagnosis itself can cause an immediate and negative response. There is no medication for it, and no clear set of beliefs among the mental health community concerning how to treat it effectively. Its symptoms do not engender empathy on the part of health care providers, and many therapists avoid working with clients diagnosed as antisocial.

Since we don't like antisocial individuals, it's quite possible for unlikable, demanding, and manipulative clients to be given a diagnosis of antisocial personality disorder, even though it's questionable whether they actually meet the criteria. If a clinician feels that a client is unworkable, the client may be labeled with the diagnosis of an unworkable disorder.

The DSM-IV is clear that a conduct disorder must have occurred prior to age fifteen in order for antisocial personality disorder to be diagnosed. Yet clients are often given the diagnosis even though the clinician has not or cannot elicit any information about the client's childhood history.

Substance Abuse

The DSM-IV states that antisocial behaviors associated with a substance-related disorder do not constitute antisocial personality disorder unless the behaviors began in childhood and continued into adulthood. This distinction is necessary because all of the traits of antisocial personality disorder can just as easily be used to describe the behavior of many drug addicts and alcoholics. According to the DSM-IV, the only means of distinguishing one disorder from the other is by age of onset. Once again, the absence of any information about a client's childhood history makes either diagnosis questionable.

Unanswered Questions

Widiger and Corbitt (1993) cite confusion about psychopathy, as well as substance abuse, as two of several criticisms of the antisocial personality disorder diagnosis appearing in recent literature on the subject. Neither the DSM-IV nor the ICD-10 define psychopathy or distinguish it from sociopathy. Chapter 5 offers an alternative to the prevailing view of the two terms; my own belief is that a career burglar is dynamically a world apart from Jeffrey Dahmer, the man convicted of sexually abusing, killing, and cannibalizing his victims.

Given the current problems with the antisocial personality disorder diagnosis, a man who lashes out in response to depression, a woman who consistently manipulates others to "get hers," an obnoxious and unlikable client who refuses to give much background information, a poor African American inmate, a chronic drug addict, and a sadist might all be misdiagnosed. The potential for such an incoherent grouping once again points to the lack of any discernible personality structure underlying the diagnosis.

And what of the clinician struggling to develop a treatment plan for any client on the basis of such a diagnosis? These traditional diagnoses describe behaviors without providing any hypotheses for why the behaviors occur. Given the differential labeling of behaviors based on a client's gender, race, and possession or lack of personal charisma, any diagnosis of antisocial personality disorder must ultimately raise more questions about a client's functioning than it answers.

4

Psychodynamic Diagnosis of Sociopathy

Freud can be paraphrased as having said that psychological health can be gauged by the abilities to love and to work. Although many may feel that this is a limited and simplistic standard, many diagnostic criteria do in fact make judgments concerning these capacities. In the spectrum of personality disorders, it is the capacity to love—to establish and maintain healthy interpersonal relationships—that appears to be the most impaired.

All eleven personality disorders listed in the DSM-IV focus to some degree on dysfunction in relationships with others. While the paranoid, schizoid, and schizotypal personality disorders in Cluster A are dysfunctional in their lack of relationship with others, those in Cluster B (the antisocial, borderline, histrionic, and narcissistic personality disorders) appear to have a different type of relational dysfunction in common. The presence of these disorders indicates an ego's inability to regulate itself and its consequent reliance on other people's ego structures as a means to cope. Common to all four is the response most people have to involvement with the individuals who suffer from them: a feeling of being used.

Borderline personalities need to ward off both enmeshment and abandonment. They are intense, demanding, and self-abusive. They use people as mood stabilizers and to protect themselves from harm.

Histrionic personalities need to be center stage. They use people to reduce their anxiety by having others constantly reassure them that they are attractive and deserving of attention.

Narcissistic personalities need to feel superior to everyone in order to reduce their pervasive sense of inadequacy. They use people by simultaneously eliciting admiration while demeaning everyone around them.

Antisocial personalities also need to feel superior in order to reduce their sense of inadequacy, but they approach this task in a different way. Antisocials use people by manipulating them and by appropriating their money or possessions.

Ego Functions in Sociopathy

The personality structure underlying the sociopath's behavioral symptoms can be understood in terms of Freud's dimensions of id, ego, and superego. Very simply, the id is raw impulse, affect, and drives; the ego provides the structure for overall functioning; and guilt and moral judgments come from the superego. This model of the personality's structure can readily be visualized as a coal-fired train, with the id providing both the coal and the furnace, the ego operating as the engine, and the superego acting as a brake.

The purpose of this three-part structure is to permit the person to negotiate the world as successfully as possible. Much as the skin is designed to protect the body's internal organs from external physical danger, this structure also serves to protect the personality from psychological threats to its integrity.

Much of this potential danger comes from the id's own material: affect, impulses, and drives. The remainder comes from the outside, from damage inflicted by the environment and other people. Too great a threat from either inside or outside can overwhelm the system and ultimately cause its destruction (through decompensation to psychosis).

It is the ego's job to ensure that this disintegration does not occur. The means used to accomplish this goal are called "ego functions"; these include mechanisms as diverse as those used to control impulses and manage feelings, anticipate consequences, and to establish relationships with others.

In sociopathy, many ego functions are simply too fragile and undeveloped to accommodate the internal and external pressures of day-to-day life.

To return to the image of the train, it is as if the engine were too small to accommodate the amount of coal being shovelled into the furnace. But here, instead of managing this problem by reducing the amount of coal, increasing the size of the engine, or dropping a car from the train, the conductor jumps off at each stop and steals cardboard boxes that he uses to store the surplus hot coals from the furnace. Of course, the boxes burn up quickly, so that the conductor has to signal for frequent stops. The train does not run well, and the conductor risks getting arrested.

Since the sociopath's ego functions are not adequate, the personality structure is unstable. To cope with this instability, the personality relies on external mechanisms to buttress areas of weakness. Thus in the area of affect management, a weak ego function in sociopathic personalities, strong feelings of any type can threaten to overwhelm the structure. One common external means that sociopaths rely on to modulate their moods is the use of drugs. Clients are typically described as "self-medicating" when they turn to this strategy.

A continued dependence on outside mechanisms means that much of the sociopath's personality structure becomes geared toward manipulating the external world. Ego functions are altered to conform to this goal and limited to accommodating and manipulating changing external conditions. Those coping skills and ego functions that are part of a healthily functioning personality, such as the abilities to soothe or forgive oneself or to moderate affect, are absent here. The environment must be manipulated to provide whatever is necessary for the sociopath's self-maintenance.

This need for external management also causes sociopaths to seek out very structured environments. Sociopaths are drawn to gangs of all types, as these generally have very structured hierarchies, lots of rules, and a punitive system of control. Sociopathic individuals also tend to do well in prison for the same reason.

Relying on external structures for self-care creates an unhealthy cycle. As these are increasingly substituted for internal structures, those same internal structures increasingly lose the ability to do their job. (Optometrists have a similar process in mind when they sometimes warn patients that wearing their eyeglasses all the time will weaken their eye muscles.) The negative impact of this cycle also explains why highly structured prison environments are incapable of "rehabilitating" sociopaths.

Frankl (1959, 129) describes another difficulty emanating from an absence of internal structures when he states that such widespread phenomena as depression, aggression, and addiction are not understandable unless we recognize the existential vacuum underlying them. For him, these phenomena indicate a lack of a sense of spirituality and meaning in one's life. It is intriguing to note that all three areas are hallmarks of sociopathy.

All of the personality disorders are so named because of this structural dependence on external mechanisms. Yet antisocial personality disorder stands apart from others, both for the very large degree to which antisocial personalities rely on the environment and other people and for the specific forms this reliance takes. These distinctions can be clarified by exploring the structure of individual ego functions typical of sociopathic personalities.

Bellak, Hurvich, and Gediman (1973, 76–79) have differentiated and categorized the ego functions. The functions from their list that are most greatly impacted in sociopathy are affect management, impulse control, judgment, use of defense mechanisms, object relations, synthetic-integrative functioning, and mastery-competence.

Affect Management

For a healthy personality, affect is experienced as different kinds of recognizable feelings on a continuum of intensity. Affect management draws on a variety of defense mechanisms, ranging from the most primitive, such as denial, to the more adaptive, such as compartmentalization and intellectualization. Skills for coping with intense affect include such diverse activities as seeking support from friends and family to beginning a regimen of physical exercise.

A sociopath, however, does not experience affect in this manner. Because they risk overwhelming the sociopath's fragile ego structure, most feelings are repressed (not felt consciously). What a sociopath does experience is a continuum that begins with tension, moves to boredom, and ends with hatred and rage.

Chapter 1 noted that sociopaths can feel humiliated by their relationships with others. In fact, without treatment, sociopaths do not consciously experience a feeling of humiliation; this emotion is too threatening for their personality's fragile structure. Humiliation is instead experienced as hatred or rage. Neither do sociopaths consciously feel anxiety, whose presence is a signal that affect is threatening to unleash itself. In its place, the individual feels an intense urge to activity of any sort.

A sociopath does not experience levels of intensity of emotion either. Affect is either absent, as it is when the sociopath's needs are being met by the environment, or it is overwhelming.

The major methods of affect management employed by sociopaths are acting on impulses, stealing, and substance use. Sociopaths are commonly described as "irritable." It is easy to see why.

Impulse Control

For a healthy personality, impulses are a threat to a personality's stability and accordingly must be managed in such a way that they do not destabilize a person's internal and external life. While impulses and affect provide individuality, motivation, and drive, they must be moderated by the ego. A healthy ego can tolerate a wide range of thoughts and feelings, even those that weaken or disturb it, without acting impulsively.

Since the sociopath acts on impulses as a means to regulate affect, impulse control would be a threat to this system. Impulsivity, in the form of the intense urge to activity noted above, provides protection from disintegration for the personality's fragile structure. Without it, anxiety would quickly become overwhelming.

Sociopaths do use impulse control to some degree in terms of planning and executing scams and other types of crimes. However, the ability to do so is quite variable, depending on how much affect each individual can tolerate.

Judgment

Judgment is the ability to anticipate consequences accurately, to avoid dangerous situations, and to learn from mistakes. People with poor judgment often find themselves in life-threatening situations, sometimes not realizing and sometimes not caring what they did to put themselves at risk. Typical examples of issues of judgment are being unaware of the potential dangers of a situation (withdrawing money from an ATM outside the bank at night in a high-crime area) or engaging in activities that are unsafe (driving at high speeds under the influence of drugs or alcohol).

Although this definition may make it appear that sociopaths are utterly lacking in judgment, the ego function must be assessed in context. Here, behaviors that discharge or reduce affect are favored, and engaging in dangerous activities does much to reduce affect for sociopaths. It is one of the few ways that they are able to soothe themselves.

As a result, judgment functions in a manner opposite to the role it plays in a healthy person. Acting out, dangerous behavior, and impulsivity are management tools, not mistakes. In this system, a past mistake and the lesson to be learned from it are likely to be the reverse of those that a healthy individual might recognize. For a sociopath, "doing better next time" after the failure of an environmental coping mechanism might mean ingesting more drugs or engaging in more dangerous behavior. What looks like increasingly suicidal behavior to others is judged for its effectiveness in helping to keep the sociopath's personality system intact and alive.

Use of Defense Mechanisms

If an affect, drive, or impulse is too threatening to the personality structure, if it will cause too much conflict, then it must remain unconscious. Defense mechanisms provide the barrier between the id and the ego and protect the ego from becoming overloaded.

Assessing the use of defense mechanisms is a two-level process. The first level identifies the type of defense mechanisms used, and the second evaluates the strength or weakness of the individual's ego structure. In other words, to what degree does the ego rely on these mechanisms? How much can it manage on its own?

Defense mechanisms are categorized as lower or higher order, depending on the distance from reality they must maintain in order to meet their goal. For example, denial is one of the most primitive defense mechanisms. When people deny something or are "in denial," they are seeking to ward off anxiety by negating what they perceive. Substance abusers rely heavily on this defense mechanism, as anyone who has ever confronted one about his or her alcoholism or drug use can attest.

Higher order defense mechanisms do not mangle reality to the degree that lower order ones do. For example, humor is often used as a means to reduce conflict or ward off anxiety. When people joke, even though they may not be consciously aware of what is making them anxious, they do accurately perceive what is going on around them and communicate what they perceive. However, they do so in a way that is less threatening and more acceptable to themselves and others.

Use of defense mechanisms is also an accurate diagnostic indicator of the level of pathology of the ego's structure. If the ego structure can tolerate greater amounts of affect, drive, and impulse, then smaller amounts need to be maintained in an unconscious form, and higher order defenses can be used. If the ego structure is weak, as it is in sociopathy, then lower order defense mechanisms must be used; otherwise, the power of the id material would cripple the ego structure.

Sociopaths tend to use the following lower order defense mechanisms to reduce anxiety: denial, projection, splitting, externalization, and acting out. Drives and impulses are often not negotiated through the ego at all. They overwhelm the ego, and the barrier between the id and the ego is compromised.

Object Relations

Object relations regulate how the ego functions in relationship with others. Healthy object relations involve the ability to establish and maintain genuine, mutual, and intimate relationships; to be flexible in establishing emotional distance from others; to recognize oneself as separate and as having perceptions and feelings different from those that others have; to differentiate past relationships from present ones; and to internalize others—that is, to be able to sustain an internal sense of others when they are not present without undue anxiety and frustration.

Sociopaths do not establish genuine or intimate relationships with others. They may appear charming, and they may in fact be very familiar with the other's strengths and weaknesses, but there is no mutuality. Reciprocity is impossible because sociopaths are limited to treating others as coping mechanisms. Other people's ego functions, internal strength, and soothing capacities have to be subsumed to maintain the sociopath's ego structure. People are experienced as one would experience a drug: something that does something for you or to you that has no needs of its own. Sociopaths engage in parasitic relationships. They draw off what they need at the expense of the other.

Childhood Victimization

How and why does this happen? The kind of relationships that adult sociopaths are attracted to are consistent with a history of childhood victimization, which is a significant predictor of a later diagnosis of antisocial personality disorder (Luntz and Widom 1994).

Sociopaths were treated as objects when they were children, in much the same way that narcissists were, and they were unable to compensate for this trauma within their environment or their internal world. Their only experience of bonding was through being used themselves.

Children who are used in this way desperately try to meet the needs and demands of their parents or guardians, but they always ultimately fail. In failing, they lose the hope of ever gaining the parent's love, and they lose the ability to feel a reality-based, internalized sense of self-esteem.

They also do not learn to distinguish themselves as separate entities from others with whom they have an emotional bond. Others' needs become one's own, and one's own needs can be experienced as emanating from the other.

As a result, sociopaths carry with them a great deal of rage and suspicion toward others. They are locked into a defensive mode that attempts to protect them from the same feelings that resulted from their childhood bonds: shame, rejection, and abandonment. Although their demeanor is one of anger and arrogance, they share the narcissist's exquisite sensitivity to humiliation.

Gallwey (1992) describes the process in this way:

> Many delinquent acts are a form of adjustment—a way of managing otherwise unmanageable emotional conflict. Emotional stress cannot be managed by solutions in fantasy which have never been properly developed. The management of emotional stress requires a system of mental buffers (unconscious defenses) that are derived from the internalization of safe nurturing experiences. Where, because of severe parental disturbances, these experiences have been erratic, hostile and anxiety ridden, no repertoire of mechanisms capable of regulating emotional stress is developed; instead, the individual constructs the kind of arrangement which in fantasy would have ameliorated emotional stress, stress which has become connected with violence, injury, intrusion, and fear of death. In this way mental equilibrium is maintained—albeit at the cost of a constructive relationship with other people. (161)

The Role of Aggression

Sociopaths are most easily identifiable by the symptoms of stealing, their main mode of obtaining narcissistic supplies, and of aggression. While aggression in sociopathy is almost its own ego function, its interpersonal nature closely links it to the ego function of object relations.

Aggression provides one of the only interpersonal boundaries available to sociopaths. Boundaries are a crucial issue, since sociopaths are so desperately dependent on others, and the vital nature of this dependency causes a great deal of primitive anxiety for them. As it does in borderline personality disorder, this primitive anxiety takes two forms. In the form of *merger anxiety*, sociopaths feel a pervasive sense of dread concerning complete loss of identity. In the form of *annihilation anxiety*, they feel a pervasive sense of dread concerning loss of life if abandoned.

As a result, sociopaths have very little ability to establish flexible interpersonal boundaries. Their dependency and its accompanying anxiety cause massive amounts of rage that overwhelm the ego structure. Aggression then provides two vital functions: (1) it protects the ego structure by discharging rage, and (2) it establishes an interpersonal boundary. Aggression keeps others at a distance, which reduces merger anxiety, and it asserts control over others, which reduces annihilation anxiety.

Lower functioning sociopaths rely on the physical expression of aggression. They will often provoke or voluntarily join fights because the activity serves several purposes. While the adrenaline rush that physical violence provokes reduces the sociopath's internal sense of emptiness, the quick discharge of a large amount of affect during the fight affords a feeling of relief. In addition, fighting permits a feeling of mastery and strength, whether or not the sociopath "wins." Sociopaths feel confident fighting, as they do stealing.

Higher functioning sociopaths fight less often, but rely on verbal aggression in a similar fashion. Higher functioning sociopaths tend to be intelligent, so that they can use their verbal skills and logic to keep the other person off balance. If words are insufficient to control and distance others, the higher functioning sociopath will resort to threats of physical aggression and will fight as a last resort.

Of course, people feel hurt and upset when they are treated as objects by sociopaths, and they rightfully blame the sociopath for doing so. Yet a part of their distress seems to result from an underlying belief that this treatment is willful on the part of the sociopath—that is, that he or she has made a choice between a genuine and a parasitic relationship. (An echo of this same belief reappears in the diagnostic criteria for narcissistic personality disorder given in the DSM-IV [661; emphasis added]: "is *unwilling* to recognize or identify with the feelings and needs of others.") Yet there is no choice here. Using people as objects is the foundation of sociopathy. Expecting sociopaths to behave differently is like feeling frustrated with blind people because they refuse to see.

Synthetic-Integrative Functioning

Synthetic-integrative functioning involves the ability to integrate contradictory aspects of the self, such as feelings, thoughts, behaviors, and values. Bellak, Hurvich, and Gediman (1973, 371) state that perceptual-motor disturbances such as dyslexia and other learning difficulties are related to this ego function and that continued frustration in this area may increase emotional explosiveness.

In addition to the ability to experience conflict and anxiety as contradictory aspects of self come into contact with each other, synthetic-integrative functioning also involves the ability to connect intrapsychic and behavioral events—in other words, to know which internal states relate to which behaviors. It is a vital component in being able to learn from one's mistakes.

Splitting is the defense mechanism that works in the opposite direction from this ego function. Splitting involves holding conflicting affects, behaviors, and thoughts as separate entities and thus not experiencing confusion or anxiety when confronted with these apparently discrepant aspects of the self. A common example of this phenomenon occurs when a suicidal client experiences no anxiety or fear about causing his or her own death.

The purpose of splitting is to ward off anxiety. However, warding off anxiety at the expense of being able to integrate aspects of self is dangerous. The inability to integrate severely limits an individual's ability to function and therefore causes a great deal of frustration, another affect that sociopaths have little tolerance for.

Here again, affect management, in the form of anxiety reduction, takes priority over personality integration.

Mastery-Competence

Mastery-competence involves the following capabilities: how well individuals perform in relation to their capacity to perform; their subjective feeling about their level of competence versus their expectations; and the degree of discrepancy, positive or negative, between actual performance and this felt sense of competence. A healthy ego is able to make a realistic assessment of its strengths and weaknesses, to use whatever capacities are present, to set expectations based on capacity, and to develop a sense of competence based on actual performance.

Because so much of their functioning comes from the outside, sociopaths are unable to assess strengths and weaknesses. Rather than acknowledging this dependency on others, which would cause massive anxiety, their expectations about themselves and their abilities tend to be quite grandiose, meaning that they believe they are capable of accomplishing much more than they actually do accomplish. Splitting and projection protect the sociopath from facing this conflict.

Sociopaths also limit themselves to pursuing goals that involve doing what they do well: manipulating people. Although their sense of competence about this area is more realistic, it also helps them to justify continuing to exploit others. In other words, if people are stupid enough to let themselves be used over and over again and the sociopath is so good at it, why stop?

In this way, criminal activity not only provides an outlet for rage and frustration, but also helps sociopaths to avoid facing their lack of accomplishment. Sociopaths can feel competent doing crime-related activities, and when confronted with the fact that they have few or no accomplishments outside the criminal world, they can reply that since they only operate in the criminal world, the judgment is irrelevant.

The Superego

Compared with the id and ego, the superego seems to be a less-well understood part of the mind. Because it depends on a number of ego functions with which it shares tasks, the superego relies on the ego functioning properly. These functions include judgment, impulse control, use of defense mechanisms, synthetic-integrative functioning, and mastery-competence.

A healthy superego is one that has the ability to assign moral values to thoughts, feelings, behaviors, and events; the capacity to label things as wrong when they cause others harm; an integrated and internalized value system; and a functional sense of guilt. (A functional sense of guilt means that a feeling of guilt is elicited when a person does something that he or she considers wrong and that this guilty feeling stops the person from continuing the behavior.)

Clearly, the sociopath's personality structure does not lend itself to a healthy superego. The ego functions most affected in sociopathy are those which determine the base for the superego. The defense mechanisms most commonly relied on, splitting, denial, and projection, do not lend themselves to self-examination, another necessary component to superego functioning.

In fact, if it is present, the superego in sociopathy is fragmented and easily overwhelmed, and it remains brittle and harsh even after successful treatment. The importance of winning and a pragmatic willingness to consider all the angles are deeply ingrained attitudes; labeling things in terms of moral values never comes easily to sociopaths, and choosing to do activities based on whether they are right or wrong often remains a lifelong struggle. For example, many sociopaths become quite concerned in treatment over the fact that they are unable to go into a retail store without "casing" it (assessing the security system) to determine how easily the store could be broken into or have merchandise stolen from it. They fear that their new found sense of right and wrong will not be strong enough to ward off the old impulse to steal.

Condensed Psychodynamic Diagnosis of Sociopathy

The DSM-IV, for any number of reasons, limits itself to lists of observable symptoms. It has avoided the use of dynamic constructs or indicators that are products of a specific theoretical orientation. Although clarity and inter-rater reliability may have improved as a result, the depth and range of the resulting clinical picture has suffered greatly.

I do not have similar constraints, and I think that it is vital to be able to take psychodynamic factors into account in making diagnostic formulations. Indications of defensive capability and ego and superego functioning must be present.

For a clinician to get a clear sense of whether or not he or she is meeting with a sociopath, I believe that diagnostic impressions should include many of the following five factors:

1. Relationships are limited to the use of other people

   a. perceives other people as all the same and as not like himself or herself

   b. uses people as coping mechanisms

   c. feels a sense of entitlement

   d. is incapable of mutuality or intimacy in relationships

   e. feels no guilt

   f. is contemptuous of others

   g. relies on verbal or physical aggression to establish and maintain interpersonal boundaries

2. Steals his or her sense of self-esteem

   a. has an extreme sensitivity to humiliation and rejection

b. feels an internal sense of emptiness

c. gains a sense of mastery through manipulating others

d. primary work activity may be illegal in nature

e. has a grandiose sense of accomplishments and intelligei

f. relies on expensive material items that are often obtainec determine self-importance

3. Primarily relies on external means (including compulsive theft and substance abuse) to achieve emotional stability. Uses impulsivity and acting out as primary coping mechanisms.

4. Has a low tolerance for the only consciously experienced affects: rage and hatred. Uses lower level defenses of denial, projection, and splitting. Has a poor tolerance, if any, for anxiety, frustration, and depression.

5. Does not perceive dangerous activities as such for himself or herself or for others.

These diagnostic criteria will alert the clinician to the defects in the sociopath's personality structure and provide a guide for an initial treatment plan. In addition, despite common traits shared with borderline and narcissistic personality disorders, these criteria should provide a means of distinguishing both disorders from antisocial personality disorder, as well as a way of distinguishing it from substance abuse disorder.

5

Psychopathy

One element missing from the criteria given for antisocial personality disorder in the DSM-IV, as well as from my own psychodynamic criteria for sociopathy, is a characterization of the disorder's relationship to what used to be referred to as psychopathy. And yet the common understanding of the two terms makes it appear as if they should be easy to distinguish. Asked to free-associate a response to the term "psychopath," most people typically think of Charles Manson or some other person who appears to obtain pleasure from inflicting physical or emotional pain on someone else. I think of the character of the enforcer in Grade B crime films—the large, stupid, cruel man who says, "Let me hurt him, boss. Please, let me hurt him." And the boss impatiently replies, "Not now, Sammy."

The boss is the sociopath. He doesn't object to violence if it serves his purpose. He uses Sammy and his psychopathy for his own ends, to maintain control of someone or to ensure repayment of a debt. He himself does not receive intrinsic pleasure from inflicting pain on someone else. But Sammy does.

I do not believe that sadism of this type should simply be considered one more trait indicative of sociopathy. I believe it deserves its own diagnosis: psychopathy.

Diagnostic Issues

The contributors to the DSM-IV do not appear to share this belief. The *DSM-IV Options Book* lists items labeled as relating to psychopathy as: "glib or superficial, inflated and arrogant self appraisal, deceitful or manipulative, lacks empathy, impulsive, irresponsible, poor behavioral controls, lacks remorse, behavioral problems as a child" (APA 1991, R:7). These traits seem to me more congruent with the DSM-IV's definition of antisocial personality disorder.

Traits corresponding more closely to the common understanding of psychopathy are grouped under the DSM-IV's listing for the sexual and gender identity disorder of sexual sadism. Sexual sadism is defined by these diagnostic criteria:

A. Over a period of at least 6 months, recurrent, intense sexually arousing fantasies, sexual urges, or behaviors involving acts (real, not simulated) in which the psychological or physical suffering (including humiliation) of the victim is sexually exciting to the person.

B. The fantasies, sexual urges, or behaviors cause clinically significant distress or impairment in social, occupational, or other important areas of functioning.

(DSM-IV, 530)

Section B of the definition seems problematic to me. True sadists would not experience "clinically significant distress" about their arousal states, although a person with some other mental illness and strong sadistic traits might. I can only imagine psychopaths experiencing such distress during those times when they are prevented from acting on their impulses.

I do believe that some of the psychopath's pleasure in inflicting pain is experienced by him or her as sexual feelings, but I do not think that this sexual component is a primary motivation. Rather, I would argue either that the perceptual capacities of the psychopath are so compromised (particularly in the synthetic-integrative ego function) that aggressive impulses are mislabeled as sexual ones, or that sexual and aggressive sensations were never differentiated from each other during development of the personality. (For a detailed discussion of diagnostic and developmental issues in psychopathy, see Meloy 1988.)

If psychopathy is viewed as the psychiatric label for sadism, the diagnostic criteria might include the following four numbered criteria.

1. There is a lack of capacity to form and maintain attachments with others except through the infliction of physical or emotional pain.

The sad truth is that the psychopath's behavior is really an attempt to form a relationship. People with psychopathic traits with whom I have worked talk about their victims in intimate ways. They feel closer to their victims than they do to anyone else. And they experience a certain feeling of reassurance that the victim had never been closer to anyone else, either. This feeling almost comes across as a deranged version of the security that couples experience when they know that their partners are faithful to them. (Note that I am referring here to psychopathic individuals who have victimized strangers or acquaintances, not family members or significant others.)

2. Causing pain or observing others' pain is a source of pleasure, excitement, and power.

3. The capacity to identify with others is absent (i.e., the pain that others feel is not recognized as similar or identical to the individual's own feelings of pain). Therefore, the capacity for remorse is absent.

This lack of remorse is very different from the sociopath's lack of remorse. The psychopath does not have the capacity for remorse, because the capacity for identification is missing. The sociopath has this capacity but does not access it, because doing so would threaten the integrity of the sociopath's personality structure.

4. There is a lack of capacity to experience internal conflicts.

Splitting, in this instance, is complete. There is no anxiety or conflict concerning regulation of affect, drives, or impulses. All affect is transformed into the impulse to inflict harm, and all energy is focused on attaining that goal. The superego appears completely disabled. In other words, there is a lack of capacity to experience guilt.

Why does this happen? Psychopaths experienced their early primary relationships solely within the dynamic of aggressor-victim. Those were the only available choices. Since psychopaths cannot tolerate the victim stance, their only choice in relationships with others is as an aggressor. Gallwey (1992) states that sadistic behavior is partly the expression of hatred, but is also a habitual defense against potentially extreme persecutory anxiety and helplessness. He notes that this defense is so efficient that addressing the feelings connected with a more normal way of relating becomes almost impossible.

Treatment Issues

True psychopaths do not seek treatment. Since they experience neither conflict nor distress, there is no reason for them to seek help. In exceptional cases, incarcerated psychopaths who experience discomfort from being unable to discharge affect do seek treatment, but it becomes clear very quickly that these individuals are not using therapy in the same way other clients do.

Clinicians come in contact with psychopaths almost exclusively through referrals for forensic evaluations. Psychopaths will tolerate these interviews if doing so means the possibility of increased privileges in the prison system or a reduced sentence. But they will consider the interview an opportunity to inflict physical pain if they can get away with it. If physical aggression is not possible or involves too much risk, the psychopath will settle for inflicting emotional pain. Seeing the interviewer in distress and causing him or her embarrassment or humiliation will become the objective.

I do not know how many true psychopaths are out there; not too many, I hope. My own experience has been that the human personality is much more variable than the diagnostic criteria suggest. The psychopath who truly enjoys violence might be viewed as one extreme of a continuum whose other pole is the sociopath who avoids all violence and may show some capacity to care for others as long as they are not interfering with his or her goals.

In the middle is a sociopath-psychopath mix: individuals who enjoy conning other people and make a living taking advantage of others, but who also enjoy inflicting some pain when they feel humiliated or rejected. Doing so makes them feel superior. For a male of this type, this is especially true in his relationships with women. He experiences his need for women as a threat to his autonomy. When he feels threatened, he relies on violence as a way to reassure himself and reassert his self-image.

Yet this is also someone who is able to assess and evaluate his own life. He may decide at some point that he does not want to behave in this way anymore. Any number of things can lead him to this conclusion. Perhaps a woman he genuinely cares for shows terror during a mild argument, and he begins to realize how violent he has been with her. Or perhaps progressing age along with multiple incarcerations begin to take their toll. For some, the turning point is the experience of "burning too many bridges," of finding out that their family no longer wants contact with them. For others, the motivation is a son or daughter approaching adolescence who is beginning to exhibit the same behaviors and traits. The decisive factor can be a diagnosis of AIDS. Or, in some cases, the reasons to change include all of the above.

6

Common Diagnostic Combinations with Sociopathy

Within each diagnostic category, a range of functioning is possible. Individuals with very different capacities to pursue work and relationship goals may still fit the criteria for a given diagnosis. At the low end of the scale for the personality disorders is the person who functions close to the psychotic level of organization. At the high end is the person who functions close to the neurotic level of organization.

For example, at the low end of the scale for borderline personality disorder are individuals who spend most of their time in psychiatric hospitals, frequently harm themselves, and regularly experience acute episodes of psychotic thought. At the high end is someone who maintains a job and a family; has extramarital affairs; experiences chronic depression, with some suicidal thoughts and minor self-mutilation; abuses prescribed tranquilizers; and is an emotionally demanding, intense, and sometimes bizarre parent and spouse.

Assessing any individual's functioning entails evaluating the relative strength and flexibility of the ego functions. For a sociopath, the amount and types of affect that he or she can tolerate before acting out are important signs. The level of chaos in the individual's lifestyle provides a good indication of this area of functioning, as a greater tolerance for affect increases an individual's ability to plan and organize his or her activities and life.

Some sociopaths do manage to maintain a dual life—for example, by keeping a legitimate job while they run scams or sell drugs. Some may even be able to maintain a family, although their home life is likely be dominated by physical, emotional, and sexual abuse. While some are able to maintain a dual life for years, others can only do so for months at a time. Still others live a much more chaotic life, spending most of their time "on the run," impulsively engaging in low level criminal activity, and finding themselves in and out of prison every other month.

As discussed in chapter 4, use of defense mechanisms is another easily observable ego function that clinicians can use to assess levels of functioning within a diagnostic category. Here, lower levels of functioning are associated with an individual's reliance on more primitive defenses and a resultingly greater discrepancy between reality and the person's experience of it.

These variations in the range of functioning within categories are further complicated by an overlap of traits between categories. I know few people who fit completely in one diagnostic category and in no others, and most of the clients I have worked with meet the criteria for several personality disorders or at least have several clusters of traits belonging to different diagnostic categories. (A mixture of traits is probably encountered more frequently in cases where the individual's functioning is closer to a psychotic level.)

As a result, I do not tend to perceive the personality disorders as separate entities. For me, all of the personality disorders imply a range of functioning in between psychosis and neurosis with similar traits grouped together. It is common to find sociopathy combined with the other Axis II categories of borderline, narcissistic, and paranoid personality disorders.

Sociopathy and Other Axis II Personality Disorders

Borderline Personality Disorder

A meld of this disorder with sociopathy produces a personality with these behaviors and symptoms: use of people, stealing, aggression, unstable and intense relationships with others, lack of a stable identity, self-mutilating behaviors or suicide attempts, wildly impulsive and dangerous behavior, and sexual acting out. With this combination, substance abuse is also quite likely to be a symptom.

Treating this type of client is generally like being in a room with a hurricane. Affect levels are intense and shift rapidly. The client makes continual emotional and material demands. Judgment and impulse control are largely absent or shift as rapidly as affect does. And the client's emotional pain is palpable. The therapist's own anxiety level grows in response to the emotional drain of simply being in the client's presence and attempting to contain him or her, set limits, and assess risk on a continual basis.

> **Case note.** Joe had completed his jail sentence when I started getting calls from him during my hours at the jail. He would call between our outpatient appointments and sometimes tell me that he

had a gun, that he was going to give up his attempt at a straight life, and that he had decided to kill a particular person. He would not reveal who he was going to kill or let me know where he was.

Joe was surprised to hear how anxiety-provoking this behavior was for me. He explained that it was extremely useful for him to "blow off steam" in this way. He stated that he felt quite relieved after these phone calls and noted that he was then able to go calmly about his business.

Narcissistic Personality Disorder

Individuals combining narcissistic and sociopathic traits are often charismatic enough to maintain a group of followers to manipulate and use to meet their own needs; many corrupt politicians and religious leaders undoubtedly meet these criteria. If some psychopathy is present, the combination produces the Charles Mansons of the world, as well as many gang leaders and mafia bosses.

This combination is also the most difficult to reach of all disorders that can be treated with psychotherapy. With this mixture of sociopathy and narcissism, the desire and ability to control people overwhelms most other aspects of the personality. And these individuals are so good at what they do that their skill at leading others meets their defensive needs. They feel little emotional pain or conflict to motivate them to establish a therapeutic relationship.

A client with this combination of traits looks for a therapist who is somehow "special," who is known in his or her field (or who very much wants to be), and who may well have narcissistic traits of his or her own. The client offers a "mutual admiration" pact: "I'll admire and idealize you if you'll admire me and not confront my problems. And I'll take care of you. You need something done, just ask."

If the therapist is narcissistic enough, that is exactly what will happen. Such a client may attend treatment for years, as long as he or she can use the fact of the therapy to buy time or leniency in criminal matters. The therapist has no idea what the client is actually doing in his or her daily life. If the client is ever caught doing whatever it is he or she is really up to, the therapist is also caught looking and feeling like an utter fool.

Paranoid Personality Disorder

This combination is one of the more dangerous ones. Paranoid individuals relate with others through feeling persecuted and attacked. A mixture of paranoia and sociopathy produces a person who spends most of his or her time alone, who is deeply suspicious of and hateful toward others, who manipulates people as a means to ward off fear, and who feels the need to lash out violently at others. People who commit arson (sometimes for profit), people who like pipe bombs and other explosive devices, and people who commit their crimes alone because they would never trust anyone as a partner can all meet the criteria for this personality mix.

Why do these clients even ask for help? Often, they do so because they are beginning to scare themselves, either by their thoughts or by their behavior. In treatment, they feel utterly vulnerable and deeply suspicious of the therapist. The therapist is left with the anxiety-provoking task of maintaining lots of emotional distance from a client with a very large capacity for violence.

Sociopathy and Axis I Clinical Disorders

In addition to a blending of personality disorders, sociopathic clients also often have more contained illnesses that affect only a single sphere of life or produce one specific cluster of symptoms. Axis I diagnoses commonly found in combination with sociopathy are substance abuse, conditions resulting from brain dysfunction, major mental illnesses, anxiety disorders, and disorders associated with sexual offenses.

Substance Abuse

Substance abusers commonly exhibit sociopathic traits, and sociopaths often abuse substances. As mentioned in chapter 3, the DSM-IV attempts to distinguish sociopathy from drug abuse not by the symptoms, but by the age of onset, stating that "when antisocial behavior in an adult is associated with a Substance-Related Disorder, the diagnosis of Antisocial Personality Disorder is not made unless the signs of Antisocial Personality Disorder were also present in childhood and have continued into adulthood" (648). I do not believe that relying solely on the age of onset to distinguish one diagnosis from another is adequate.

Since sociopaths rely so much on the environment for coping mechanisms, drug and alcohol use seems an almost inevitable course of action for them. Substances are generally more reliable and comprehensible than people are, and they do not respond with hurt feelings or a desire to retaliate when they are used.

Lower functioning sociopaths tend to use substances with more abandon and are more likely to become addicted. Drug use may help to contain and moderate feelings, but drug addiction creates a very unstable lifestyle.

The higher functioning sociopath may "dabble" in drug use, but his or her main mode of drug involvement is usually through selling, not using. It does sometimes happen that sociopaths who have sold drugs for years without regularly using them undergo a life crisis—loss of a steady intimate relationship, being forced to give a child up to the foster care system, or the death of a close family member—that they are unable to cope with through other means. Even higher functioning sociopaths may then become addicted.

I have found that addicted sociopaths are generally easier to treat than those who can limit themselves to selling drugs. People who use drugs to "self-medicate" tend to be more conscious of their feelings and experience more emotional pain and conflict than those who do not need to use drugs. In addition, their personalities are more unstable. While instability normally indicates a poor prognosis, in the sociopath's case (as well as in the narcissist's), the less effectively aggression is used to maintain interpersonal boundaries, the more able the client is to establish a therapeutic relationship.

Brain Dysfunction

For some sociopaths, brain trauma may result from childhood malnutrition or neglect. Raine (1993, 195) states that head injury may play a much greater role in predisposing an individual to delinquency and criminal behavior than was previously realized. Central nervous system damage may be present due to abuse if the person was raised in a violent home.

For others, memory impairment and other disturbances can come about as a result of the kind of lives that sociopaths typically lead. Substance abuse will have a damaging effect on the brain, particularly if it involves long-term use or experimentation with substances such as glue. AIDS can eventually cause dementia. Sociopaths are also likely to have accidents that impact the brain, for example, high speed collisions with cars and motorcycles. They also like to fight. Given all this, it is logical to speculate that most sociopaths have suffered some amount of brain trauma in their lives.

Although a detailed account of the various types of brain dysfunction and their related symptoms is beyond the scope of this book, clinicians should note that brain trauma can affect cognitive capacity and impulse control. Accordingly, a sociopath with brain dysfunction is likely to have memory problems, a limited capacity to think in an abstract manner, and less impulse control than other sociopaths.

Less intelligent sociopaths tend to get caught more often and to spend more time incarcerated. They also tend to be more suggestible and are often preyed upon by more intelligent sociopaths, who set them up to be caught both inside and outside of prison. As a result, sociopaths with brain dysfunction often have more motivation for treatment than clients with some of the other diagnostic combinations. Such clients need a lot of limit setting, reality testing, and judgment from the therapist to help them avoid danger to themselves from others.

If sociopathy, brain dysfunction, and psychopathy combine, you get Sammy, the grade B movie "enforcer" from chapter 5. This is another combination that is very difficult to treat, again because the client has little motivation to change his behavior. Violence is often his only protection against being victimized or teased, and it makes him feel good when little else does.

In order for treatment to occur, this type of client must be away from his "boss." Treatment has an even better chance of success if the boss has sacrificed Sammy to the criminal justice system in order to avoid incarceration himself and then made no effort to look after Sammy once he was locked up. The more extensive the degree of psychopathy involved, however, the more the prognosis deteriorates.

Clinicians may also encounter developmentally delayed individuals with sociopathic traits. Such clients prey on other developmentally delayed people that they meet and associate with through group programs and residential settings. Clients such as these tend to be angrier and less cooperative than other people with significant cognitive impairment.

Major Mental Illnesses

In describing the diagnostic features of antisocial personality disorder, the DSM-IV states that the antisocial behavior must not occur "exclusively during the course of Schizophrenia or a Manic Episode" (651). For someone with bipolar disorder, it should be fairly simple to determine whether antisocial behavior was part of a manic episode or a symptom of the personality disorder. If it was a symptom of a manic episode of bipolar disorder, then the antisocial behavior would not occur during the depressive phases of the illness. In this case, antisocial behaviors could be treated in the same manner as other behaviors that occur during the manic phase. Since schizophrenia does not have the clear ebbs and flows of bipolar disorder, unless the illness is in remission, this determination is not so easily made.

Formal mood and thought disorders are so named because cognitive processes are drastically altered. Accordingly, major mental illnesses such as schizophrenia combine with sociopathy in ways similar to disorders associated with brain dysfunction. People suffering from hallucinations and delusions who have sociopathic traits usually victimize other mentally ill people that they encounter through the programming that they share. They are also often victimized themselves, because they prefer to socialize with higher functioning sociopaths with whom they have something in common and whom they admire. As a result, they often put themselves in dangerous situations in the company of people who will not help them when a crisis occurs.

Bipolar disorder. Individuals with bipolar disorder and sociopathic traits present a difficult management problem during their manic phases. Although the impairment of their thought processes is likely to make their attempts to victimize others relatively easy to detect, a lack of success will not stop them from continuing to try. During depressed phases, they may continue to use others as a means to increase their self-esteem and to ward off the depression. Depletion of their possessions during manic phases may also provide a motivation to continue to steal.

Some sociopaths also have distinct manic-like phases, sometimes in combination with traits associated with borderline personality disorder. Here, a sociopath will have episodes of increased activity and grandiosity, during which acting out reaches a maximum level. Such an episode will be followed by a crisis of sorts and then a period of depression with suicidal thoughts or gestures. The administration of lithium tends to achieve results in this case, as it does with bipolar disorder.

Schizophrenia. The most dangerous combination of a major mental illness and sociopathy results when the paranoid type of schizophrenia is joined with sociopathic traits. This diagnostic picture is very similar to the combination of paranoid personality disorder and sociopathy, with the crucial difference that individuals suffering from a thought disorder such as schizophrenia cannot test reality and are therefore unable to determine their level of safety around others.

It is usually this diagnostic picture, coupled with psychopathic traits, that creates the person who kills (or attempts to kill) large numbers of strangers. Determining whether such individuals belong in prison or in a forensic psychiatric facility is a continuing source of confusion for the legal and mental health systems. When they end up in prison, they tend to be victimized by other inmates and to experience a sharp increase in their symptoms, and unless the prison has a setting for housing the chronically mentally ill, they become a major management problem for correctional staff. When they end up in a forensic hospital, they are more able to victimize others.

As clients, these individuals are seldom able to tolerate therapy without medication, as they find it too threatening to even sit in a room with a therapist. They may believe that the therapist is reading their thoughts and brainwashing them. They might then feel an urgent need to act out violently to reduce their rage and gain control of the situation. Even with medication, it takes a very long time to establish a relationship with a client with this type of illness.

Anxiety Disorders

Posttraumatic stress disorder. A significant number of Vietnam veterans who suffer from PTSD became addicted to substances during the war and continued in a drug-addicted lifestyle on their return. Another sizable population of men and women who developed PTSD as a consequence of being sexually abused in childhood also have sociopathic traits.

People who fit this criteria tend to live lives that are quite chaotic. For the most part, they do not buy into the value system of the career criminal, and so they attempt to hold jobs, with varying levels of success. They have less success in interpersonal relationships, as demands for intimacy may prove overwhelming and result in spousal and child abuse.

As clients, this group is among the more motivated for treatment. They experience great distress from their PTSD symptoms, as well as from the original trauma. Sociopathic tendencies are clearly used here as defense mechanisms, and once these clients find other coping mechanisms, their need to act out in antisocial ways dwindles.

Anxiety-related symptoms. Sociopaths who suffer from anxiety-related symptoms often are substance abusers, carry a diagnosis of antisocial personality disorder, and describe themselves as experiencing dissociation. They have two selves, so to speak. One self uses drugs, steals, and uses people. The other self is sober and "wouldn't steal a pack of gum." The sober self cannot set limits with people or confront them. It is quite passive and permits itself to be victimized. It also suffers from a great deal of anxiety. All the while, the rage is boiling up inside.

At some point, the rage becomes overwhelming, and the drug user takes over. This self is quite sociopathic in its treatment of others. At some point, this self gets caught. It is then up to the sober self to make amends and repair the damage that the drug-using self caused. These clients often wonder if they are schizophrenic, in the belief that a personality split such as this is a diagnostic criterion for schizophrenia.

Anxiety may also surface in the form of panic attacks and somatoform disorders. Sociopaths tend to experience those types of anxiety reactions that need soothing and reassurance from the outside. Medical staff often label these symptoms as "manipulative" and "drug seeking," and they sometimes are. But they are also products of real anxiety. An angry confrontation from health providers will exacerbate the symptoms, thereby increasing the anxiety and the demands. A little empathy and some effort to reassure the individual will usually work well to decrease this type of symptom.

Sexual Offenses

Sociopaths do often coerce others into having sex or sexually victimize individuals in other ways. However, this behavior differs from the way in which sex offenders who do not have sociopathic traits commit their crimes.

Sociopaths who sexually victimize others tend to do so in an opportunistic fashion. They are not likely to fixate on sexual offending as a main coping mechanism, nor will they victimize in a planned and organized fashion. For example, when a rape occurs during the course of a burglary, it is likely that the burglary was planned, and the rape was not. Traditional sex offender treatment programs do not work at all well for sociopathic sexual offenders of this type.

Male sociopaths who rape women will often be unable to distinguish this type of sexual behavior from consensual sex; the consent of the sociopath's sexual partner is simply irrelevant. This type of person will also rape men in prison and experience no conflict over the issues of either consent or bisexuality. (In his mind, he maintains his heterosexuality because he did the penetrating.)

Not much is known about female sexual offenders. Female sociopaths do tend to use sex as a means to material gain. For example, those who work as prostitutes will be alert for opportunities to cheat or rob their "johns."

The widespread use of crack cocaine has produced an environment permeated with opportunities for sexual exploitation. Male sociopaths who sell the drug will demand various forms of sex in payment for it, and male and female sociopaths will prostitute themselves for drugs or for money. Again, sex does not have much to do with intimacy. It is one more thing that can be bartered with or taken from someone else.

Beyond the Diagnostic Continuum

Unfortunately, it is quite possible to see all of these diagnostic combinations in one person—for example, someone with a major mental illness who abuses drugs, suffers from some PTSD symptoms, has borderline and sociopathic traits, and has incurred some amount of cognitive impairment. It is less common to encounter an example of antisocial personality disorder as a fixed cluster of symptoms without indicators of other types of disorders.

This section has provided the information necessary to formulate a full diagnosis. This is the first of the two tasks of the beginning stage of treatment. The following section on countertransference undertakes to provide information necessary for the clinician to accomplish the second task: to ensure the establishment of a working therapeutic relationship.

Section II

Countertransference

7

What Is Countertransference?

I began this book by noting that the bare mention of the term sociopathy is enough to elicit very strong reactions from mental health professionals. When I tell other clinicians that I have had more experience working with sociopaths than with any other population, I get a variety of responses:

"How can you stand it?"

"What do you do with all of the lying?"

"God bless you. I sure wouldn't want to do that."

Sometimes the response is a litany of questions about serial killers or other types of psychopaths.

Many clients are also aware of the power of the term, even if they do not know its correct meaning. Fairly often, I hear clients labeled with a diagnosis of antisocial personality disorder say things like this: "People say I'm antisocial. I'm not, you know. I *like* people. I don't spend all my time by myself."

From the diagnostic perspective of the previous section, it is clear that the many quite negative responses to sociopaths within the mental health profession come in multiple layers. While some of these responses may technically belong in the category of societal prejudice, all of them will be included within this section's examination of countertransference.

In order to form a therapeutic bond that can withstand the onslaught of sociopathic pathology, countertransference must be given special attention. In this section, types of countertransference responses will be detailed, along with the typical defensive responses that therapists use to manage them.

The crucial next step is to relabel the countertransference material. Instead of viewing it as a source of shame or something that the therapist should try to ignore or eliminate, the focus will be on viewing countertransference feelings as *the most important source of information the therapist has about the client*—and, consequently, as the most powerful and potentially effective vehicle for bringing about therapeutic change.

With this focus in mind, strategies for accessing countertransference material will be presented.

Changing Definitions

"Countertransference" is a term specific to psychodynamic theory whose meaning has evolved over the years since it was first introduced. Originally, transference and countertransference were both considered to be "neurotic" responses (in other words, unhealthy ones) that clients and therapists have toward each other.

Transference reactions were those thoughts and feelings that a client has for a therapist that are not based on who the therapist actually is, but on how the client has been treated by others in the past. As a very simple example, consider the case of the man raised by parents who never said anything negative directly; as a result, a compliment from them was more often a lie than an expression of their true feelings. Thirty years later, his therapist praises him, and the client immediately labels the compliment as a lie—even though he has previously found his therapist generally truthful in their interactions.

Countertransference was similarly defined as those neurotic reactions that an analyst has for a client that are based on the analyst's own past, not on who the client is. As such, countertransference was considered to be the byproduct of an unsuccessful personal analysis. As they still do, analysts then underwent their own analyses as part of their training, and it was believed that a successful analysis would result in the elimination of the vast majority of the analyst's conflicts— leaving no unresolved neurotic conflicts behind for the client to "pull" from the analyst.

As these definitions suggest, in the early days of psychoanalysis countertransference was considered bad. The stated ideal was an analyst without unconscious internal conflict. Such an analyst could function as a mirror or some other type of blank slate for the client (Fromm-Reichmann 1960, 11). Those analysts with sense enough to know that they had plenty of unresolved conflicts were left to worry whether they were themselves too ill to be effective psychotherapists.

While this definition of countertransference may have been workable theoretically, it was quite difficult to apply in practice.

Rethinking the Concepts

As a result, for years therapists using the traditional definition focused almost exclusively on transference as the main therapeutic vehicle. Fortunately, over time and after many therapeutic failures, theorists began to rethink transference and countertransference as concepts. This new approach may have resulted from the realization that successful personal analyses do not wipe out all unconscious conflict, or perhaps from a belated acceptance of the fact that many therapists do manage to practice psychodynamic psychotherapy successfully without going through a personal analysis. Whatever the reasons may have been, it was established that therapists are as human as their clients.

Another major factor behind this rethinking of the definition of countertransference had to do with changing ideas regarding the application of psychoanalytic psychotherapy. When psychoanalysis was first introduced, Freud made it clear that it was not to be used with anyone who presented any type of symptom more severe than those within the neurotic range (Boyer and Giovacchini 1990, 2). By 1980, professional opinion had shifted to such an extent that the newly published DSM-III simply eliminated neurosis as a category of mental illness. (Perhaps the ideal human personality is free of neurotic symptoms, but neurosis is so commonplace that any definition of mental health based on statistical incidence has to consider those symptoms "normal.")

These changes had their origin in the 1950s, when some therapists began to insist that psychoanalytic psychotherapy could be effectively used, with some adjustments, in the treatment of severely mentally ill people. (For the works of pioneers in this area, see Fromm-Reichmann 1960; Searles 1965; Winnicott 1972; Kernberg 1975; Balint 1979; and Boyer and Giovacchini 1990.) By now, it is completely acceptable to treat certain types of character disorder with psychodynamic psychotherapy. Yet efforts to treat people with major mental illness and severe character problems from this perspective have revealed that the concepts of transference and countertransference are a good deal more complicated than they were previously thought to be.

New Complexities: A Chess Analogy

The old definition made it sound as though transference and countertransference were as easy to distinguish from each other as the black and white pieces in a game of chess. The therapist's thoughts, feelings, and reactions were one color, and the client's were the other. Black makes a discrete statement, and white makes a discrete response. While it's doubtful that things were ever this clear even with neurotic clients, therapists working with clients with severe character problems soon found that their emotional reactions were much stronger and that there was more of a merger of the therapist's and client's personalities throughout the course of treatment. (See chapter 12.)

Therapy is like chess, in the sense that both client and therapist do strategize, based on the response of the other "player." But a board that accurately represented a therapeutic relationship would look rather different from a normal chessboard. At the beginning of the game, both players would hold more pieces off the board, in reserve, than on the board and in play. Although the number of pieces on the board would increase over the course of the game, some pieces held off to the side would never be played. Because the pieces that were played could be used by either side, they would change color from time to time. In fact, each player would actually volunteer to give some pieces to the other (although each would also expect to get those pieces back at some point in the game). The power of the various pieces would change over the course of the game.

Toward the end of the game, many of the pieces on the board would start to take on a new, more permanent color, of a shade that looked like a blend of the original two. The pieces that were never played would remain their original color, in stark contrast to the pieces on the board. At the end of a successful game, each player would be left with just about the same number of similarly colored pieces—with the pieces on both sides drawn up close to the middle of the board, but not trespassing over the center line to the other side.

Fortunately, understanding of the nature of the therapeutic relationship in psychodynamic psychotherapy has increased tremendously. Many theoreticians now focus their work solely on the nature of the relationship itself (Hedges 1992 provides an excellent example). Their work makes it clear that the game of alternative chess just described can only begin to suggest the complexity of the interrelationship between therapist and client.

The Current Definition: A Broader Understanding

Transference and countertransference are now generally defined in their broadest sense: as what each person, the client and the therapist, brings to the therapeutic relationship and how each reacts to the other. The old expectation that therapists are conflict-free has disappeared, replaced by an understanding and acceptance of the fact that therapists do have feelings about and respond deeply to their clients. (The only therapists who do not are the ones who don't care.) The two terms are no longer limited to the resurfacing of past conflicts; rather, therapy is seen as a real relationship, based in the present, between two people whose feelings reflect both personal history and the here-and-now of their interaction.

In the past, theorists could study countertransference in a vacuum because it was so narrowly defined. (Some might argue that it was the theorists' own countertransference that motivated how narrowly defined it was.) If we accept that countertransference has to do with aspects of a real and present relationship, then we need to look at therapy in a much broader context. This context involves multiple levels, including the traditional psychodynamic view of countertransference, the therapist's own feelings about personal and professional relationships, attitudes and biases resulting from his or her training, and still wider social concerns.

Psychodynamic Applications

At the root of the traditional view of countertransference is the simple observation that therapists do react to their clients. Often, and particularly in working with the severely ill, a client's regression, affect, and demands will evoke especially strong reactions in the therapist.

Some of these reactions are based on unconscious and unresolved issues from the therapist's past. When this happens, the therapist may consciously experience the client's behavior in the same way that he or she would react to the behavior of a significant other. At other times, this perception of the client's behavior may occur at an unconscious level, and the therapist's only conscious experience is an immediate and compelling affective reaction and an impulse to respond. To a neutral observer, it looks like the therapist is either overreacting to the client's material or missing its point. Often, the therapist will not remember the content of his or her response or will seriously distort it in recollection.

Some countertransference reactions are based on the personality structure of the therapist. For example, if the therapist has difficulty tolerating certain types and levels of affect, then he or she will need to defend against them when they appear. This mechanism functions at an unconscious level, and the therapist will neither experience the feeling nor be aware that the defense has been used.

Such issues become particularly pressing in work with severely ill clients, where therapists must contain both their own and their clients' affect, and clients have few, if any, interpersonal boundaries. Such extraordinary emotional demands require adequate coping mechanisms, and some of these mechanisms will inevitably be unconscious ones. (A classic exploration of these issues is presented by Searles (1965) in his description of his work with schizophrenics.)

In her work with schizophrenics, Fromm-Reichmann (1960) observed what she describes as the effects of insecurity in therapists. One reaction on the part of therapists is the need to assert themselves at the expense of the client. In this instance, therapists do not help clients search for their own answers, but rather expect them to accept or work out the same solutions for their personal problems as those that the therapists have adopted in their own lives (16). Another common response is an inability to cope effectively with clients' hostility (22). Fromm-Reichmann states that a prerequisite in working with clients who are severely mentally ill is the therapist's capacity to respect the client, and that this respect is not genuine unless it derives from a realization that the client's difficulties in living are not very different from the therapist's own (xi).

Traditional discussions of countertransference normally end here. However, therapists do not emerge from a cocoon to begin their practice. They are raised in a given society, trained by its schools, and paid by its institutions, either directly or indirectly, for the work they do. In addition, they enter into their own relationships and have their own experiences with people outside of their clientele.

The Role of Dependence, Autonomy, and Responsibility in Relationships

Therapists generally have strong feelings and opinions about the nature of mental illness long before they actually see their first client. One of the quickest ways to find out how strong and how divergent these opinions can be is to get a group of therapists in a room together and bring up the issue of forcing schizo-phrenic clients to take medication. The group will usually divide into two camps.

One camp points out that the nature of their illness prevents schizophrenics from being capable of self-care. Since they cannot make a competent decision whether to take medication, others (who are hopefully more competent) must make that decision for them.

The other camp argues that schizophrenics have the same right to self-determination that everyone else has. Certainly, if they put themselves or others at risk, then they must be cared for against their will. But in the absence of such a risk, schizophrenics' thoughts and opinions about themselves and their treatment need to be made as large a part of their care as is humanly possible.

At its core, this debate raises questions about the nature of dependence, autonomy, and responsibility in relationships. And how these questions are answered has a great deal to do with determining how therapists approach their clients.

Cycles of dependence. Some people approach relationships looking to find someone who will do things for them that they do not want to do for themselves (or feel that they cannot do for themselves). Others approach relationships looking to find someone who will foster and nurture their capacities to do things for themselves.

These are two extremes. Most of us (therapists included) fall in between.

Dependence on others often leaves individuals of the first type feeling out of control and inadequate. How can they avoid these painful feelings? Since they usually assume that others are like them—that is, others also do not want to (or cannot) do things for themselves—one way to feel better and more in control is to look for ways to meet others' needs. (This process is sometimes referred to as counterdependence.)

Note that it does not matter whether the other person is actually capable of meeting his or her own needs. The relationship itself is what matters. Its basis can be summed up like this: I will be responsible for you, and I will maintain the fantasy that you will be responsible for me.

Unfortunately (or fortunately, depending on how you look at it), these kinds of relationship do not work. Since no one can read anyone else's mind, one person's attempts to meet another person's needs will never be quite right. And since self-esteem and a sense of adequacy are ultimately based on one's own abilities, trying to increase either by "caring for" someone else is an exercise in futility.

Surrendering one's own needs inevitably causes depression, fear, and rage. Attempting to compensate by controlling someone else rarely decreases these emotions. And since no one can control anyone else's behavior (for long, anyway), trying to do so is a stopgap measure at best.

Taking responsibility for the client. A therapist who operates from such a relational stance tends to feel that clients cannot manage the problems that they have brought to therapy; therefore, it is up to the therapist to manage their problems for them. Over time, the client will become increasingly dependent on the therapist. The client will also experience increased amounts of depression and anger, but will not be able to direct these feelings toward the therapist for fear of the therapist's withdrawal.

Some clients in situations like this will stabilize; the result is one of those therapy relationships that never changes and never ends. Those clients who cannot manage their increasing depression and anger will deteriorate. In response, the therapist will increase his or her "helping" behavior. And the client will continue to get worse.

At some point, since his or her efforts are not being rewarded, the therapist will begin to get frustrated. The client takes the blame (often, the therapist will conclude that the client is not a good candidate for therapy), and the therapist has his or her world view validated: "See? These people can't manage. They need more controls and more structure."

These dynamics should seem at least vaguely familiar: both are examples of mutual-use relationships. The first one is stable and enduring. The second is not.

Supporting client autonomy. At the other extreme are people who conceptualize optimal relationships as environments where each member can develop to his or her fullest capacity. Therapists who operate from this relational stance view clients' inability to manage from a very different perspective. If someone cannot do something, what is missing? Can the person gain that skill? In other words, there is an expectation that clients retain primary responsibility for their own lives.

In this stance, it is the therapist's job to help clients increase their capacity, not to take over that function for them. Clients often get angry at therapists who do this, because many have come from relationships that were based on mutual use. However, in this case, clients feel freer to verbalize the anger. As clients' skills and capacity increase, their self-esteem increases, as does their autonomy. They manage more of their own lives, learn to make more decisions, and realize that they have more choices available to them about the kind of life they want to lead.

As I said, these stances are at either extreme of a continuum. Most therapists fall somewhere in the middle. But no matter where one is on the continuum, it is the therapist's own experience with and view of relationships that will determine how he or she approaches any future relationship, therapeutic ones included. No matter what size or shape their problems are, all clients will be viewed from within this same perspective.

Professional Prejudice

Therapists-to-be bring their experiences with relationships and opinions about the nature of caring to school with them. Ideally, professional schools exist to impart information about specifics relating to treatment. But in doing so, they inevitably impose perspectives and attitudes that become part of the way a therapist assesses clients.

Some of these perspectives are formal categories, such as ways of classifying mental illnesses and the theoretical orientation of the teaching. Some of them are more like a shared common knowledge (for example, the attitude that borderlines are a pain in the neck to work with). Some of the information is presented less overtly. For example, I learned in school that borderlines are almost always female. No one ever told me that fact, but in every case example of borderline personality disorder presented to me, the subject was a female.

Some diagnostic categories were never even mentioned. Antisocial personality disorder was one of these. From this exclusion, if one had no experience working with antisocials, one might conclude that they do not exist. I knew that they existed, and so what I learned about them was that no one wanted them to exist.

Most diagnostic categories that include the severely ill, such as schizophrenia, psychopathy, or borderline personality, evoke a swift and specific set of responses among mental health care providers. These responses are a combination of the therapist's own background, training, and experience. They are different from the traditional ideas about countertransference because they are in place before the therapist ever meets the client. In that sense, they are a type of psychiatric prejudice.

All of these various personal and professional factors contribute to a therapist's response to any given client. When that client is a sociopath, an additional level comes into play. Here, the therapist's response to an individual with a specific personality disorder is also necessarily colored by the therapist's reaction to the sociological subculture with which that disorder is associated.

The Social Context

Many types of psychiatric diagnoses and problems do not necessarily correlate with a particular subculture. However, some do. In the case of transvestic fetishism, there is a society within our society comprised of cross-dressers, transsexuals, and their loved ones. Those Vietnam veterans with posttraumatic stress disorder provide a rather different example. In their case, the war itself created a group of people with a shared and disturbing history, and many have become marginalized citizens because of their inability to make sense of the war and their role in it.

Subcultures of these types are generally closed to outsiders. They were formed in the first place because their members felt that they did not belong and were not wanted within the larger society. Since these groups do not usually welcome curious nonmembers with open arms, a therapist will find it difficult to learn about one of them without the help of a client willing and patient enough to explain it. (For classic explorations of subcultures, identity, and American society, see Goffman 1961 and 1963.)

Subcultures are generally perceived as threats to the order of the larger society. (That is why they were marginalized in the first place.) Sociopaths are identified with and often belong to a specific subculture that evokes very strong feelings in anyone who is not a street criminal. Therapists are no exception.

As most of us do, therapists also have their own political views and cultural biases, including opinions and feelings about how society manages its criminals and its problems with crime, as well as about issues of drug addiction, race, and poverty. Many therapists have also been victims of crime or know people who have.

In work with many different types of clients, these areas of the therapist's personal life never become relevant to the process of psychotherapy. With sociopaths, however, this is not the case. The therapist's feelings about these social concerns will inevitably play a role of some kind, regardless of whether these issues are ever actually discussed during the course of therapy.

Fully comprehending the impact of countertransference when working with sociopaths means exploring this concept in its broadest sense. At its base is the psychodynamic definition, which brings into focus the feelings and responses that the therapist has toward a specific client. In addition, the therapist's feeling about the nature of intimate relationships and about client autonomy in general play a part. Learned responses to diagnoses provide another layer. The client's own subculture and the therapist's responses to it must be explored. Finally, the therapist's feelings about the social, political, and economic structure of his or her society will strongly influence countertransference reactions with this client population.

8

Specific Countertransference Responses to Sociopaths

This exploration begins with traditional countertransference issues and goes on to consider three additional levels: the individual therapist's notion of autonomy, factors related to the attitudes and economics of the mental health field, and larger socioeconomic issues that influence the shape of the therapeutic relationship.

Traditional Countertransference: The First Level

One way to begin exploring how the traditional definition of countertransference applies to work with sociopathic clients is to start with Searles' observation that regression in clients causes regression in therapists (1965, 211). If this is so, then it follows that a client's reliance on primitive defenses and ego functions is likely to cause a similarly regressive response in a therapist.

To summarize the discussion of ego functions in chapter 4, the sociopathic character structure is based on the following features:

- Externals are acquired for internal management.

- Feelings of tension, boredom, hatred, and rage have precedence over other affects.

- Impulsivity is used to regulate feelings.

- Denial, projection, and splitting are relied on as defense mechanisms.

- Other people are perceived and treated as objects.

- Aggression is heavily used to discharge feelings of rage and establish interpersonal boundaries.

- The superego is unformed.

We know what this combination of factors will produce in a personality. If we accept the idea that unconscious identifications are occurring between client and therapist, what would the therapist's reactions be like?

When a client expects a therapist to drop everything to serve the client's demands, the therapist might well respond by becoming tense, angry, bored, or perhaps resentful. If the therapist is blamed for doing an inadequate job of solving the client's problems, the therapist might start feeling rather indignant and defensive, or even perhaps aggressive in response. When clients appear to have no understanding of right and wrong, the therapist may impulsively respond by lecturing them about the therapist's own values, and even go on to insist that those standards become the yardstick that clients use to make judgments of their own.

In other words, therapists commonly become quite controlling and demanding in response to controlling and demanding clients.

Accordingly, therapists typically respond to sociopaths with these feelings: tension, anger, boredom, hatred, defensiveness, indignation, and aggression. The impulse to control the client is strong. If all of these factors are combined, the end result that they produce in the therapist is similar to the one they produce in sociopathic clients: the objectification of the other person.

Types of Regression

A therapist's regressive urge to dehumanize the client can be caused by any number of different aspects of sociopathic presentation. The specific source is determined by those areas of the therapist's personality that are most vulnerable to attack, whether as a result of unconscious conflict or unresolved trauma. These "sore spots" or weaknesses are characterized by increased reliance on lower level defenses, lack of flexibility in ego functions, and an inability to tolerate the full range of feelings associated with the given areas of pain.

Since sociopaths so often cause interpersonal damage, it is understandable that countertransference reactions with them will be strongest when centered around emotions related to being objectified by another: feelings of powerlessness, lack of control, and of being victimized.

Some general guidelines describe the relationship between the therapist's affective response and the type of regression that he or she might experience. At the extremes, when people have been overwhelmed by feelings of being victimized, they react in one of three ways. One group identifies with and experiences the pain, suffering, and humiliation of the victim; those who find these feelings intolerable respond by either perceiving the aggressor as a fellow victim, or by identifying themselves with the offender and experiencing feelings of power, control, and sadism.

Identifying with the victim. A therapist who identifies with the victim will typically respond to the sociopathic client with revulsion, disgust, and rage, and will tend to blame the client for any problems that arise during their interaction. Since therapists do not generally harbor such hateful feelings toward others, particularly toward clients, and since it is contrary to their self-image to do so, negative feelings at this level often cause unconscious conflict for therapists.

In this situation, the most effective way to dispel these feelings and avoid the conflict they present is to get rid of the client. Given the client's apparent lack of remorse and refusal to take responsibility for what he or she does, it is easy to justify this response. The therapist reaches the conclusion that this person should be treated differently from other clients. This client isn't quite human; he or she acts more like an animal or a predator. The services that the therapist provides to others will not be effective with this client, and so they do not have to be offered. Ultimately, the client is objectified in order to preserve the therapist's emotional equilibrium.

Perceiving the aggressor as a victim. In this case, the therapist simply cannot tolerate the feelings of powerlessness and incompetence that result from being victimized. He or she responds by denying the client's rage and predatory impulses, so that both the therapist and the client can be perceived as victims, and responsibility for the sociopath's behavior can be projected onto others. Since this means that large aspects of the client's personality are denied, the therapist "fills in the blanks" left by such massive denial with his or her own unconscious projections and identifications; in true counterdependent fashion, what the therapist now sees is mostly a product of his or her own needs. The invariable result is that the therapist ends up as the client's victim.

The denial of danger that Meloy (1988, 328) notes as a common countertransference response in work with psychopaths plays a role here. A counselor I knew could simply not accept that an inmate she was working with had the capacity to hurt her; he sexually assaulted her when she met with him alone in a secluded area of the prison. Despite this brutal outcome, she still refused to press charges against him.

Identifying with the aggressor. Although this response occurs less frequently, it is equally ingrained, and it causes the most damage. Instead of feeling empathy for the victims of the psychopath's exploits, this type of therapist may end up "identifying with the exhilaration and contemptuous delight of patients as they recount their fantastic, perhaps fantasized, history" (Meloy 1988, 328). Therapists who make this response typically fall into one of two groups.

Those in the first group are basically quite sociopathic themselves, are aware of this tendency, and identify with the client's behavior for that reason. In this case, they may become involved in illegal behavior in concert with their client. These clinicians do not label such behavior as a boundary violation; rather, they see themselves and their client as "taking charge" of a situation. Whether the client or the therapist ends up as the ultimate victim is determined by which of them is the better sociopath.

When I worked as a literacy volunteer in a New York prison during college, the coordinator of our program was caught smuggling in plans of the prison buildings so that some of the inmates could escape. He was not being coerced by the inmates; he simply believed that it was acceptable for them to escape. Counselors I have known in other settings have been caught dealing drugs with clients.

A second group joins in a sociopathic stance through a combination of counterdependent defenses and identification with the aggressor. These counselors will deny the client's responsibility for his or her behavior, but will also deny their own rage and sociopathic impulses. The result is that while they do not deny the seriousness of the client's behavior, they feel that it is justified and enjoy it vicariously. Although they usually will not engage in any illegal behavior, they also make no effort to stop the sociopath from continuing to do so.

Again, although these workers invariably end up as victims, they blame neither the client nor themselves, and instead project the responsibility elsewhere. I recently learned of a sad and troubling case of this type where a worker aided an inmate in an escape. He was her former client, and she had become romantically involved with him

Notions of Autonomy: The Second Level

The second level of countertransference is an overlay that rests on the foundation established by the first level. Accordingly, therapists' unconscious identifications with either the victim or the aggressor must be kept in mind when thinking about their beliefs concerning responsibility, autonomy, and dependence.

A related issue central to work with this population is that of punishment. A therapist's views regarding personal responsibility relate directly to the issue of punishment whenever client behaviors are as consistently out of acceptable bounds as those of the sociopath invariably are.

When the Therapist Finds Punishment Unacceptable

If a therapist feels that clients should not be held responsible for their behavior, then it follows that they should not be punished for their actions. While this point of view may be helpful for some clients, with a sociopath this attitude can only end up letting the proverbial bull loose in the china shop. When a therapist enters into such a relationship with a sociopath, sadistic and masochistic impulses quickly surge to the forefront. Both parties feel sadistic toward the other; the sociopath because of the free rein to thoroughly use someone else, and the therapist because of the rage and helplessness that result from being so thoroughly used.

If the therapist cannot tolerate these sadistic impulses, he or she will quickly terminate with the client. If the therapist has low tolerance for feelings related to being a victim, then this counterdependent dynamic will lead the client and therapist to alternate in playing the aggressor and the victim roles. The client will act out. The therapist will not punish him or her and will feel like a victim. The therapist will then act out a sadistic impulse in an indirect manner toward the client. The client will feel victimized and respond in a sadistic fashion, and the cycle will continue to repeat itself.

When Punishment Is Seen as the Only Appropriate Response

At the other extreme are those workers who see punishment as the only appropriate response to sociopathic behaviors. Many times people enter into the fields of corrections or criminal justice because they find something intrinsically comforting in taking on the role of the one who keeps the world safe for humanity or for the "good guys." Generally speaking, these people feel a strong need for order and for control of "bad" impulses, and a significant amount of projection is at play here.

In this context, it has frequently been noted that police officers and sociopaths are often opposite sides of the same coin. It is revealing to learn that kids who end up becoming either police officers or career criminals often come from the same group of delinquents.

Therapists who unconsciously project their own unacceptable impulses and urges are often drawn to work with sociopaths and other types of criminals. Therapists such as these are not looking to help sociopathic clients learn to accept responsibility for their behavior; rather, they are punishing their clients for their own unacceptable impulses.

Since these therapists cannot accept their own unconscious identification with the aggressor, they must also perceive themselves as the victim—but they do so in a peculiar way. They do not experience any of the victim's passive feelings of grief, humiliation, or depression; they only experience the rage. So even though they may express sympathy for victims, claim to be operating on their behalf, or portray themselves as having been victimized, they still don't look like victims; they look like aggressors.

As a group, these therapists are the most controlling and punitive, using very much the same defenses that their clients use. They see their clients as "scum" and "animals" who would use, hurt, or kill someone at the drop of a hat. They do not believe that therapy is a useful tool for sociopaths, nor do they perceive themselves as doing therapy with them. They see themselves as agents of social control who have been given the job of protecting the rest of us from these "slime." They have no objection to any type of punishment for sociopaths, including physical or psychological torture. Essentially, these workers have found a way to manage their own sadistic and psychopathic impulses by acting them out on a socially acceptable target.

The Mental Health Field:
The Third Level

The first two levels of countertransference are comprised of aspects of personality that are largely unconscious. The third level expands this base by including the therapist's conscious feelings and thoughts about clients and by moving beyond the client-therapist dyad. Opinions and reactions of groups will be addressed at this level: what is commonly known about sociopaths as a diagnostic category and how those in the field of mental health view those who provide direct care to sociopathic clients.

Negative Diagnostic Preconceptions

Section I made it clear that the diagnosis of antisocial personality disorder is psychiatrically ill-defined, pervaded by moralistic judgments, and often used as a "throw away" diagnosis. Although the most common verbal association to the term "antisocial" is a variation of the phrase "remorseless criminal," the visual image that typically comes with the thought is something along the lines of a gang member in an urban ghetto. When a clinician does not know what the diagnosis should be and the client is male, black, poor, and intimidating, antisocial personality is usually one of the first diagnoses considered. All of these traits are either easily visible or quickly discernible. And once the assessment is made, all the negative feelings and attitudes associated with it are conjured up as well.

The field itself reinforces this process. When professional workers with little or no experience treating sociopaths learn that I believe that they are treatable through traditional psychotherapy, the responses are generally quite negative. Traditional psychotherapy is currently unfashionable anyway, and even in its hayday no one considered it an option for this population. Only someone incompetent or naive or just plain weird would possibly suggest that traditional psychotherapy can work with sociopaths now.

One result of these attitudes is that beginning workers or students who have an interest in working with this population often meet with incredulity or suspicion. Those who do enter the field often sit down for their first session with a sociopath with a whole set of negative thoughts and images already formed. Students I have supervised, who often found themselves with me not because of an interest in correctional mental health but because the placement was convenient, have reported that they were often the center of attention in their classes. Yet all of them ended up concluding that the clients were not nearly as horrific as they had originally thought, and they all were able to make genuine connections with at least some of their clients.

Treatment Settings

The field itself marginalizes the treatment of sociopaths. Sociopaths are not usually treated in traditional mental health facilities. The treatment they receive comes to them through jail or in drug counseling centers or in domestic violence programs. These agencies all have several things in common.

In correctional settings, most of the workers who provide the direct care are not required to carry credentials, and workers in state facilities are usually exempt from state licensing laws. Seniority is customarily substituted for training. It is not unusual to find that job titles requiring an MSW or other graduate training in a mental health classification need only a bachelor-level degree in a correctional setting. Despite this discrepancy, "therapists" in both settings are given the same duties, including assessment, referral for medication, therapy, and treatment evaluation.

Drug counseling programs generally require only certification in drug and alcohol counseling, and training for such certification does not teach anything about mental illness. Recovering addicts who work as substance abuse counselors are rarely required to receive any training, as the experiences they have undergone in recovering from their own addictions are thought to be adequate preparation for counseling others in similar circumstances.

Finally, substance abuse counseling centers and providers of family services are often private nonprofit agencies. These organizations characteristically operate on a shoestring budget and must offer very low salaries. These economic limitations preclude any expectation that line staff will have graduate-level preparation in a mental health field.

How the field sets up and operates the care provided to sociopaths sends a message about their value and treatability. The lack of clinical training is part of that message, and it also perpetuates the cycle. Formal clinical education, even if not specifically focused on work with sociopaths, would provide clinicians with the basic foundation for how to approach and treat clients. Without this foundation, counselors working with sociopathic clients are at a double loss: they do not have the basic skills, and they are dealing with one of the most difficult of all client populations. The chance that a successful clinical encounter will occur in this situation is poor. And when the treatment does break down, the sociopath is then blamed for being a poor candidate for therapy, and the field's negative preconceptions about the diagnosis are validated once more.

Socioeconomic Structures: The Fourth Level

Therapists are usually aware that their own ethnicity and socioeconomic status have an impact on their work with clients. Most know (at least at an intellectual level) that clients should be free to develop their own moral code and should not have to mimic the therapist's own personal beliefs or those of the therapist's background or class. And few would disagree with Fromm-Reichmann (1960) when she assesses the danger that ignoring these issues can have:

> [T]he psychiatrist may consider the changeable man-made standards
> of the society in which he lives to be eternal values to which he and

his patients must conform. . . . This may render him practically incapable of guiding certain types of patients. (32)

Although Fromm-Reichmann had schizophrenic clients in mind, her words apply equally well to any client population whose attitudes or behavior differ substantially from the therapist's own. Current economic and political trends give these concerns a special significance when clients are sociopaths.

Recently, these trends have made daily life harder for all strata of society except for the very wealthy. Therapists, who tend to fall within the range of the middle to upper middle class, have been directly affected by related changes in our health care system and by governmental budget cuts. While these developments have an impact on how therapists treat all of their clients, sociopaths are particularly vulnerable.

Sociopaths are usually poor and often incarcerated; these circumstances alone leave them at the mercy of changing social policies. But sociopaths are not just poor people; they are also perceived as an enormous social problem. In fact, they probably constitute the most politically volatile social issue in this country. Politicians' careers have been made or lost over their views on street crime alone, and sensationalized media coverage colors nearly everyone's feelings and thoughts about crime and criminals. All of these factors require careful attention and a special sensitivity from the therapist.

Changing Views of Crime and Punishment

In particular, the past several decades have brought enormous changes in the way we think and talk about incarcerated criminals. The word "punishment" drew critical looks back in the 1960s and 1970s; the prevailing view then was that correction was an appropriate goal for a correctional system. The whole concept of "rehabilitation" draws bitter laughter now. Polls tell us that the majority of Americans are "fed up with crime," convinced that inmates are "coddled," and in favor of making our prison system as punitive as possible.

These changing feelings about crime and punishment would be easier to explain if a major increase in criminal activity had occurred during the same period. On the contrary, statistics suggest that we should be feeling safer, as the crime rate is actually down, and the segment of the population presenting the greatest risk for criminal behavior (age 15–25) has decreased significantly since the 1960s. Since these facts argue that rehabilitation can be successful, why has public opinion turned so thoroughly against it?

The Economic Context

These changes have not taken place in a social vacuum, nor are they isolated events. Over the past two decades, a change in this country's economic structure as far-reaching as that of the Industrial Revolution has occurred. We are changing from a manufacturing economy to a service and information economy. At the same time, we are struggling to compete in a global marketplace that no one quite understands. Neither the government, corporate management, nor our workforce are prepared for this shift.

Governmental policies have not helped to manage the transition. Instead, legislators have eagerly cleared the way for a "deregulated" marketplace where hyperaggressive tactics prevail and short-term profits outweigh every other concern. At the same time, working conditions have seriously eroded for most American workers as corporations turn to "downsizing" and substitute no-frills employment contracts for full-time jobs. Because the new jobs that result do not pay nearly as well as the jobs that were lost, many of the displaced workers caught in this crunch have had to take two or even three jobs simply to make ends meet. And those who have kept their old positions have still had to subsume work previously done by others.

During the same period, federal and local governments have tried to cope with mounting budget deficits by cutting back on social programs—in effect, reducing the cushion for the very people who have been cast aside in this economic upheaval. Even in those agencies where direct services have not been slashed, client workloads have multiplied and working conditions have deteriorated. Among other changes, the excellent benefits packages that private nonprofit agencies previously offered to compensate for low salaries are no longer possible. Many of these jobs are now "fee for service," meaning that therapists are paid only for the hours during which they see clients.

Given the impact of all these developments, it's not surprising that many Americans feel traumatized. Those who were cast aside feel victimized by their previous employers; those who remain feel oppressed by their current work environments. Unhappy as they are with their work situations, most are terrified of losing their jobs. And it is a terrifying prospect to have so little sense of security about the future.

Blaming the Poor

The mechanism of countertransference tells us that when people are objectified, they tend to objectify in response. When people are victimized and overwhelmed by powerlessness, they often identify with the aggressor as a defense mechanism.

While few in government or in the business world are willing to admit responsibility for the damage that they have done, many are quite ready to divert attention to a group with little ability to fight back: the poor. Overwhelmed by their own feelings of helplessness and despair, the working, middle, and upper-middle classes have provided a willing audience for a flood of campaign speeches and media commentary attacking the shortcomings of America's "permanent underclass" or the "undeserving poor." I have heard Michael Lerner refer to this process as one of viewing people as "the demeaned other" (in a March 1995 lecture at the Rowe Camp and Conference Center, Rowe, Massachusetts).

While rhetoric of this kind often makes it sound as though poverty and crime are synonymous, when the others in question are actually sociopaths, and not just anyone whose income falls below a certain level, an additional factor comes into play. The sociopath's aggression and lack of remorse also raise troubling moral questions about our society's values and attitudes toward personal responsibility.

The Face in the Mirror

Although social critics have been bemoaning the deteriorated state of American values since the days of Cotton Mather, in recent years popular sermons of this kind seem to have reached a new level of intensity. Despite varying political agendas, those commentators who condemn our "culture of narcissism" or who lament the loss of "traditional values" do appear to share a common unease. Underlying many such complaints is a perception that our national obsession with consumption and profit has significantly eroded the boundaries between objects and people, and that we have come a long way toward reducing all ethical issues to a deceptively simple question: How much will it cost?

Accompanying this disdain for our own materialism is a sense that those who do get caught breaking the rules are not held accountable. Even when individuals acknowledge culpability for some personal failing or violent action, the admission invariably comes with a built-in alibi: the real culprit is an abusive childhood, or a psychological "addiction" of some kind, or even poor eating habits (as in the infamous "Twinkie defense").

To a surprising extent, these complaints about American society as a whole sound very much like the DSM-IV's diagnosis for antisocial personality disorder. In this sense, the sociopath is a somewhat exaggerated mirror image for everyday life in a consumer society. And indeed, sociopathy would be the logical end result if one were to base one's life completely on consumption.

How do people respond when faced with such a disturbing image? They deny it, and they project it. They deny the greed and materialism of their own lives and project these qualities onto the sociopath. They overlook their own self-centered relationships and recoil at the sociopath's willingness to exploit and manipulate others. And rather than acknowledge their own evasions of responsibility for what happens to them, they react with outrage toward the sociopath's alibis and excuses and lack of remorse.

As therapists, our lives are affected by these same political and economic trends. As is the case with the other three levels of countertransference reaction, the socioeconomic context interweaves the themes central to sociopathic character pathology: objectification of others, victimization, aggression, and denial of responsibility. All four levels combine to create a formidable obstacle to establishing a working therapeutic relationship with sociopathic clients. And since most major aspects of the therapist's personality are affected by these clients, the task of managing these reactions can seem daunting.

On the plus side, a primary benefit of experiencing a strong negative transference is that it is hard to miss, and thus the material it provides is readily available for the therapist to use as a therapeutic tool. The next chapter explores how these powerful emotions can be harnessed for a useful purpose: to promote the health and well-being of the client.

9

Solutions

In order for any therapeutic relationship to be tolerable, much less effective, structures must be in place to contain, order, and make use of transference and countertransference material. The framework for doing so is comprised of three factors:

1. Therapeutic neutrality

2. Clinical training and supervision

3. An understanding of the concepts of the repetition compulsion and projective identification

This chapter will explore these three components, the application of this framework, and how to formulate assessments from countertransference material.

Therapeutic Neutrality

Therapeutic neutrality is one form of those therapeutic boundaries that Modell (1991, 15) describes as establishing a border between therapy and everyday life and as providing a frame that contains the treatment. Appointments are one very basic example of a professional boundary. Why do we need appointment times with clients? Why couldn't we accomplish the same therapeutic goals with a drop-in center?

First, an appointment is a contract for client and therapist to spend exclusive time with each other, and a commitment that each party will give the other his or her undivided attention. Second, an appointment permits each party to prepare for the meeting. For the therapist, this means that some thought can be given to treatment-plan issues and goals, how the past several sessions have gone, and ideas the therapist has for the general direction of the next session.

For the client, an appointment indicates that the process of dealing with his or her problem will not take place in an impulsive fashion. Since the therapist cannot be seen on demand (except in crisis situations), the client cannot use him or her as an immediate self-soothing mechanism. Nor can the therapist be easily avoided when the client is feeling resistant or defensive. And even though specific issues or events may not be critical for the client at the moment, a set appointment time also means that the client must come to therapy prepared to access and present them.

These consequences for clients also happen to correspond to three very important ego functions: impulse control, internalization of the object, and affect management. None of these functions would be affected if clients were given permission to simply show up and see the therapist whenever they wanted.

Therapeutic neutrality is the one professional boundary that is crucial to the management of countertransference reactions. In this context, "neutrality" does not resurrect the old definition of the therapist as blank slate, but instead refers to the ability to listen to clients' material without interference from the therapist's own personality. Several of the concept's many facets are particularly relevant here.

Moral Judgments

The most commonly known and understood element of therapeutic neutrality is the idea that the therapist's judgments, values, and moral system must be withheld when clients are describing their feelings, opinions, or behaviors. This is not to say that therapists should be without values or morals, nor that they should never make a moral judgment about anything that their clients do or say. It is to say that these beliefs must not prevent the therapist from accurately taking in what the client is communicating.

Personal Information

Another aspect of therapeutic neutrality is the rule that therapists must only disclose personal information about themselves to the client when doing so serves a clinical function. Again, this is not to say that clients should never be told anything about the therapist's personal life, but only that such disclosures should not be made simply to meet the therapist's needs. For example, when a warm and friendly client asks personal questions at the beginning of treatment, and the therapist's answers will do little to move the therapeutic process forward, the therapist who does respond is essentially serving his or her own need to avoid a potentially painful conflict with the client about boundaries.

Splitting Experience and Observation

By definition, therapeutic neutrality means that the therapist's observable reactions and responses to the client derive from diagnostic formulations and a treatment plan, and not from the therapist's own personal feelings. In order to establish and maintain this stance, it is necessary for therapists to develop an additional ego function.

Sterba (1934) describes this process as one of learning to separate one's observing ego from one's experiencing ego. Modell (1991, 18) adds that it is the ability to discipline oneself to inhibit affective responses, but not affective perceptions. It is critical for the therapist to be able to experience the full range of feelings that occur during the course of a session. It is even more critical for the therapist to be able to store these feelings. The place to share them is in clinical supervision.

The ego function of splitting experience and observation is a product of relevant training, experience, and supervision. The concept is first introduced to most beginning workers in school and nurtured and developed in supervision. Once the basic skill is in place, the clinician can then hone it over time as he or she gains experience.

Clinical Supervision

Clinical supervision is an essential component in the development of therapeutic neutrality in work with any client population. It is a prerequisite in work with sociopaths and other clients who have severe personality disorders (Gallwey 1992, 168).

Unfortunately, given the second-class status of these diagnoses in the mental health field, adequate clinical supervision is often not available. However, for countertransference responses to sociopathic clients to be effectively managed during the course of therapy, direct-care staff must have access to clinical supervision. Further, as examples in chapter 8 have shown, inadequate clinical supervision not only undercuts the effectiveness of any treatment program, but also poses a real danger to both clients and staff.

None of the staff mentioned in these examples are bad people; I believe that all of them had the best intentions. However, they were unable to maintain a psychological equilibrium when working with this clientele. As a result, they experienced massive trauma, and, in some cases, their careers and lives were destroyed. Clients were also damaged because their overall functioning deteriorated as a result of work with these individuals.

Although safety concerns in work with sociopaths are more fully addressed in chapter 14, it is worth mentioning here that concerns about mental health workers' physical safety have recently been on the rise. Clients are becoming more violent and are hurting staff, themselves, and others. Clinicians who are unprepared for such encounters have been unable to defuse and control these situations.

Some of these incidents would not be preventable by the provision of clinical supervision alone. Yet if an agency makes a consistent effort to offer clinical supervision by a licensed and experienced supervisor, disasters such as these should be greatly reduced. Clinical supervision is one of the most effective means of helping direct-care staff learn how to monitor client communications and prioritize interventions to maintain the well being of all the participants in the therapeutic process.

The Repetition Compulsion and Projective Identification

The third aspect of the foundation for the therapeutic use of countertransference is the understanding of the mechanisms that fuel it: the repetition compulsion and the defense of projective identification. These two mechanisms play a crucial role in countertransference responses because both involve the individual's significant others.

Other familiar defenses, such as denial or intellectualization, are solely internal defenses. When an individual's unconscious feelings are overwhelming or in conflict, these defenses provide protection by either changing the way the individual experiences those feelings, altering his or her perception of self, or modifying the way he or she sees the outside world. In contrast, the repetition compulsion and projective identification both attempt to protect the ego's stability from internal threats by engaging someone else in the re-creation of a traumatizing situation.

The Repetition Compulsion

Paul Russell (1987) eloquently describes the experience of the repetition compulsion as such:

> [T]he repetition compulsion is the repetition of that which, so far as we know, we would rather not repeat. This covers a lot of ground. It can be a very simple affair, or extraordinarily complex. It can be of such complexity and power that one has the impression that it is an act of an intelligence that is more than a match for one's own. It can at times operate like a doom, a nemesis, a curse. The same thing will happen, despite one's best efforts at avoidance, prevention, or control. In fact, it gets its name precisely on this account; that despite the apparent wish to avoid the pain, the cost, the injury of the repetition, one finds oneself repeating nonetheless, as if drawn to some fatal flame, as if governed by some malignant attraction which one does not know and cannot comprehend or control. It has, in other words, all the external earmarks of a volitional act, and yet

the person is unaware of wishing any such thing. In fact, quite the contrary; he or she would wish to avoid it. (5)

Why do people do this? Why would someone unconsciously recreate the worst and most painful conditions of his or her life?

The repetition compulsion serves two vital functions: it successfully communicates the affect, and it provides the only opportunity to heal the trauma.

Trauma is defined as such because it irreparably damages some vital aspect of self. Since the feelings associated with it are overwhelming and because the person usually cannot conceptualize the nature of the damage, this kind of pain cannot be described in words alone. For example, people in the throes of grief often cannot speak; if they do try to communicate their feelings, their words sound empty and inadequate. The pain surrounds them and consumes them. Only later, when the grief has become bearable, can they explain and describe in words the impact of their loss.

People with personality disorders have a character structure that is based on the repetition compulsion. They are in a constant state of trauma, and they rely on the repetition compulsion as their primary defense and coping strategy. These clients communicate to the therapist how overwhelmed they are by recreating the conditions of the trauma within the therapeutic relationship.

In other words, a therapist who experiences the full range of the client's feelings during a session will invariably end up feeling as the client did when the trauma was at its worst. In this way, the repetition compulsion delivers the most accurate and comprehensive rendering of a client's problem that a therapist will ever have. As such, it is both the most difficult aspect of the therapeutic relationship for the therapist to manage, and the most effective vehicle for helping a client to heal.[1]

One very clear illustration of this process is provided by a counselor whose clients responded quickly and deeply to him; this response was particularly evident with clients who had borderline traits and who were overwhelmed by loss. In the counselor's own childhood, he had been abruptly moved from several homes where he had established attachments to the foster-care families who raised him. During the course of the eighteen months that he held two positions at one agency, he recreated these conditions by resigning four times. The clients with whom he had established the closest relationships were especially devastated on two such occasions when he abruptly announced that he was quitting and then disappeared. Essentially, he had recreated the conditions of his own unresolved trauma in such a way that his clients were left to experience the devastating loss.

Projective Identification

Projective identification is a game for two (or more) players that provides a mechanism for the repetition compulsion to occur. Simply put, one person *projects*

---

1. The material in this section is indebted to several unpublished articles by Paul Russell, M.D., that translate the complexities of the repetition compulsion into understandable and familiar concepts.

his or her overwhelming or unacceptable feelings, and the other person *identifies* with those feelings and responds by recreating a role from his or her own past.

For example, a housewife complains that her husband never helps out around the house. She keeps everything very neat and orderly and asks him to be responsible for certain tasks, but he does not do them. She will wait for a short period of time, get frustrated, and then do them herself. When she then accuses her husband of ignoring her needs, he acts perplexed, as if he does not know what she is talking about. He claims that every time he tries to do one of the chores, he finds that she has already done it. No matter how hard he tries, he cannot succeed.

The wife is projecting her own impulses to be messy and to have her surroundings in disorder onto her husband. These impulses are unacceptable to her because their presence would indicate that she is not a good housewife.

The husband was raised by a mother who did all of the cleaning and did not require him to be responsible for household tasks. This childhood experience taught him that if a female loves you, she will clean up after you. Being messy, then, is an indicator of manhood, and this association makes it easy for him to identify with a role consistent with his wife's unacceptable impulses.

In the woman's case, the repetition compulsion at work might be the residue of a childhood history of feeling ignored and having to provide much of her own self-care. This very painful experience is now recreated in her marriage.

Her husband, on the other hand, may have grown up with a father who competed with him. Every time the boy wanted to learn a new skill, he would invariably be given a demonstration of his father's superior competency. These childhood experiences of failure and inadequacy are now recreated in his marriage.

She projects, and he identifies. Both repeat painful experiences from their childhoods. And neither can figure out a way to get this process to stop.

Bonding Mechanisms

It is important to keep in mind that projective identifications are not signs of dysfunction in and of themselves. In fact, they are the most powerful capability for bonding with each other that we have. Projective identifications operate in all of our relationships, and the more significant the relationship is, the stronger the projections and identifications are. What is critical is the type of projections and identifications that are occurring.

In any relationship, whether healthy or unhealthy, both members project their own impulses and identify with the projections of their partner. If these identifications strengthen and gratify each partner's ego, then the relationship will be stable. If the identifications are positive (care giving, nurturing, protective) then the relationship will be strong and healthy. If the identifications are negative (aggressive, passive, sadistic, controlling) then the relationship will be very well balanced but quite dysfunctional.

Without projective identification, we would not have repetition compulsions. (Of course, we would also lose our capacity to form any kind of relationship at all.) In action, this quite ordinary bond can become extremely complex: two people who each have their own set of repetition compulsions join together, projecting their own unacceptable impulses onto each other and identifying with the impulses that the other projects.

It is this mix that creates the common presenting complaint in therapy: "I can't seem to find the right man (or woman). I keep getting into the same sort of terrible relationship with the same type of creepy person over and over again, and I don't know why, and I can't seem to stop it." This same combination of dynamics also creates those abusive and dysfunctional families who persevere in retaining every possible symptom that they can while simultaneously expressing outrage over the therapist's inability to "help."

Implications for Therapeutic Relationships

Repetition compulsions and projective identifications are also the bonding mechanisms in therapeutic relationships. They are the paths on which transference and countertransference travel. The source of most therapeutic errors, impasses, and inappropriate terminations can be traced back to problems in the management of countertransference: namely, the therapist's difficulty with the underlying repetition compulsions and projective identifications.

All of the levels of countertransference previously discussed in this section can be understood in greater depth if these concepts are applied. For example, the aggressor-victim dynamic that operates at all four levels of countertransference in work with sociopaths is a product of both the therapist's and the client's repetition compulsions concerning trauma about having been victimized. The roles of aggressor and of victim are ascribed and accepted based on intense levels of projective identification.

Accessing and Managing Countertransference Responses

Thankfully, all of this material can be harnessed to provide diagnostic and assessment information for treatment planning purposes. In order to achieve this result, the therapist must apply at least as much skill and care in attending to countertransference responses as he or she applies in attending to material that the client produces.

The ego function of separating affective experiences from affective responses must be present. The therapist is then free to observe, accept, and explore his or her own thoughts and feelings during the course of a session in the same way that he or she accepts and explores the client's thoughts and feelings. Here, too, moral and value judgments need to be suspended; in effect, the therapist internally free-associates a response to the client's words and presentation. The process feels a bit like dissociating: as if one part of the mind is observing another part's perceptions and responses.

Sociopathic clients rely so much on the defense mechanism of projection that many times the only way to discover what they are feeling about something is to search for an affective response in the countertransference. For example, if the therapist is feeling angry with the client, it is likely that the client is feeling an overwhelming amount of rage (even if his or her outward appearance is calm).

Unfortunately, the process is not so straightforward, since countertransference material also occurs in response to the therapist's own personality weaknesses. How can one tell the difference? Particularly for beginning workers, there is no way to do so without the help of a third party. Affective responses toward clients need to be brought to clinical supervision for the supervisor to help sort out the therapist's own emotions from the client's projected feelings.

Over time, the therapist will learn that one's own affect and defense mechanisms feel different than someone else's. When I am not sure "whose pathology is operating" (the phrase is from Casement 1991, 81–82), I will free-associate until I can determine whose affects I am experiencing, mine or the client's. While this process can feel a bit bizarre at first, once it becomes familiar, it provides a wealth of information. (Casement provides an in-depth discussion of how to access countertransference material in this fashion.)

Applications and Assessment

These steps provide a channel through which to access, manage, and understand countertransference reactions. The next step is to be able to apply this understanding. The most effective way to do this is to use the information to paint a mental picture of the client's personality structure. The therapist can then step into this picture and try to experience what the world actually feels like to the client.

From this operational stance, sociopathy and psychopathy become much more understandable as character structures. This stance also makes it relatively simple to predict some of the client's responses.

For example, in the course of telling me how he ended up relapsing, a client describes an enabling relationship he had with a woman who was helping him to "shape up." Given my sense of his personality, I might respond by remarking how frustrating it can be trying to relate with someone who takes over everything all of the time. The client will normally be surprised (and relieved) to hear his own underlying feelings recognized. I might then encourage him to explore other affects. Does he feel guilt over resenting someone who was taking such good care of him? Does his inability to explain his anger to the enabler make him feel powerless? If the therapist can recognize and truly understand how easy it is for a sociopath in a situation like this to start stealing, it becomes infinitely easier for a sociopathic client to be honest.

Using countertransference responses for assessment purposes makes the client's strengths and weaknesses become more apparent to the therapist. The therapist can then begin to form some hypotheses about the nature of the traumas underlying the client's repetition compulsions and gain some understanding and empathy for the nature of the sociopath's struggle.

The complexity of the process makes it a demanding one. In working with sociopaths, the therapist must be able to move about freely in the client's emotional world as well as his or her own. Once achieved, among the gifts that countertransference can provide are a truly affective understanding of the client's world and the opportunity for the therapist to explore his or her own moral system. It is the key to unlock the potential for the emergence of a meaningful therapeutic relationship. Without it, no treatment strategies will be effective.

Section III

Treatment Strategies

10

What Does Not Work

Therapist: What brings you here to this agency? What can I help you with?

Client: My wife said I had to come.

Therapist: Why is that?

Client: I don't know! There's something wrong with her!

Therapist: (*getting irritated with the level of projection and denial*) Well, what reason do you think she had for telling you to come here? Obviously, she had something on her mind.

Client: She says I've got problems. But I don't. It's her fault. She's the one with the problems.

Therapist: (*getting angry and impatient*) What kind of problems does she say you have?

Client: I'm telling you . . . there aren't any except that she's always bitching and moaning. Look, she said if I don't come here she's going to throw me out—so can you call her up and tell her I came like she said I should?

Therapist: *(feeling defensive and judgmental)* Well, no. I don't see any reason to do that. I still don't know why you're here.

Client: Look, why did you bother to ask if you could help me? You aren't interested in helping me.

Therapist: *(now indignant)* I *am* interested in helping you. You're just not telling me anything that I can help you with!

Client: This is a waste of time. Are you going to call her or what?

Therapist: I said no. Now if you can't understand when people say no to you, then I would see that as a problem we can start to work on.

Client: *(sneering)* I got me one of the all time great counselors here. Thinks he knows what problems I got. It's been real nice talking to you. *(And out he goes.)*

The client can now walk away from this meeting feeling free to tell his wife that he did what she said to do while still ensuring that he does not have to follow through with treatment. The therapist was manipulated to react as he did, and he obliged.

After a meeting such as this, the therapist typically feels anger at all of the client's denial and projection, some amount of concern about whatever was happening with the client's marriage, defensive about the claim that he is not interested in helping people, and relief that he no longer has to deal with this demanding and obnoxious person. He might have some concern that he could have dealt with the client more effectively, but their interaction makes it easy for him to tell himself that this client clearly did not want help, that he just wanted to "get over" and was being manipulative.

Section II noted that sociopaths elicit strong feelings of anger and outrage in most people, and that clinicians are no exception. Although such countertransference feelings can be an unfailing guide for the therapist, they must be experienced and used solely as a source of information. If a therapist impulsively responds to a sociopathic client on the basis of these feelings, the result is usually that the therapist becomes confronting, judgmental, and authoritarian toward the client. The client ends up gaining more information than the therapist does, and the meeting breaks down into a power struggle.

So what approach can we take to avoid such an outcome?

Current Treatment Strategies

Unfortunately, all of the current treatment strategies that I am familiar with are based on the belief that sociopaths are fundamentally untreatable through any conventional means. Essentially, these strategies respond to the manipulative and combative course that sessions with sociopaths are likely to take by offering the therapist a means either to avoid any confrontation or to rigidly control the interaction between client and therapist. These approaches tend to take one of three general paths.

One strategy is simply to refuse to treat them. If a sociopath ends up on the caseload of a clinician such as this, the client is generally ignored except when his or her behavior has to be confronted.

The second strategy is based on the belief that sociopaths are incapable of establishing a genuine relationship in therapy or anywhere else. (This is the clinical way of saying that they are basically untreatable.) Here, clinicians will provide a very structured, time-limited, controlling, and punishment-oriented format.

Therapists who approach sociopaths in this manner talk a lot about how important it is "not to let these people get over." Their belief is that "getting over" is all the client wants to do. The therapist takes a defensive and threatened posture that I call "The Fort Knox School of Counseling." The therapist has the valuables, and the object is to prevent the client from stealing them. Treatment is considered successful if the therapist can foil the client's attempt at manipulation and keep the gold safe in the vault.

Yochelson and Samenow (1977, 117) provide an example of the cognitive interventions that this method often favors. They state, "Crimes are the outcomes of thinking processes and it is the thinking processes that are our focus." Their instructions to clinicians for the first meeting with a sociopathic client contain the following advice:

> Early in the meeting it is essential to inform the criminal that
> complaining about and blaming his criminality on the circumstances
> of life is an exercise in futility when used with us. We go on to say
> that the room is too small for two crybabies. (117)

The third stance is not an overtly defensive or punitive one. Here, therapists take a rather helpless approach. While they still believe that almost everything they have to offer is useless to a sociopath, they do want to provide something— albeit something that involves the least possible effort on their part. (Of course, offering as little as possible limits the client's opportunities to manipulate the therapist.) Typically, these clinicians will focus on a particular topic in a time-limited, highly structured, cognitively-based group format. The intention is to make the treatment as close as possible to an educational class.

None of these approaches are successful. The first does not even attempt to make an effort. The second does protect the clinician, but sociopaths are usually familiar with this stance and tend to react to it with anger and frustration. The third approach comes close to the sociopath's mutual-use pact. The therapists offer something to assuage their sense of obligation. Clients receive a certain amount of information, some of which may be useful in an intellectual sense, and are reassured that they will not have to engage in any self-examination or to change.

Recent New Perspectives

Two theorists have recently offered different perspectives in order to open new avenues of intervention in work with psychopathic clients. (Their work is directly relevant to sociopathic clients in that both authors criticize current diagnostic criteria and use the terms "psychopathy" and "sociopathy" in quite general ways.) In Britain, Hodge (1992) proposed conceptualizing psychopathy as an addiction to violence that has more links to posttraumatic stress disorder than to a personality disorder. And in New Zealand, Mullen (1992) suggested that psychopaths have a conduct disorder of adulthood that was caused by a disturbance in learning social and moral codes of conduct in childhood.

These attempts are laudable, and work like this is vital if the treatment of sociopathy is ever to enter the mainstream of mental health care. Unfortunately, neither study focuses specifically on the sociopath's disturbed ability to relate with others; both essentially provide a new framework for analyzing some of the symptoms associated with these disorders.

"Talking the Talk"

All of the current interventions maintain maximum emotional distance between therapist and client. Although theoreticians clearly indicate that sociopaths need the most work in the area of relationships with others, all of these approaches avoid establishing a therapeutic relationship, based on the familiar justification that sociopaths are incapable of forming one.

Cognitive interventions alone will not help a sociopath correct his or her "thinking errors." Sociopaths know perfectly well how to think. What they don't know how to do is feel. This, in my opinion, is the source of their thinking errors.

Sociopaths continue to deny and to lie because they are unable to realize that they are causing other people pain. They hear it said that they are, but the statement does not make any sense to them. As long as they are unable to identify truly with others, sociopaths will have no way to correct their thinking errors. They will just go through the motions of parroting whatever the treatment person says so that they can get whatever it is they are trying to manipulate. They will "talk the talk" without "walking the walk."

The same point can be made from a more theoretical stance by citing the many authors who make the argument that psychodynamic therapy is the treatment of choice for preoedipal conditions. (See Balint 1968; Kernberg 1975; Meloy 1988; and Boyer, Bryce, and Giovacchini 1990.) Balint describes clients such as these as being in a primitive preverbal state in terms of their capacity to form relationships with others. Further, he states:

> [M]ost important . . . is to help the patient to develop a primitive relationship in the analytic situation corresponding to his compulsive pattern and maintain it in undisturbed peace till he can discover the possibility of new forms of object relationship, experience them, and experiment with them. Since the basic fault, as long as it is active, determines the forms of object relationship available to any individual, a necessary task of the treatment is to inactivate the basic fault by creating conditions in which it can heal off. (167)

Although it is quite possible that the high failure rate of treatment for sociopaths can be attributed to the fact that the underlying character pathology is not addressed in most interventions, this type of treatment is rarely attempted with this population.

Other Treatment Settings

Since sociopaths are considered by and large to be incapable of establishing relationships, they have been shut out of traditional mental health treatment. While they have not been closed out of self-help and support groups, even the best intentions of these groups do not work—not because such groups label sociopaths as hopeless, but because basic diagnostic information is not used in the interventions they provide.

Since so many sociopaths have substance abuse problems, Twelve Step groups are often a source of help that they will seek out or to which they are mandated. And this program will accept sociopaths as it does everyone else. However, sociopaths cannot use the program in the same manner as others do without the accompaniment of some effective psychotherapy. Without therapy, this situation can have tragic consequences.

One common outcome is that people with sociopathic and narcissistic traits who become involved with a Twelve Step program end up becoming "stars." They say all the right things and appear to do all the right things. Others in the program assume that these individuals are functioning as well as they seem to be and start to look to them as role models. Their participation in the supervisory aspects of the program is increased.

The problem is that people with this diagnostic combination cannot internalize the work. Once again, they are gaining their self-esteem from an external source; its whole basis is what "the program" thinks of them. Since anything that would tarnish that approval has to be avoided, they are unable to admit any problems they are having or draw on the program for meaningful support. When events become overwhelming, they are essentially on their own; to ask for help would threaten the external source of self-esteem.

At this point, sociopaths caught in these circumstances begin to live a double life. They feel angry and humiliated because they once again cannot get what they need, and these feelings often lead them to begin stealing from the program itself. Other program participants feel betrayed—and yet the sociopaths had really been stealing all along, even though no one knew it and the theft did not involve material items.

This failure is as tragic for the sociopaths as it is for the program. They believed as sincerely as everyone else did that they were doing well. Since they are unable to make assessments about their own internal functioning, they relied on others to do so—others who were supposed to know.

When they lose control, they not only lose the program as a support system, but they also see themselves as failures. This is a terrifying outcome, particularly since this type of person has usually sought help unsuccessfully in the past. If the Twelve Steps won't work, then nothing will; this is the end of the road. And events occurring in this sequence will often culminate in a suicide attempt.

So how can a therapist establish a therapeutic bond with such a difficult client? How can one successfully enter and complete the first stage of therapy with sociopathic clients?

The next three chapters describe the stages of therapy, from the first session to termination of treatment, as they apply to individuals with a preponderance of sociopathic traits. To the extent that other personality disorders and Axis I diagnoses are part of the client's personality structure, treatment will need to focus to a greater degree on those areas; however, the interventions presented here can be used in response to sociopathic traits in conjunction with many other types of therapies and treatments.

These three chapters are supplemented by a clinical workbook (appendix C). The workbook focuses on tasks that the clinician and the client can do, individually or together, to help gain clarity and to better articulate the various aspects of the treatment process. Given the complexity of that process, you may find it helpful to refer to the corresponding sections of the workbook as you work through the beginning, middle, and end stages covered here.

11

The Beginning Stage

There are three basic goals for the first phase of therapy with any client:

1. The establishment of a working relationship
2. The formulation of a diagnostic/psychosocial assessment
3. The development of an initial treatment plan

The establishment of the relationship and the diagnostic assessment occur simultaneously. The formulation of the initial treatment plan occurs toward the end of the beginning stage.

The Starting Point

From the first session on, there are four levels of material to listen for throughout the course of successful therapy. These are the manifest content, the latent content, the client's coping patterns and emotional cycles, and the dynamics of the treatment relationship.

Manifest content is simply what is said. At this level, the client's words need to be heard at face value.

Latent content is defined as what the client's words symbolize or represent, what the unconscious message is.

As therapists listen to clients and begin to gain a sense of what they do to manage their lives, individual coping styles and emotional cycles become apparent, similar to the routines that guide people through their days. These patterns provide important insights for the therapist.

Finally, transference and countertransference need to be monitored continually.

All of these levels of listening will be explored in greater detail throughout this section.

From the Client's Perspective

At the start of establishing a treatment relationship with sociopathic clients, it is vital to keep in mind how clients perceive the first meeting. Typically, a sociopathic client's previous experiences with service providers will have been negative and unsuccessful. These clients arrive with the belief that the therapist will not want to help them; they expect to encounter a graduate from the Fort Knox School of Counseling who will need to be manipulated into providing any help at all. While these clients would normally be looking forward to the challenge, in this instance the humiliation is too overwhelming, and so they arrive feeling angry and resentful and suspicious.

Almost immediately, clients will begin assessing the intelligence of the therapist and scouting for "do-gooder" traits. This assessment will determine how much manipulating they can do.

Manipulation will make the relationship into something that is familiar, understandable, and manageable for sociopaths. In this context, Madden (1987, 62) notes that violent patients accept nothing at face value. Hypervigilance of this type is a defense that protects violent patients from possible danger; since such patients do not trust themselves or their own resources, they cannot trust others.

The next greatest need for sociopathic clients is to reduce their humiliation. They attempt to do so by controlling the interaction as much as possible; they make demands, and they do whatever they can to keep the therapist off balance. They also lie about almost everything they say about themselves. They try to present themselves as they think the therapist wants them to be.

The Therapist's Opening Stance

My own experience is that a sociopathic client will normally walk out of a successful first meeting feeling calmer and slightly more confused—and also a little hopeful that some real help may be gained. Accordingly, I look forward to the meeting. I approach the client in a warm and comforting fashion, and I look hard for something to like in him or her.

I use the diagnostic impressions that I glean as the meeting progresses to adjust my level of engagement. Warmth can be threatening to some clients, and if I sense a significant amount of paranoia, I will become more emotionally distant as quickly as possible. In contrast, if the client appears to be a sociopath with borderline traits, I try to be as warm as I can sincerely manage to be.

The first meeting is also the time to begin assessing countertransference responses and reactions and to start creating a portrait of what the world feels like from the client's point of view. In doing so, remember that sociopaths understand situations and relationships only in terms of what they can gain from them.

Interventions made from this perspective will be successful even if they are wrong. For example, if a male client says that he enjoys fighting, it is appropriate for the therapist to ask him if he sees fighting as a way to keep control of situations. Even if the client disagrees, he can still relate to the "What's in it for me?" context of the question and go on to explain what he does feel he gets out of fighting. If the therapist instead responds that it is not healthy to enjoy fighting, or asks the client to think about how the other person feels getting beaten up, the client will not be forthcoming with any more information about his feelings.

It is vital not to lie to sociopaths—not only because they can sense lies in ways that only chronic liars can, but also because the powerful repetition compulsions and projective identifications at work in their lives stem from experiences of having been lied to (and stolen from) when they were children. In attempting to heal a trauma protected by a repetition compulsion, the relationship that is established must not re-create the trauma. In order for it to be safe for the sociopath to change, the therapist must not behave as the sociopath does: he or she must not objectify the objectifier, steal from the thief, or lie to the liar.

It is also crucial not to show fear. Sociopaths are already afraid of themselves. If the therapist also becomes afraid, the therapist's fear will cause greater anxiety for the client at a time when his or her level of tolerance for anxiety is already overwhelmed by the meeting itself. Fear on the part of the therapist will cause anger from a sociopathic client.

Sociopaths can sense genuine concern as easily as they can sense dishonesty. They will initially interpret concern as weakness and take it as an indication that the therapist is someone who is easily taken advantage of. But if genuine concern is present and the therapist is not easily manipulated, the sociopathic client will not know how to respond. The discomfort that the client feels comes from being forced to experience a relationship that is outside of his or her limited range. This experience is the very beginning of the process of change.

Components of the Sociopathic Initial Presentation

Sociopathic clients do a number of things during the first few meetings that are generally quite effective at unravelling any engagement process. Foremost among these are lying, reliance on denial and projection, making demands, attempting to control the session and to break the rules, and asking questions about the therapist.

Lying

One of the most fervent complaints heard about sociopaths is their chronic lying, and clinicians can get very caught up in attempting to discern whether something a sociopathic client says is a lie. Trying to formulate an assessment from this perspective means that everything the client says has to be filtered through a "truth lens." If a statement is determined to be a lie, then it is rejected; only if it is determined to be the truth can it be accepted as part of the assessment. A clinical assessment cannot be formulated in this piecemeal way, and the interview will quickly deteriorate if the clinician is as suspicious of the client as he or she is of the clinician.

Experienced therapists know that there is no absolute truth. I would add the corollary proposition that there are no absolute lies, either. A 1992 article about lying in *The Utne Reader* included the following exercise:

> The next time you are in a group of three or more people, ask each
> person to introduce herself or himself by lying. Tell them to lie wildly,
> exorbitantly. Then notice what follows. The stories that bubble out
> are obviously bald-faced lies, often greeted by the group with gleeful
> laughter. But as you listen, notice how lying often discloses hidden
> truths. Old wounds and unfulfilled wishes come rushing to the
> surface. Frustrated athletes fib about their glory days with the Green
> Bay Packers. If truth and lying are as simple as black and white,
> how are we to make sense of these disclosures? (Tollefson 1992, 58)

Working with sociopaths has taught me wonderful lessons about how to hear what all clients say. Essentially, I make no attempt to determine "truth" until the middle stage of treatment. In a sense, I assume that almost everything about the beginning stage is a "lie," but making this assumption is simply to recognize that clients at this stage are relying more heavily on unhealthy defenses and will not be able to admit many things that they will be able to acknowledge later in treatment. Clients will try to present themselves in the best light; if attempting to do so is "lying," it is also a trait that most human beings share.

How then can the sociopath's lies be heard in a way that will help to establish a treatment relationship and to formulate a diagnostic assessment? First of all, it is useful to eliminate the entire categorization of truth as an assessment. Let the client paint the picture in whichever way he or she chooses. Asking the client to clarify what color something is or what object a shape represents is appropriate. Stating that the picture is not an accurate representation of the clinician's idea of reality is not.

Seen in this way, all of the client's statements are symbolic. They have some truth, and some untruth as well. They communicate something about the given topic (manifest content) and about other unconscious topics (latent content). The more that a client relies on denial and projection as defenses, the greater the amount of "truth" that will be communicated through latent content. When lower functioning clients lie, they reveal a great deal about themselves.

One of the reasons that sociopaths use lies in the course of treatment is to deflect the clinician from the purpose of the meeting. (This is especially true for lies of the bald-faced type.) Lies are used in this way at times when humiliation is becoming painful. I now take note of lies in the same way that I used to observe when clients would light cigarettes. Such behavior is both an attempt to reduce affect and a delaying tactic.

When clients are desperately trying to deflect my attention, they will sometimes demand that I tell them whether I believe them. My answer is usually similar to the one I make when clients want to know whether I believe their protestations of innocence: I say that I don't know, I wasn't there. If they become indignant, I then state that I accept how they are describing themselves. If that response is insufficient, I shrug and say that is the best I can do. It is difficult for them to continue to argue at this point.

For therapists who are unsure of themselves, this stance may be an uncomfortable one to take. Beginning therapists want to frame problems quickly and then fix them even more quickly. But that is not the way therapy works. If the solution were that simple, clients would not have needed to become clients; they would have figured the problem out for themselves. Any anxiety the therapist feels about this issue must be contained and shared in supervision.

Once the concept of honesty has been put aside, sociopaths' lies become extremely revealing. They are a statement of old wounds and unfulfilled wishes, as Tollefson said, and they are indicators of affect overload. But they are also something else: a statement of what the sociopath thinks that the clinician wants to hear. In other words, the lies will tell you what the client thinks you think a nonsociopath looks like and sounds like. Two valuable indications emerge from this information. One is the assessment that the client has made of the therapist (the initial transference), and the other is the client's hopes, expectations, and fears about change.

> **Case note.** During the course of our first meeting, a client told me four times that he had made $250,000 by the time he was 25 years old. My initial assessment was that this statement had probably served him well as a deflector in the past; I also suspected that he was not adept at thinking on his feet (since he did not come up with an alternative statement when his claim twice failed to elicit any response from me). In addition, his statement told me he believed that I would think that making that much money was an important achievement, and that if he got help, he either could or would be expected to achieve something similar.
>
> What did these indications suggest about his transference? I speculated that he felt he would have to do something spectacular in order to gain my positive regard—something that he was not capable of doing. Accordingly, his feeling from the outset was that he would try, but not succeed, to win my admiration. From his point of view, he not only had a problem that he felt utterly ashamed of, but

also had to talk about it to someone who would never accept him.

The "facts" behind the $250,000 were that he had stolen a good deal of money from his father's business and had used his business contacts to sell drugs. Yet I would have learned a good deal less about his inner life if he had been "honest" at that point and simply told me the "truth" about the money.

Reliance on Denial and Projection

"I didn't do it. It wasn't me. How come no one believes me?"

Denial, projection, and a little whining thrown in for good measure are usually extremely effective ways for the sociopath to anger others, therapists included. And sociopaths are experts at leveling blame. Whatever happens, it is never their fault. Anyone or everyone else is always responsible.

Since denial and projection are so closely related to lying, the clinician's stance can be much the same. Again, it is not helpful at the beginning of treatment to confront denial or projection; all that will ensue is an argument. However, just as you would not want to agree with a schizophrenic's delusional material, neither do you want to give a sociopath the impression that you believe material that you actually find doubtful or insupportable. And besides, he or she will know that you are lying.

A simple way of listening for projective identification patterns and repetition compulsions is to replace the pronouns that clients actually use with either "I" (to listen for what they think of themselves) or "you" (to listen for what they think of me). For example, imprisoned clients will often complain about prison staff during their first few meetings. A client will say that the disciplinary report he received was not his fault, that the staffperson was not being fair, that he's vengeful and jealous and racist and enjoys the power he has over inmates. All this may be quite true. But the description is also a true picture of the client's own psychopathy, as well as of his conscious perception of me and his unconscious expectation that I am also a sadist.

Listening in this manner eliminates the commonly voiced frustration that sociopaths do not talk about themselves to their therapists (except to lie, of course). It's true that sociopaths would much rather focus their attention on others, specifically to point out others' inadequacies. Aside from what such projections reveal about the client's self-perception, they also are true in another way. Sociopaths characteristically attempt to meet their needs through the environment, and these attempts inevitably do not succeed. Although the mechanism of relying on externals is the underlying problem, the fact of the matter is that the others in their life have not been able to come through with the level of support that sociopaths require.

For my part, when a sociopathic client complains in the beginning of treatment that it is all someone else's fault, I do not challenge that statement. I ask for details. I want to know more specifically what the failure was, how exactly it happened, and how the client reacted to it. I'll often ask the client to speculate about what was going on in the other person's mind. A diagnostic assessment can begin through evaluating the levels of affect and impulsivity presented through material of this kind.

This exploration is also the basis for the therapeutic relationship. Clients of this type may have never had anyone respond to them in this way before. They will find themselves telling the therapist things that they hadn't planned to talk about. Doing so will make them nervous. They will assume that they are being manipulated, but they won't be able to figure out how. Every time they try to create distance and regain control, they end up disclosing more. As their anxiety increases, they will try to reestablish control by other means.

Making Demands

Sociopaths are also famous for making demands of therapists. Some demands are outrageous, and some are quite subtle. All of them serve a twofold function: (1) to gain a sense of mastery and control, and (2) to create distance.

For sociopaths, one of two things will happen when they make a demand. Either the demand will be granted and they will win, or the demand won't be granted and they will then be free to blame the therapist for his or her lack of willingness to help. In the client's mind, he or she wins either way.

However irritating demands may be, they are still requests for help, and it is useful to hear them from that perspective. Sociopaths are requesting what they need based on their personality structure. There is much that they cannot do for themselves, and so they have to ask. At the same time, they will need to distance themselves from the other person. The dependence inherent in the demand causes humiliation, which must be discharged somehow. Angering the person whom they are making the demand of simultaneously permits the discharge of affect and prevents the person from getting too close.

This is not to say that the demands should necessarily be granted. However, a request is an important opportunity to lay some groundwork in the therapeutic relationship.

In the beginning, requests should always be treated with respect, no matter how provocative or outrageous they are. A significant amount of anxiety is behind any request, and clients are as likely to remember how the request was handled as whether it was granted.

Negotiating a solution or a compromise of some kind is the critical task for the therapist here. Sociopaths do not know how to negotiate. They demand. They threaten, or they fight. They lie or manipulate. But they don't negotiate. Showing the client how to approach a situation honestly and say no and mean it, or say no and then offer a compromise, or say yes and then follow through, are all valuable lessons and new experiences for a sociopath.

Whenever I say no in the beginning stage of treatment, I *always* try to offer an alternative. I offer something that I would be willing to do even if I am certain that the client will reject the offer. I do this for several reasons. Rejecting something that I have offered reduces the client's humiliation and permits him or her to feel some level of control. And making the offer shows respect for the person doing the asking.

Case note. An incarcerated client who had denied everything concerning his offense during the two meetings that he had attended demanded that I attend his parole hearing and recommend that he be released. I said no, but I offered a compromise. I would write a letter to the parole board stating the truth—that the client recently applied for treatment and that he had attended two sessions thus far—but I would not give the board any indication that I thought he was appropriate for release. I knew that the parole board would draw its own conclusions from the fact that the parole hearing date and the request for treatment coincided so closely. (A related note: I do not believe that treating therapists should do evaluations that are supposed to be objective in nature, such as for parole or for furloughs, for their inmate clients.)

Case note. An incarcerated client began each of our weekly sessions with a request to call his wife. (Pay phones were available in the cellblocks for personal phone calls.) I had no viable alternative, and so I simply explained our department policy (therapists' phones were to be used for inmates only in cases of emergency), reminded him that making phone calls was not the purpose of our meetings, and so on.

Nothing I said made a difference. Every time I said no, the client responded that he believed that I was trying to provoke him into a rage. (This man had killed someone. Why he thought I would want to provoke his rage was beyond me.) He would get extremely angry and stare coldly at me, but he would go on to discuss other things and would stay for the hour. And he always came back.

I had no idea what any of this meant, and I had no idea what to do other than what I was doing, so I kept doing it. After seven or eight months had passed, he came in one day and began the session with his usual request. I looked at him sadly and shook my head no. He said, "I guess the reason I'm down here is to talk about myself and not to make phone calls, huh?"

I realized that it had taken him the entire seven or eight months to be sure that I really wanted to talk to him. In this instance, giving in to his demand would have been a terrible mistake because he would have taken my doing so to mean that I wanted to avoid talking with him.

Attempts to Control the Session and to Break the Rules

Breaking the rules. Sociopaths have a love-hate relationship with rules and external structure. As they continually find themselves in situations where their lives are regulated by an external agency, they continually attempt to shape the rules to fit their needs and wants. The agency in question may be a prison, a court, a hospital, a halfway house, the parole department, the welfare department, or those government agencies that oversee families and monitor them for child abuse and neglect.

Therapists who treat sociopaths are continually placed in positions of authority, of interpreting and enforcing rules. Those therapists who feel uncomfortable acknowledging the power inherent in their position can find it extremely unpleasant to continually struggle with sociopathic clients over the rules. This struggle may seem more palatable if it is seen in clinical terms rather than legal ones.

As noted in chapter 4, sociopaths' need for external management and annihilation anxiety cause them to seek out very structured environments. At the same time, their dependence on others produces humiliation and a pervasive sense of dread concerning potential loss of identity. The sociopath's need to bend or break the rules is an attempt to maintain a sense of self in the face of this merger anxiety.

In this context, power struggles over rules can be seen as a reflection of clients' massive ambivalence about containment—and the sociopath's means of communicating that he or she is overwhelmed. In effect, the amount of anxiety and frustration attached to the need to break the rules can be correlated with the intensity of the client's need for the rules themselves: the more that a sociopathic client insists that the rules should not apply to him or her, the greater the need is for an external structure. And the more intense the need for structure is, the more intense the humiliation about the need.

Accordingly, rules need to be enforced in a way that does not destroy the sociopath's sense of self. Doing so is always an interesting balancing act, and a combination of interventions seems to work best in the beginning stage of treatment. (More flexibility can be introduced at a later stage.)

First, it is once again vital to remember that the sociopathic client's only concern is how something will benefit him or her. This stance cannot be argued with at this point in the treatment process; the therapist must approach from this perspective and focus on pointing out the benefits that the client will obtain for following the rules.

Second, it is equally vital to reinforce positively anything that the client is doing right. No matter how infuriating a battle over the rules becomes, encouragement is critical. Sociopathic clients need to feel that their therapist is on their side and wants them to succeed.

Third, enforce the rules fairly. Avoid any temptation to use the rules to get back at clients for all the trouble they are causing.

And last, when a sociopath needs to be told that he or she did something wrong or that a rule is going to be enforced, do so in a neutral tone of voice. Approach this task as though you were simply passing on some information that the client needs to have.

I see the whole process as akin to dealing with a troublesome adolescent who needs to be told that the rules are in place for a reason and cannot be set aside. Explain the reason if it seems appropriate or useful to do so. Clarify which rules can be negotiated, and which cannot. If a system of privileges is in place, point out what the client can do to earn any relaxation of the rules. Offer limited choices if any are possible. If the client rejects the alternatives that are offered, then describe some options that the client would definitely not want and reoffer the limited choices. Validate feelings of anger and frustration, but set limits if the expression of them becomes inappropriate. Do not become patronizing or condescending. Try to keep in mind something likable about the client and hang on to it for dear life.

War stories. Another of the varied ways that sociopathic clients attempt to control therapists and sessions is to tell "war stories." These are recitations of past events that the client has repeated many times. They are related with little feeling, and the therapist's capacity to interact with the client is limited while they are being told. Their recitation gives the client an opportunity to enjoy the activity being described all over again and is a means of forcing the therapist to experience the activity. Since they are a related type of communication, I deal with war stories the same way I deal with lies.

Intimidation. Sociopathic clients will also try to use a little intimidation to control sessions. The more subtle forms are discussing violence or sex in graphic detail or leaning over the desk to intrude on the clinician's personal space. This is one form of control that needs to be addressed directly and immediately or it will escalate.

> **Case note.** A large, well-muscled inmate covered with tattoos requested treatment. He had never asked for help before and clearly felt quite humiliated doing so.
>
> During our first session, he used a nickname to address me and reached over to touch me on the forearm as if to make a point. He was behaving as if we were old friends chatting over coffee. Even though I knew that he had served a lot of time and was well aware that inmates are not permitted to touch staff, I gave him the benefit of the doubt and moved my arm away without saying anything. The next time he had to reach further over to touch me, and I responded by asking him to please not touch me. He looked surprised and said, "Of course." His facial expression indicated that he felt it was I who was overreacting.
>
> He made no more attempts at physical intimidation, but it took him months to be able to talk about this incident. If I had not confronted him, the behavior almost certainly would have continued and escalated.

Overt attempts at intimidation, such as verbal or physical threats, need to be dealt with swiftly. The therapist must make an immediate determination about his or her safety level. If he or she is not feeling safe, then the meeting needs to be terminated. If the therapist feels that the client will not attack him or her, then the client needs to be approached in a calm, direct fashion, and limits need to be spelled out. (See chapter 14 for detailed discussion of safety considerations.)

Flirtation. As the previous case note indicates, sociopaths will also attempt to flirt and to engage in dating behavior to shift the balance of power in the room. Clients also engage in this behavior simply because they do not know any other way of relating. Using their sexuality makes them feel less humiliated as well. It is something that they know they have and that they think they know what to do with.

Flirtation occurring in the beginning of treatment can usually be ignored unless it is quite overt or causes significant distress for the therapist. If setting a limit is necessary, it is best to frame it as a short, simple reminder of the purpose of the meeting.

Questions about the Therapist

Sociopathic clients, especially ones with narcissistic traits, are experts at getting therapists to talk about themselves. They appear to be genuinely interested and concerned. One client put this "concern" in perspective when he remarked during the middle stage of treatment that knowing things about me at the beginning would have helped to make up for all the things I knew about him. His curiosity didn't mean that he cared; it meant that he wanted some information to hold over my head.

The more that sociopathic clients know about the therapist, the more room they have to manipulate. The more questions the therapist answers, the more questions they will ask. The questions may be intrusive and personal ("Are you married? Do you have children? Where do you live? Do you own your own home?"), or they may be more subtle. The client may ask how the therapist deals with a particular issue that is being explored or if the therapist has ever experienced anything like what the client is describing. A still more subtle approach opens with a concerned look at the beginning of a session and the question: "How are you? How is it going? You seem a little down today."

The therapist should defer exploring which of these questions he or she might want to answer until the middle stage of treatment, when the client is beginning to be able to identify with others. Before that, any information that the therapist provides will only be used in an attempt to shift the balance of power.

I will answer two types of questions at the beginning of treatment. One type is any question the client asks about my professional training and background. All clients have a right to know this information. The other type of question is one that is frequently asked in prison: "Why do you do this? What do you get out of it? Why are you working in a prison?" (Or my favorite variation: "Can't you get a job anywhere else?")

What these questions seek to uncover is the source of the therapist's motivation. If the therapist responds that working in prison pays well, sociopaths will readily understand this explanation—but they will then feel free to perceive the therapist as they do other sociopaths. I state that I do the work by choice, and that I do it because I like helping people. (Clients immediately label me as a "do-gooder" and assume that they will be able to take advantage of me.) Note that I would not make this statement if it were not an accurate reflection of my motivation. Therapists who have not chosen to work with sociopaths or who are committed to the work for other reasons should say so (and expect that the sociopath will then find another label for them.)

Sociopaths can ask what appear to be very innocent questions. The therapist can best gauge whether to answer them by observing his or her own immediate affective response when the question is posed. If there is a twinge of anxiety or a fleeting sense that something is not quite right, then the question should not be answered. At the beginning of treatment, in the course of describing the process and my expectations, I also discuss confidentiality and its limits. I note that if I ask a question that the client does not want to answer, all he or she needs to do is to say so and I will respect his or her reluctance. I then add that I may also choose not to answer certain questions. If I then later decline to answer a question, my refusal does not come as a complete surprise.

When male sociopaths attempt to derail a session by flirting with a female therapist, they often begin by asking about the therapist's marital status. If the therapist won't answer, the client typically feigns indignation and says something like "How can I know if you can help me with my marital problem if I don't know whether you're married?"

This struggle can sometimes lead to a productive discussion about differences between the therapist and the client. As stated before, African Americans and poor people are overrepresented among clients diagnosed with antisocial personality disorder. Therapists tend to be white and middle class. Sociopaths tend to be male. Social workers, who work more often with sociopaths than other mental health providers do, are largely female. Differences in marital status are insignificant compared with these other differences.

At the beginning of treatment, I welcome an opportunity to recognize the obvious fact that the client and I have lived very different lives and to acknowledge differences of gender, race, criminal history, drug addiction, gang affiliation, experience with incarceration, and so on. I admit that there are many things that I do not know about their experiences, culture, and belief system, and let them know that I will be asking a lot of questions in order to learn from them. I encourage clients to ask questions about my values and beliefs and to compare them with their own. I then talk about my basic belief that although people come from very different places in life, they all have feelings in common—for example, that anyone from any walk of life would feel sad and alone when incarcerated. I add that even though I have not had comparable firsthand experience, I have listened to many people tell me about their lives and I use this knowledge to try to understand others. (For a more detailed discussion of the management of therapist-client differences, see chapter 15.)

A conversation like this is a strange one for sociopaths. At this point, they are so unaware of their feelings and so incapable of identifying with anyone else that these ideas are absolutely foreign. But even if they have no idea what I am talking about, they still tend to respond well to a tone of genuine interest and concern. Most also appreciate the therapist opening the door for them to talk about racism and how it affects them. For the most part, clients will not bring these issues up on their own unless they are reasonably sure that the response will be an accepting one.

Some clients, and particularly those who participate in Twelve Step programs, will state that they cannot get any meaningful help from someone who is not in recovery. Although I do not share that belief, if the client genuinely feels that way, then I will tell him or her that I have never been addicted to anything other than to cigarettes and that I quit those many years ago. If there is no room for compromise, then I will refer the client to a therapist who is in recovery (if one is available) or back to Alcoholics Anonymous or Narcotics Anonymous.

However, some clients who raise this issue are not expressing a genuine concern. In this instance, the conversation tends to go something like this:

Client: If you are not in recovery, then you can't possibly understand what I'm going through and you can't help me.

Therapist: I work with a lot of people in recovery or struggling with an addiction, so I don't share your belief that I can't be helpful.

Client: Oh, come on! Didn't you use drugs as a teenager? Don't tell me you've never smoked marijuana. How much do you drink?

A litany of questions like these can be very irritating—and if the sociopath senses a great deal of irritation, then the questions are achieving the purpose of derailing the session and reducing the sociopath's humiliation, and he or she will continue asking similar questions. The best response is simply to remind clients that the point of the meeting is to give them an opportunity to talk about themselves. If this point is made politely and respectfully, clients will generally move on. (Of course, if the therapist sounds sarcastic or impatient, the struggle will continue.)

Basic Interventions and Approaches During the Beginning Stage

Most of the interventions and approaches used in the beginning stage of treatment with a sociopath are the same as those for any other type of lower functioning client.

- Try to perceive from the client's point of view.

- Stay where the client is.

- Approach in a respectful and genuine fashion.

- Contain countertransference reactions.

- Don't lie.

- Listen to everything that is said with the goal of gaining the most clinical information possible.

- Know when to set limits.

- Acknowledge cultural and racial differences.

- Offer alternatives to demands.

- Provide positive reinforcement for appropriate behavior.

- Ignore provocative behavior (except when setting a limit is necessary).

- Remember that someone's behavior is a more valid indicator of "truth" than are his or her words.

Obviously, many of these approaches apply to work with higher functioning clients as well.

As section II indicated, countertransference management is a bit more complicated with this population than it is with some others. No matter how obnoxious the client's behavior seems, the therapist must remember that it functions as a coping mechanism and is there for a reason. Similarly, it is important to stay focused on the reason why interactions with this client are taking place: namely, in order for the clinician to learn about his or her coping mechanisms and their purposes.

All this will seem easier if therapist can find something likable about the client and keep in mind that he or she has the potential to behave quite differently (that is, much better) than he or she is behaving at the moment. It is also useful to remember that sociopathic clients are just as frightened and humiliated during the beginning stage of treatment as other clients are. They are there for help. Their lives are falling apart in some major way; otherwise they would not be knocking at the therapist's door.

If all of this works reasonably well, then the client will want to enter into a "mutual-use pact" with the therapist. The therapeutic relationship has to be framed in this way at this point because the only other connection that makes any sense to the client is one in which the therapist gets victimized. Here, however, the therapist can set the terms for the mutual use. The pact is best communicated as such: "I have something to offer you, but it is not what you think. And yes, you have something to offer me, but, again, it is not what you think." The client will think that this is some sort of game and that he or she will probably win it.

Another look at the session that went wrong at the beginning of chapter 10 should help to bring out the basic elements in establishing a strong therapeutic foundation with a sociopathic client.

Therapist: What brings you here to this agency? What can I help you with?

Client: My wife said I have to come here.

My first thought is that this is a good sign. If this man is following through with something his wife told him to do, then it means to me that he is showing some level of commitment to her and that he is interested in getting help. Note the need for external management inherent in the client's reason for making the appointment.

Therapist: Why is that?

Client: I don't know! There's something wrong with her!

From this touchy response I can assess the man's capacity for humiliation (not much), which indicates to me that I have to approach in a way that will not feel like a threat to him. So I do not pursue the discussion of what is wrong with him, and instead go on to ask him to tell me what is wrong with her. I get two results in this way. (1) He relaxes at a conscious level; he thinks he is off the hook. (2) At an unconscious level, he is freer to tell me what is wrong with him. Note that I not only hear the projection in his second statement as denial of his responsibility, but also as projection: something *is* wrong with him, and this is how he is telling me that there is.

Therapist: What do you sense is wrong with her?

Client: Oh, she's just crazy. She can't make up her mind about anything. First she says one thing, then she says another thing. You know, I'm trying to make her happy, but I can't because she's always changing her mind. Plus she spends money! You wouldn't believe the shopping she does. Of course, you probably would, being a female and all.

Therapist: And then she blames you?

Client: Yeah! And I didn't do anything wrong! I just work my job and get my paycheck and give it to her, and she blows it and then blames me! I don't know what's with her!

From this I hear that he is experiencing anxiety levels that are too high for him to manage and that he's probably using a good deal of the household money for himself (for drugs, gambling, or whatever). He isn't sure whether I'll take her side ("being a female and all"), and so he attempts to cover up his own responsibility and flirt simultaneously.

These are pertinent indications, but I would ignore them at this point and focus on the history of their marriage: how long they have been together, whether there have been separations, where they live (on their own or in a parent's home), and so on. From this relatively unthreatening context, I would then go on to ask how he is feeling about the difficulties in their relationship.

My guess is that his response would reveal a downward spiral typical of those many sociopaths experience. He is utterly dependent on her, but still cannot manage day by day. She is getting increasingly upset with him and escalating her demands and expectations while his capacity is actually diminishing. His anxiety and humiliation levels are growing, and I would be concerned about the risk of violence.

Since I have made no statements that confront the client directly, at this point he thinks that I am either a potential ally or someone who can easily be manipulated. Either way, he will be willing to attend another appointment.

Toward the end of the meeting, he would make the request concerning the phone call to his wife.

> *Client:*   She said if I don't come here, that she's going to throw me out. So can you call her and tell her I came here like she said?
>
> *Therapist:* Absolutely. I think it shows a lot of commitment to her and to your marriage that you did come here. I'll need you to sign a release of information to permit me to speak to her.
>
> *Client:*   Sure.
>
> *Therapist:* The other thing is, if you think it might be useful at some point, she is welcome to join us here.

I pose the possibility of meeting with them as a couple in this manner because it increases the client's sense of control over the meeting. I have no expectation that he would want his wife to join us at this point, because she would then be free to give her version of what is going on. But he can keep the option in mind for the future, and I still have access to his wife through the phone call, which will give me a chance to assess her level of risk being with this man.

If this session had taken place in an outpatient clinic, then I would not know at this point whether he will attend the next appointment. Nor would this single meeting have given me a thorough sense of his level of functioning. If he were to show up again, that development would indicate that he has some significant capacity to use treatment.

Formulation of a Diagnostic/ Psychosocial Assessment

During the course of the first several meetings, the therapist will normally be focused on four crucial tasks:

1. Identifying the nature of the crisis that brought the client to treatment

2. Assessing the client's environment and its impact

3. Evaluating the client's capacity for treatment

4. Formulating a diagnosis

The Crisis That Brought the Client to Treatment

Even when the precipitant to treatment is clear (as it is when the client is mandated to treatment or is admitted to an inpatient treatment program), it is still important to assess what the nature of the crisis was *for the client*. Invariably, the client's description of events will be different from the official records or from friends' and relatives' accounts. If the client feels that everyone else is at fault, then what is the crisis for him or her? Although dealing with the client's provocative behavior during an initial session can make it easy to lose sight of this question, the answer is a critical indicator in making a diagnostic assessment.

The Client's Environment

Although assessment of the environment is important with all clients, it provides more information in the case of sociopaths, again due to the level of dependence on external factors. As a general rule, the more restrictive the environment, the lower functioning the client.

An assessment can also indicate, to some degree, how much the client will have to rely on the environment for containment in order to tolerate treatment. Many incarcerated clients have told me that they had attempted treatment on the outside but either did not follow through, could not afford it, or were turned away. They often felt that they might not have committed their crimes if they had been able to "get some help on the street." My assessment is usually that clients such as these would have been unable to manage treatment without the structure of some sort of residential setting.

The Client's Capacity for Treatment

Motivation to change behavior is an important factor to assess within the first few meetings. If the client is comfortable with his or her current situation, then there is little incentive to do anything differently.

The client's capacity to verbalize is also a factor in determining suitability for treatment. If there is a large amount of organicity and violent acting-out behavior, then it may not be possible for the client to contain affect well enough to tolerate sitting in a room and talking about painful and humiliating subjects.

Although the amount of psychopathy is difficult to assess in the first few meetings, it is also an important indicator of the client's capacity to use treatment. Psychopathy becomes clearer to see in the middle stage of treatment. Meloy (1988, 316–324) states that use of an assessment scale for psychopathy developed by Hare (1985) along with Meloy's own structured interview format will aid in assessing psychopathy in the beginning of treatment.

Formulating a Diagnosis

The components of the sociopath's initial presentation can be assessed as a means to formulate an initial diagnosis. Level of reliance on provocation and lower level defense mechanisms give an indication of ego strength and capacity to tolerate affect. Material that the client lies about can be evaluated for knowledge of the client's internal states and transference reactions. Levels of intrusion (shown by attempts to get the therapist to break the rules and by asking personal questions) indicate difficulties with interpersonal boundaries. Assessment of all of these traits will give a picture of the types and level of personality disorder.

If the client presents with a suicidal crisis, then chances increase that he or she is a person with a sociopathic and borderline mix. Another indicator of evidence of borderline traits is when clients steal compulsively but do not keep what they steal, and instead either immediately give the items or money away or create a situation in which it is stolen from them.

Symptoms of Axis I disorders such as substance abuse, major mental illness, PTSD, and organicity should become clear during the first few meetings as well. Sexual offending may take some time to assess as the sociopath will avoid discussing this issue in the beginning (unless, of course, he or she has been mandated for sex offender treatment).

Although diagnostic assessment should begin with the first session, the therapist should remain alert for diagnostic indications and continue assessment throughout the course of treatment.

Formulation of the Initial Treatment Plan

As the diagnostic impressions become clearer, so should issues for the treatment plan.

Although it is not necessary to sit down with the client and go over every detail of a formal written plan (unless this procedure is mandated in the given agency), the client does need to participate in the planning process. I ask clients what they think the problem areas are, try to give them some idea what the middle stage of treatment is like, and elicit their view of where to go from here.

At this point, clients will have a basic idea of how the meetings are structured and what goes on in them. They now need to make an informed decision about whether they want to continue.

Some clients say no. Some honestly admit that they do not want to make the effort. Others simply say that they are not ready to give up their lifestyle, or acknowledge that they do not feel they are capable of going through the process. I always praise these clients for being honest and invite them to come back whenever they do feel ready. And many do return.

Other clients who say that they want to continue are not really interested in treatment. For some inmates, treatment just provides a welcome chance to get out of their cells and stare at a female. In other mandated situations, continuing is the simplest way to avoid the ramifications of not continuing. Here, I make it clear what the guidelines are and offer to write a letter to the referring authority explaining that the attempt was valid but will not go forward. I want to leave the door open for these clients as well; if the end is handled well, they will also often return. Successful treatment with sociopaths generally happens in fits and starts.

The treatment planning discussion can be a strain for some clients; these individuals tend to be those who have already formed an attachment to the therapist and are ready to start the middle stage. If the discussion makes the client anxious, the therapist should not push to continue it. Determining the client's attitude toward the details of the plan is much less important than evaluating the client's motivation to continue the work.

> **Case note.** Bill, a 22-year-old African American serving a life sentence, requested treatment. Although he claimed to be looking for help adjusting to the prison, he mentioned that he has served multiple sentences in the past and could not be any more specific about the kind of help he needed. My attempt to get some history from him met with charming evasion. He reported no distress or anxiety. He stated that he was married and that this relationship was going well.
>
> At the end of a second similar meeting, I told him that therapy was like going to the doctor's office: the doctor can't help if the patient has no complaints. He was still unable to state a specific problem, so I concluded by inviting him to contact me in the future if anything did come up that he wanted to work on.
>
> His records indicated that severe behavioral problems had caused his transfer from an out-of-state facility. Yet he made no reference to this fact and was unwilling to ask for whatever it was that he wanted.

> **Case note.** John, a white male, was 24 years old and serving ten years for sexual assault. Although this was his first incarceration and his first sexual assault, he had been involved in compulsive drug abuse, burglary, and various sorts of criminal mischief since preadolescence.
>
> Although he clearly met the criteria for sociopathy, John also met the criteria for paranoid, schizotypal, and narcissistic personality disorders, and he had psychopathic and borderline traits as well. He had been in therapy on and off since age 7, with several hospitalizations during his adolescence, but this was the first time he had voluntarily requested treatment; on all of the other occasions, his parents had insisted that he begin treatment. As soon as he was referred to me, his parents began calling almost daily to monitor our progress and tell me how to treat him. They were clearly terrified of what might happen to their son in prison.
>
> During his first several meetings with me, his basic presentation was that I could not help him. He was terrified for his life because he was refusing to "sign into PC," that is, to live in an area of protective custody segregated from the general population as most (particularly white) sex offenders ended up doing. He was clear about the help he wanted: he wanted to stop committing sexual offenses and be able to get by day by day in the prison. Yet he would not tell me anything about himself, and he refused to sign releases for summaries of his past treatment experiences. (Although I normally refuse to see individuals who refuse to sign releases, I

made an exception in his case.) He stated that he could not remember anything about the sexual assault.

In addition to this gap in his memory, John was also experiencing some severe sensory distortions. He reported having hallucinations, and any frustration, humiliation, or fear caused a cascade of extremely violent ideation. Although he stated that he had an IQ of 170+, he was clearly unable to think through even the most basic plan for how to approach daily management. At the same time, he was capable of quite detailed plans for making bombs, setting fires, and other types of mayhem.

My initial impression was that he was a walking time bomb. Although many clients in prison express violent thoughts and fantasies, 95 percent of what is said is never done. However, given this man's history of acting out violently, I was convinced he was more than capable of following through on any of his ideas, and my first assessment was that he would be better served by a placement in a cellblock for mentally ill inmates. He was somewhat agreeable until he realized that this plan would mean that he would have to return to a maximum security prison. (I also learned that the program would not take him because he was too violent.) So I was left to try to monitor him through weekly hour-long appointments.

Understandably, John approached me during the first several months as if I were an enemy. Given his paranoia, I did not try to argue with him to convince him that I was not. He subjected everything I said and every question I asked to an intense scrutiny and then usually concluded that he would not tell me what I wanted to know. When I suggested ways to manage within the prison, he would sneer at me and tell me how unworkable the strategies that I was suggesting were. He constantly blamed me for my lack of help and did his best to make me feel incompetent and uninformed.

I realized that one of the first things I needed to do was to reassure his parents that he was okay (or as okay as he could manage to be) so that they could approach him in a calmer fashion. He was very dependent on them, and their panic was terrifying him. Although I was able to enlist his parents' help, this development caused still another problem. His parents had hated the one former therapist whom he had liked, and so when his parents began to feel comfortable with me, their trust made John even more suspicious of me.

That was how the beginning went: everything I did to address a massive problem caused another equally large problem. I began to understand why he could not plan anything; the effort could easily seem pointless. Yet although he was deeply suspicious of me, and remained very sarcastic and hostile, he never made any attempt to intimidate or frighten me. He was so needy and so scared that he bonded to me almost immediately. It was a bond fraught with intense and conflicting demands.

Case note. Ted was an African American inmate in his late twenties, doing "life on the installment plan." He had a long history of IV drug abuse and nonviolent criminal activity. He requested treatment for "anxiety," stating that he had received Valium in another facility and that it helped a great deal. I made an appointment for a medication evaluation with a psychiatrist (who eventually placed him on an antidepressant). Although he wanted me to help him convince the doctor to prescribe Valium for him, I refused; I explained that Valium is not the prescription of choice for clients with histories of drug addiction. But I did make sure he had access to the doctor.

Ted reported that he did not want to return to prison anymore. He remarked that he would start out very motivated to change, but then lose his motivation as the sentence dragged on. His recidivism, he said, was the court system's fault; if he received smaller sentences, he would be able to remain drug-free.

I asked him where he was in his sentence; he was approaching the middle of it and once again losing interest in working on issues. That development appeared to be the precipitant that brought him to treatment.

I pointed out that he could not change the sentence and went on to ask him what he could change about himself that might increase his chances of remaining sober on the street. He couldn't think of anything and asked for any guidelines that I could recommend. I suggested that he begin to attend NA. I also asked him to think back to the times when he had begun to use again after a period of sobriety and try to see what had made him start to use again. He acknowledged that that sounded like a very useful way to start and agreed to do a lot of thinking about it. He requested weekly meetings.

He did not show up for the following three meetings. I wrote to him telling him that his case would be closed and his medication would stop if he did not show up for his next scheduled appointment. Two days before that appointment, a block officer called to tell me that Ted had asked to see me on an emergency basis. I called for him, and he came in.

His emergency was that he had received a disciplinary report earlier that day; he wanted me to go to the disciplinary board and state that his medication made it impossible for him to follow the rule that he had broken. I said that I would not do that. He argued with me. I then agreed to go, with the condition that I would also recommend that he lose his prison job. (Since the job entailed following the same rule, then any medication that made it impossible for him to follow it would prevent him from performing the job as well.) He laughed, put up his hands, and said, "Okay, okay."

We talked about how he could approach the disciplinary board in a way that would decrease his chances of losing his housing or job. I also made it clear that I respond poorly to requests for emergency meetings when clients don't show up for the regular ones.

He left the meeting relieved and calmer, and he went on to handle the hearing well enough to negotiate successfully for the smallest punishment. Previously, an incident such as this would have ended with him in segregation.

During the next few meetings, he described being unable to tolerate the frustration engendered by a routine day in prison. My assessment was that dealing with sobriety on the outside was significantly beyond his present capacity. The treatment plan became to focus on his day-to-day management of himself in the prison: affect tolerance, impulse control, and decision-making skills.

12

The Middle Stage

Therapy would be a much more convenient process if its stages moved in a logical linear progression from beginning to middle to end. In reality, clients move back and forth from stage to stage in response to transference and countertransference work and according to the ease or difficulty of various tasks. Clients' internal states and problems that they encounter in their daily lives can also speed up or hold back the progress of the treatment.

The First Phase of the Middle Stage

The middle stage of the process has three distinct phases of its own. The first of these is reached when the beginning stage ends and a therapeutic relationship has been established.

Clients now have some sense that the therapist cares about their welfare. They can tolerate some amount of confrontation and can confide in the therapist to some degree. The relationship feels as if something solid were there, although it does not remain so consistently, and disclosure or confrontation can still often cause clients to regress, withdraw, and become suspicious.

The beginning of the middle is stage is particularly rocky. Clients test the therapist a good deal during this period, although the purpose of the testing differs from that of the beginning stage.

Following a successful beginning, clients experience some reduction in their levels of anxiety and frustration. They recognize that the therapist has learned some things about them, perhaps more than most others in their lives know. Clients may even feel some hope that they will actually be able to change. At this point, testing is an attempt to find out if the therapist really can tolerate and accept all of the "bad" that clients feel that they are and have done. Seeking this information is frightening for clients, and they often revert to questioning the usefulness of counseling.

Testing also continues in the form of demands. Clients still expect the therapist to fix whatever mess they have created. The things that they complain about the most are generally the things that they most need to have in place. Thus clients frequently complain a great deal about external structure, insisting that they do not want to have an agency determining their behavioral boundaries. Yet if the therapist were to succeed in advocating that the structure be reduced, its lack would actually cause increased chaos for the client.

The therapist can usefully hear such complaints as suggestions for what needs to remain in place. For example, if a client in a residential program is loudly complaining that he needs to get a furlough or a pass, particularly if giving him a pass at this point would break the rules, chances are that the client is experiencing a significant amount of anxiety about being outside, and the therapist should hear the demand in this way. When the appropriate time for the pass comes, the client will not sound so demanding when he makes the request.

Cognitive Structures

Continuing work in object relations—the development of a relationship that does not repeat the client's past relationships—must be balanced with an equal amount of emphasis on cognitive work. Sociopaths are usually quite intelligent, and so are capable of using thoughts and concepts to organize and understand their feelings. The whole concept of feelings and the idea that relationships between people do not have to be exploitative can be introduced at this point in the treatment. As long as the therapist avoids sounding condescending, he or she should not be afraid to approach these very basic ideas as though they were completely unfamiliar to clients. In many ways, they are.

Cognitive information must be framed in a way that is meaningful to the sociopath. In other words, clients need to be clear how learning these ideas will benefit them.

In the beginning of the middle stage, much of the work tends to focus on skills that clients can use to manage their daily lives. Since clients' lives are usually falling apart, and recovering clients are generally newly sober, feelings of any sort are a disturbing and disorganizing experience. Cognitive structures need to be introduced with an emphasis on decision-making skills, impulse control, and the like. As the therapist helps clients to slow down to a pace that will let options be discussed before decisions are made, chances are that clients will experience a better outcome than they would have without the use of the thinking process. Simultaneously, ego functions are being shored up.

Struggles during the first phase are also products of the therapist and client working out a common language. In the beginning, it is often the case that therapist and client quite literally do not understand each other. They may come from very different cultural backgrounds and are likely to have had very different experiences. And each approaches therapy from a different perspective. The therapist has some knowledge of a theoretical stance and an understanding of the therapy process. Clients have a sense of self and a history of experiences that they are often quite ambivalent about sharing.

Twelve Step programs can be extremely useful resources in this endeavor. These programs approach recovery from a cognitive perspective, and their writings are clear, simply written, and well structured. If clients refuse to attend meetings, or have attended in the past and did not find the program useful, or do not meet the criteria for attendance (if the client's compulsion is theft, for example, and not substances or gambling), then I borrow the Twelve Step structure. I use the workbooks and introduce ideas from the program during sessions. If this material proves useful, I then inform clients where it came from and again encourage them to attend.

Note that it is as vital with this population as it is with any other that the therapist not "enable" clients by doing things that clients are capable of managing on their own. Enabling engenders dependence, rage, and poor self-esteem in everyone; in sociopaths, it also reinforces all of their existing defensive systems. It tells them that something or someone external to them will "take care of it" and takes away any fledgling ideas they have about responsibility.

Managing Regression

When clients regress to lying, denying, and provoking, these behaviors can now be approached a bit differently than they were in the beginning stage, before a therapeutic relationship was established. Everything that the client says no longer needs to be accepted as if it were the truth. Clients can even tolerate some laughter or an "Oh, come on" from the therapist, as long the therapist's disbelief is expressed with warmth, and not anger or derision. Bear in mind, though, that it is still too early to introduce the therapist's value system or attempt to get the client to identify with others.

At this point in treatment, clients usually feel some conflict about telling the truth. They want to be truthful, but they still feel that they need to lie. One compromise formation that clients use results in a blend of half-truths and projection. It is very common to hear clients say things like: "My friends seem to be doing a lot more drugs lately. They offer them to me all the time, but of course I turn them down." This type of statement generally means that the client is still using, but is making an effort to avoid drugs. Rather than directly confront the client, I prefer to respond, "It's hard to stop using, huh? It's really a struggle."

This statement is also an example of another type of intervention. When a client is regressing and the therapist is relatively certain that the client has more capacity than he or she is exhibiting at the moment, it is possible for the therapist to speak to the healthy part of the client. Such a conversation actually takes place between the therapist's and the client's observing egos. Although a dialog of this type might sound rather strange to a third party, clients will understand it perfectly well, even if they are unable to articulate what it means at the time.

> **Case note.** Richard, a white male who was a member of a motorcycle gang, repeatedly told me of an incident that occurred when he entered the gang's clubhouse to find several club members raping a woman who was an acquaintance of theirs. (He stated that the men commonly used gang rape as a means of eliciting submission in women who wanted to "join" the club.) The client claimed that he had stopped them, telling them that what they were doing was wrong. Years later, he was able to tell me that the conclusion of the story was not true. In fact, he had joined them in the gang rape.
>
> This vignette told me a number of things about him. In terms of his transference, the client was feeling a need to control me and some conflict about the impulse to rape me. By altering the story, he was trying to present himself to me as someone who could distinguish right from wrong, who would defend a woman who was being hurt, and who was powerful enough to stop several gang members who were in the middle of a rape. He honestly wanted to tell me something about himself, but stopped when the truth became too uncomfortable.

Establishing Stability

Work in the first phase of the middle stage should increase clients' level of stability in their day-to-day lives. It should also expand their capacity to think through decisions and to tolerate some anxiety and frustration. As their trust for the therapist grows, clients will rely on the therapist's judgment and decision-making system to shore up their own. James Sacksteder, M.D., has referred to this process as the therapist's "ego function lend-lease program" (in a July 1986 lecture at the Smith College School for Social Work). All of these elements need to be in place before further work can continue.

Near this point in the process, clients come to the realization that the therapist is not the foolish "do-gooder" they originally perceived, but a person with genuine, if unfamiliar, abilities and strengths. Clients will be both relieved and frightened by this discovery. It is a sign that the foundations of a nonexploitive relationship are being established as the first phase of the middle stage of treatment evolves into the second phase.

> **Case note.** Bob was a 31-year-old divorced white male with a long history of drug abuse and criminal behavior, multiple incarcerations,

and several recent serious suicide attempts. He requested treatment because he felt like he was going crazy.

For the first several months, every session began with a crisis. Bob would enter the room and announce that he was either going to kill a particular person or himself. He would tell me that he had a well thought-out plan and that nothing I said or did was going to stop him. Once these developments were out in the open, he would want to sit down and discuss why he felt he was going crazy and why he had attempted suicide.

I did not show much interest in those topics, but chose instead to return to his current crisis. We would go over how he got to the point where he was ready to commit homicide and then discuss other options and possible interventions. He would tell me that none of them would work. I would ask if he would try. He would say that he would, but that he could not give me any guarantees about anything. I worried a lot. He didn't.

Each week, he would come in and tell me that the crisis had been resolved without violence, sometimes as a result of my suggestions, sometimes not. And he would produce a new crisis.

The crises became less severe over time, and eventually I was able to ask him if people truly deserved to die for the things that they had done. He was adamant that they did. Over time, he was able to label that thought as a feeling of rage. Still later, he was able to explore the possibility that his homicidal impulses were actually attempts to ward off his suicidal impulses.

Many months later, as we were terminating, he told me that my original responses had been utterly perplexing to him. In the past, counselors would either have him locked up or get into power struggles with him over his threatened behavior. He remarked that it really used to piss him off that I would remain so calm.

The Second Phase of the Middle Stage

Work in the second phase is focused on internal difficulties. Clients' outside lives should not be in chaos at this point, because this work will cause a significant amount of internal chaos.

An additional indicator that work has progressed to the second phase is that clients begin to use their acute observational skills in new ways. They now begin to observe their own internal states and to study others' actions and reactions in order to understand their emotional world. They spend much less time complaining about external events. Instead, clients are filled with questions, confusion, and anxiety. It is as if they have discovered a world that they had previously known nothing about.

This part of the process reminds me of a well-known story about Helen Keller, who was born both blind and deaf long before educators knew how to teach people with this double loss. Her teacher made a long and patient effort to establish a connection for Helen between sign language and the world. Finally, the moment came when Helen first realized that the fingers drumming on her palm were communicating a symbol for water from the well. Helen went on to race joyfully around the yard, touching everything in it so that her teacher could label it all for her (Davidson 1965, 124–129).

Before this moment, Helen had never been able to communicate with anyone around her. In addition to being Helen's liaison to the world of things, her teacher was also her introduction to relationships with other people. It was a very powerful bond.

Cognitive Structures

Once again, the learning process is best approached from a cognitive stance. Thoughts must be used to contain feelings. The first step in doing so is to help the client identify, label, and distinguish feelings from each other.

It is often helpful to start with clients' physiological reactions and extrapolate the emotion from there. Male clients can begin to identify physical cues such as sweating, flushing, or a rapid heart beat as precursors to rage (Madden 1987, 61). One female sociopathic client I worked with found it useful to borrow children's books about feelings from the library.

Clients will attempt to understand others as well. Here, the therapist can help clients apply skills that they already have in place. Clients who successfully manipulate others have tremendous assessment abilities, perhaps better than the therapist's. The goal is to teach clients to use the skills for a different purpose.

For example, an incarcerated client might notice that another inmate is feeling vulnerable or afraid. Although this insight would normally provide an opportunity to manipulate the other person, if that impulse can be contained, then client and therapist can begin to explore other uses for this kind of information. The first kind of change the client might be willing to make is to resist taking complete advantage of the other person and to substitute an intervention that would benefit both parties. For example, instead of using the inmate's fear as a chance to extort some protection money from him, the client might consider locating the person who is intimidating the inmate and telling him to lay off. Although this move might appear genuinely altruistic, it would also serve the client's purposes (by making him feel powerful and by avoiding trouble in the cellblock that would bring down "heat," that is, attention from the custodial staff.)

The Role of Advocacy

At this point, the therapist may want to advocate for the client with various agencies. Any such attempt must stay within the limits of the client's current capabilities; otherwise, the therapist's efforts will be enabling.

If the therapist advocates for clients when treatment first begins, clients see these efforts as an opportunity to take advantage. Interventions in the middle stage differ in that clients have established a relationship with the therapist, and the therapist is more of a real person to them. Clients have also begun to take responsibility for their own lives, and advocating at this point reinforces and validates that behavior. In the very beginning of treatment, there is nothing in clients' behavior to reinforce or validate.

In a prison setting at this point in the treatment process, for example, I would contact members of the disciplinary staff on a client's behalf. My intent would not be to argue that my client should not be punished for whatever he did, but to let the staff know that he is in treatment and that I would like to know the conditions of the punishment, including what the client has to do to regain any privileges that he has lost.

Such an intervention serves an additional function. If the client is a lower functioning sociopath, chances are good that custodial staff are becoming vengeful and punitive, because this type of inmate makes them angry and frustrated. By getting in touch, I let them know that someone outside of their department is aware of the decisions that they are making, and I also give them the opportunity to blow off a little harmless steam.

For higher functioning clients, intervening serves an opposite purpose. In this case, the inmate is usually very well liked, and the custodial staff's response is to want to let the man slide for whatever he did. Here, I encourage them to hold him accountable by disciplining him in exactly the same way they would discipline other inmates. (This kind of advocacy is often ineffective, either because the inmate does favors for the staff, or because they have established a mutual-use relationship: the inmate will not "snitch" on the staff as long as the staff does not "snitch" on the inmate.)

Establishing a Holding Environment

All of these developments—the therapist's advocacy, the nonexploitive nature of the therapeutic relationship, and the observations about other people that clients make—will cause clients to ponder why people do things when there is no apparent motive other than to help someone out. This is the time when the therapeutic relationship is able to contain the client and therapist well enough to let the relationship itself become a major vehicle of healing. Winnicott (1972, 163) refers to this phenomenon as "the holding environment."

This is also the time when the concepts of identification with others and moral values can be introduced. These concepts could not have been introduced successfully earlier.

In the beginning stage, clients are not capable of recognizing that anyone would do anything for them without a hidden (or not so hidden) agenda. In addition, clients at that stage do not know much about and have little tolerance for their own feelings. If clients are introduced to these concepts too early, they justifiably feel that they are being asked to talk about something that they don't understand and to do something that they don't know how to do. At the same time, they sense that these are things that the other person does understand and is capable of doing. This inequality makes them feel as though something were being held over their head and so reinitiates the familiar cycle of humiliation, rage, and acting out.

Introducing these concepts too early enables clients to continue to experience the world through the sociopathic lens. This experience once again reinforces the client's view that everyone, including the therapist, has a hidden agenda. (In terms of object relations, the therapist is reenacting the trauma that the client's repetition compulsion is attempting to manage.)

Identification with Others

As clients learn to identify their feelings and observe similar reactions in others, they begin to realize that other people also have feelings similar to their own. Although the practice of observation provides this information, the vehicle for identification with others does not come from observation; it comes from the therapeutic relationship. At this point in the treatment process, clients idealize their therapists, introject some of their traits and attributes, and use them as role models.

Identification is just such a process of internalization. It creates a genuine connection between the client and others. It will leave the client feeling less empty internally.

Even in its most fragile and unstable form, the capacity to identify indicates a major shift in the sociopathic personality. Consequently, it causes significant conflict for the sociopath. Male and female clients describe themselves as suddenly feeling "like marshmallows inside." They feel weak and too sensitive to everything and everyone. They sit down to watch a television show and feel tears welling up—for the first time in their lives. They find themselves becoming upset when they see others—total strangers—being physically or emotionally hurt. These reactions make them feel as if they are going crazy.

On a more positive note, clients also describe feeling immensely relieved about this change. Many say that for years they had thought of themselves as "monsters." How could they be human if they never seemed to feel all the things that others reported feeling?

Even so, clients usually find the process overwhelming and end up longing for their truly sociopathic days when nothing bothered them. If they attempt to turn to drug use or to reactivate their old defense mechanisms, they are horrified (and relieved) to discover that these strategies are only somewhat effective. Clients typically report that they got high (or acted out in some other fashion), but that doing so didn't make them feel any better. They feel terrified at the loss of their major coping mechanisms. They blame that loss on the therapist. And they feel guilty about disappointing the therapist. It scares and confuses them to realize that they could not lie to the therapist about what they did and that the therapist's judgment is much more important to them than they thought.

As the identification process continues, clients usually start to describe what they experience as a good/bad split inside of themselves. They categorize all of the behaviors and traits associated with sociopathy as "bad" and everything else as "good." Clients will often ask their therapist if they are schizophrenic, thinking that the disorder involves a "split personality" similar to what they feel. The therapist should encourage this process of labeling parts of their personality and may even find it helpful to suggest that each part be given its own name. (In fact, in cases where clients are sociopathic and dissociative, these aspects of their personality may already have names.)

These new feelings lead clients to begin to struggle with the concept of control. The client may find Twelve Step materials helpful here; since control is such an intrinsic part of addiction, Twelve Step programs discuss it in great detail. I like to introduce their idea that the client's previous definition of control is actually the opposite of true control. Sociopaths generally think of themselves as "in control" when they are controlling others, even though their own behavior is actually out of control. When they begin to take responsibility for their own behavior and to contain impulses, they describe themselves as feeling "out of control"—that is, vulnerable to others, anxious, and unsure of themselves. Although this paradox may sound confusing, clients generally find it helpful to hear that all the vulnerability and anxiety they are feeling are actually the markers of true control.

The effect on past relationships. At this point, clients usually get a lot of grief from past associates and crime partners because of this change. Men are frightened of being labeled as a "wuss" or a "wimp" or some other term of derision about the "feminine" traits of sensitivity and caring. Some men experience gender panic at this point, even to the point of fearing that having and expressing feelings means that they are homosexual. For a male client, modelling himself on a female therapist will increase this panic.

As the pressure increases from past associates, clients begin to explore those relationships as well. They realize that making a real change in their lives will mean that they will have to find new people to socialize with—people who are sober and not involved with criminal activities. Clients also become aware that past associates who try to undo their attempts at straightening out have motivations of their own that are not necessarily in the clients' best interest.

Clients often feel quite hurt and betrayed when they discover that someone whom they had considered to be a lifelong friend (a relationship typically described by males as "I'd kill or die for him, and he'd do the same for me") does not want them to succeed. The appearance of these feelings is the first time that clients truly experience the anguish and pain that they have caused others to feel. It is important *not* to seize the opportunity to encourage remorse for past behavior. Affect tolerance is still low and fragile. This feeling simply needs to be identified, labeled, and expressed along with other feelings.

Clients usually describe experiencing significant depression at this point. As they explore this feeling, they generally come to realize that they have suffered from chronic depression for most of their lives. But this depression feels different; it is more acute, and more closely related to feelings of grief. Suicidal thoughts and impulses must be monitored at this point. Clients can generally manage them, but may need some structuring and cognitive interventions from the therapist to do so.

The effect on the therapeutic relationship. This whirlpool of emotion and internal change causes increased dependence on the therapist. Clients feel as if no one else understands them (which at this point is probably true). They usually look forward to appointments and arrive having spent the week formulating a list of things to discuss and explore. Therapy is no longer an armed battle or a chess match.

The continuing "lend-lease" of ego functions, along with the emotional support that the therapist provides, causes some blurring of boundaries between therapist and client. Clients at this point in the therapy process may feel as though the therapist can read their minds. They will say that they had every intention of not bringing up a certain issue, but still found themselves "spilling their guts" in a way that feels almost out of their control. Clients will become indignant if the therapist is unable to distinguish lies from statements that are true.

During the time that clients are experiencing this merger with the therapist, the therapist feels as though he or she and the client are symbolically joined at the hip. However, this bond should not feel unpleasant or as if it were a demand on the part of the client. It should feel intimate, warm, and close. Balint (1968, 136) describes this boundary merger as similar to the relationship people have with air: it is very difficult to separate the two entities during the breathing process. He also describes the therapist as carrying the client as water carries a swimmer.

Clients with narcissistic traits. Clients with a preponderance of narcissistic traits will attempt to circumvent the identification process and use observation alone to promote internal change. Clients who take this route end up looking as if they were just going through the motions, which is, of course, exactly what they are doing. In general, sociopaths with narcissistic traits tend to take longer than clients with other types of diagnostic combinations to approach identification. Such clients need more testing, more distance, and more patience from the therapist.

Clients with psychopathic traits. True psychopaths can succeed at going through the motions of the therapy until the process of identification begins. At that point, if a client has a preponderance of psychopathic traits, the identification process will not happen, or it will be fleeting or inconsistent.

How can a narcissist, who is just a "late bloomer," be distinguished from a client who is incapable of identification? Narcissists will move through the stages at a slower pace, while psychopaths will move through the stages at a normal or quicker than normal pace. To the therapist, it appears that the treatment is proceeding according to plan. But when the time comes for the client to begin experiencing the therapist as a human being, that development does not happen. What does happen is that psychopathic clients continue to make inappropriate demands on the therapist, just as they did at the beginning of treatment. And when these needs are not met, these clients typically act out toward the therapist.

For me, it is a sure indicator of psychopathic traits when clients state that they gain sexual or emotional pleasure from making me angry. This behavior is very different from the kinds of provocation that sociopaths use in order to reduce their feelings of humiliation.

Sociopaths make people angry in order to create distance and to make themselves feel more in control of an interaction. This behavior diminishes from the beginning to middle stage of therapy and then may spike again in the end stage. When it occurs in the middle stage and the therapist begins to show any real distress, sociopathic clients will stop, because causing the therapist pain is not the point. These clients are beginning to care about the therapist as a person.

For psychopathic clients, this kind of behavior begins to occur midway through the middle stage, at the exact point when a real relationship is supposed to be forming. It is also clear that these clients are using the therapist's bad feelings in order to arouse themselves. This experience feels worse to me than a rape. A nonpsychopathic rapist will simply ignore the victim's pain and distress; for a psychopath, the pain and distress cause the arousal. In other words, sociopaths use other people, and psychopaths use other people's pain. In terms of countertransference reactions, I do not just feel irritated and frustrated as I do with a sociopath. I feel vulnerable and panicked inside when I am used in this way by a psychopath.

Meloy (1988, 338) writes that the syntonic nature of this sadism toward the psychotherapist is a key to treatment prognosis: in cases where the sadism is not conflictual and no dependency is evident in the transference, expressive or supportive therapy should not be continued. Meloy states that such individuals are not treatable and that efforts to do so will usually result in a profound dehumanization of the treatment process and may place the clinician in actual danger.

> **Case note.** Michael was a 34-year-old white male with a long history of incarcerations, drug abuse, and violent and nonviolent criminal behavior. He also appeared to have some brain dysfunction that caused increased difficulty with impulse control. His relationships were primarily based on intimidation. Inmates were afraid of him due to his violent and erratic behavior.
>
> After some initial testing of me, he seemed to settle down. He stopped getting disciplinary reports. He got a job. He began to talk about what kind of future he wanted to have. He talked about his past with apparently genuine affect. However, he continued to have difficulty relating with others.
>
> After many months of treatment, he decided that his problems would all be solved if I were to become his girlfriend. We talked and talked about this, but nothing I said to discourage him made a difference to him. He began to talk about sexual encounters that he had in the past in graphic detail. When I set a limit with him about this material, he began to try to engage me in arguments. At one point in the process, he stated that if he could not succeed at sexually arousing me, pissing me off was the next best thing.

When he realized that a sexual relationship between us was not going to happen, he began to make threats that he would kill me. I had him transferred off of my caseload. I alerted the custodial staff, and I tried to make sure that he was not near me when I was walking in the facility.

Eventually, he calmed down, and we were able to meet together many months later with other staff present. I apologized to him for not providing him with the proper treatment. He apologized for all the threats. I did not have any further problems with him.

I know of no means of treating a psychopathic client through traditional individual therapy. Traditional therapy operates from the principle that the attachments people make with others are a combination of both rage and love, with the rage contained within the love. A psychopath's primary attachment to others is through rage (typically with a sexual component), and the rage ultimately overwhelms the love. Unfortunately, as societal conditions continue to deteriorate, these sorts of attachment disorders are likely to become increasingly prevalent—and the task of finding new ways of treating them will become increasingly urgent.

If a predominance of psychopathic traits is uncovered by the middle stage of treatment, the therapist will find it prudent to inform the client that traditional individual therapy will not be effective. It may be best to have another worker present, perhaps the therapist's supervisor, during this discussion. Other treatment options should be explored at this point, together with the possibility of facilitating a transfer to any of these that appear viable. If no treatment alternatives are available, I offer the psychopath a letter of some sort stating that although the client was cooperative, therapy was terminated because it was not the treatment of choice.

Establishing a Sense of Self

In sociopaths, the capacities to rage and to love are both present. Sociopathic clients begin to explore this "split" in their personality in more depth at this time in treatment. They begin to realize that as much as they might like to surgically remove the "bad" part of themselves, it is not possible nor desirable to do so. They come to realize that an ability to assert themselves is wrapped up in their aggression and that they will need to learn how to apply skills that they have used for criminal or manipulative purposes in other spheres of life. For example, when male sociopaths first attempt to approach women honestly, they feel utterly vulnerable. It is a revelation to them that they can use their assessment skills to determine if a woman would be a suitable partner.

Many sociopaths with borderline traits will initially attempt to approach others as if everyone is going through the same process that they are. They sometimes assume that because they are trying to be more honest, everyone else is, too. As a result, they open themselves up to victimization and a great deal of disappointment. Clients discover that "straight" people can be just as hurtful, manipulative, and dishonest as the best sociopath. (Their naivete reminds me of the way that developmentally delayed individuals assume that all people of average intelligence are geniuses.)

As the therapeutic relationship deepens, clients clearly recognize that this is a relationship unlike any other that they have experienced. The therapist has become a person to the client, and as they begin to express the full range of their emotions, clients begin to pay great attention to behaving in nonexploitive ways. The client becomes intensely curious about everything about this other person. The processes of merger and introjection are in full force.

It is now that some of the questions that clients ask in the beginning of treatment can be answered in a meaningful way for the client. "Why do you do this work?" is asked from a very different perspective than it was during the first meeting. The therapist's sense of right and wrong can be successfully introduced here, as long as the therapist is clear that clients are not expected to mimic them. If clients are religious, I refer them to clergy for help with concepts of right and wrong. For clients who are not religious, if they are capable readers, I refer them to philosophical works. If clients participate in AA or NA, this phase of work can coincide with work on the steps of taking a moral inventory and sharing it with someone.

Clients will begin to pursue questions concerning the meaning of their lives and the meaning of life in general. Frankl (1959, 133) states that the meaning of one's life can be discovered through three spheres: one's deeds, one's relationships, and one's attitude toward unavoidable suffering. This third sphere is particularly relevant for those clients serving long sentences. Clients begin to discover that the internalization of a value system leads to developing a sense of meaning in life.

It is important to work on superego functioning simultaneously with transference work, because as clients begin to label various behaviors and attitudes as "wrong," they will feel overwhelmed with self-hatred. The therapist has to model appropriate guilt and shame for clients. Clients often express their self-hatred as a feeling that they are "unlovable." The therapist needs to walk the tightrope of helping clients feel accepted while assuring that therapeutic boundaries are such that clients can struggle with the issue of self-esteem without relying entirely on the therapist for the answer.

Effective Use of the Transference

The work of the middle stage will now go along fairly smoothly for a period of time. It is as if all of this time has been spent peeling back layers of an onion. The core has now been reached, and the client and therapist together begin to formulate new layers with which to protect the core.

Clients now begin to experience their attachment to the therapist at its most primary level. Clients appear to feel all of the rage, grief, love, neediness, and joy that infants feel for their primary caregiver. However, these feelings occur in an adult person who has a well-defined cognitive system in place.

Other significant relationships. It is at this time that clients who find their attachment to the therapist too overwhelming to experience directly report that they have "fallen in love" with someone outside of the therapy relationship. Much of the discussion and the work then focuses on how to manage these feelings, how to understand and meet the other person's needs, how to maintain safe boundaries, and so on. At this point, client and therapist are working through how to establish and maintain two intimate relationships: the outside relationship that the client is describing, as well as the one between therapist and client.

It is crucial to remember that whenever clients are discussing other significant relationships, they are also communicating aspects of their transference. Whatever clients say, either positive or negative, about any other important person in their lives also applies to the therapist. Beginning therapists tend to respond to this principle with denial ("That's ridiculous! How can everything someone says about everyone else in his or her life be about me?") and a feeling of dismay at the thought of having to add still another level to all the other kinds of listening that they are supposed to be doing.

In order to listen for transference material and to observe the projective identification that is in process, I follow the same procedure I use in listening to lies and other projected material. I simply substitute my own name (or the pronoun "you") for the name of the person the client is discussing (or the pronoun used to refer to him or her). If the resulting sentence sounds as though it might also apply to me, I can then choose how to proceed. I may not make an intervention at all, and instead continue to listen. I may make an interpretation, usually by asking, "Does this apply to you and me as well?" Or, most often, I will respond with a statement that could apply to the manifest content (the relationship being discussed) as well as to the latent content (the transference).

For example, if a client is talking about feeling overwhelmed by all of the emotional demands of her new relationship, I respond by asking to hear more about the nature of those demands and more about how it feels to struggle with learning how to respond. The client might then talk about feeling angry or afraid or withdrawing. I might then ask how it feels to have this person whom the client feels so close to and wants so much from make these demands. Throughout this conversation, we are talking about both relationships.

Clients will often come to the realization that similar issues apply to both relationships. If the therapist has to point out material like this, the client is most likely not ready to hear it. A client's spontaneous realization indicates the optimal time for internalizing the material.

If the transference is not worked on in this way, several results will follow. First, clients will not learn the skill of applying the dynamics of the therapeutic relationship to other types of relationships that they are starting to establish. Second, clients' character pathology will not be addressed directly through the therapeutic relationship, and the focus of the therapy will instead remain solely on thoughts and cognitive interventions. And third, as a result, full integration of clients' new coping skills and personality structures will not take place. In order for effective therapy to happen with clients who have severe character defects, work must be largely focused on relationships, and it must be accomplished through relationships. The rest of what goes on is just words.

The therapeutic relationship. If it is necessary and tolerable for clients to experience their feelings for the therapist directly, they will do so. And if the client-therapist relationship seemed rocky before, those earlier days will feel calm in comparison.

In an April 1993 lecture at the Boston Institute for Psychotherapy, Tracy Mac-Nab, Ph.D., described love as a disorganizing affect (compared to hatred, which tends to organize the personality). Clients' loving feelings for their therapist will leave them feeling more out of control, and they will struggle with these feelings at several levels.

If clients are in the lower range of functioning, then becoming sexually involved with others occurs as an act of merger. A sexual identity, whose development demands that clients be able to experience themselves and others as separate entities, has not yet been established. (Note, though, that clients experience these feelings as attachment to and desire for a separate love object.)

Clients' feelings of love and attachment for a same-sex therapist can feel disorganizing even if clients have had same-sex physical relationships in the past. If the therapist and client are of opposite genders, then the feelings will cause regression on the client's part. Clients will feel that a love relationship or marriage with the therapist would solve all of their problems. Many clients, particularly those with a significant number of narcissistic traits, will also not understand why the therapist does not appear to jump at the opportunity. Other clients may struggle for quite a while about whether to tell the therapist about these feelings. These clients may start to seem more withdrawn, or all the internal chaos they are dealing with may cause some acting-out behavior.

The therapist's response. Psychodynamically trained therapists understand the feelings of love and desire for attachment that lower functioning clients experience toward them as primary maternal attachments. These feelings are products of the merger between therapist and client. Yet even though therapists may understand the source of the attachment, the strength of the client's feelings (to say nothing of their own) often makes therapists uncomfortable. This is especially the case when the therapist and client are of the same gender. Homosexual panic may ensue for heterosexual therapists. For homosexual therapists, concern about managing sexual feelings for their clients may occur.

How the therapist responds when clients express these feelings will determine the remainder of the course of the treatment. Many therapists are unprepared for these declarations and respond in ways that do not help the therapy process. New therapists often unconsciously ignore many such signals that clients give; when clients finally take a risk and state their feelings clearly, the therapist is shocked and taken aback. Clients will understand this reaction as one of rejection. New therapists will feel as though they did something wrong to encourage these "inappropriate" feelings from their client. They may also not know what to do with their own feelings of closeness toward the client, and a feeling of embarrassment may hold them back from telling their supervisor what is going on.

More seasoned therapists may give the client unconscious signals to avoid discussion of this topic. Clients will heed the signals. They will not take the risk unless they are fairly sure of a positive response.

When clients first discuss their feelings for the therapist, it is best to listen as one would to any other type of feelings that clients express toward therapists. Therapists learn early in their careers how to tolerate clients' angry feelings and how important it is to hear and accept these feelings without reacting to them impulsively or as if they are a personal attack (even if they are). The same guidelines apply here as well. I find that it works well to accept the feelings and label them for the client as a gift. I usually say that these feelings are the most precious things people have to offer one another and that I am deeply flattered that this person feels this way about me.

Since clients with many borderline traits are more capable than others of discussing the nuts and bolts of the therapeutic relationship, a discussion of their feelings for the therapist can often take place as objectively as though someone else's feelings were under consideration. Other clients may be more protective of their feelings and not want to examine them in detail. These clients typically think that a discussion will end up neutralizing their feelings for the therapist, in much the same way that previous sessions had dissipated their feelings of rage. I support and respect this reaction, particularly because it is a client-created and healthy interpersonal boundary.

Establishing an interpersonal boundary.   At this point in the process, clients may want to know if the feelings they have for the therapist are mutual. If this question is mishandled by the therapist, the client will conclude that he or she really is unlovable and the progress of the therapy will be derailed.

Mishandling tends to occur in two opposite ways. Therapists either give the client the impression that a romantic relationship is possible, or they reject the client by stating either through words or tone that the feelings are not mutual.

Sometimes, even though therapists are clear that they do not want to pursue a romantic relationship, their discomfort with the question and their uncertainty about how to answer it deter them from giving clients a definitive response. Clients may then interpret the therapist's discomfort as a sign that the therapist does have romantic feelings for them. Should this occur, clients will regress to believing that their problems have been solved and conclude that the therapy process no longer needs to continue. Such a series of events only delays the discussion and makes it more painful for the client.

If the therapist responds by reciprocating the client's feelings or by becoming sexually involved with the client, the therapeutic relationship is destroyed, and the therapist will be using the client in one of the worst possible ways.

Why is this so? Why can't therapists really show clients how lovable they truly are by entering into a romantic relationship with them?

The critical flaw here is that once such a relationship begins, the therapeutic boundaries are gone. At this point in the therapy process, clients are in the midst of a massive personality change and are in no shape to do anything except to continue the work of the therapy. Once those boundaries are breached, work cannot continue, and the client is left hanging, having lost his or her guide in the process. And since a genuine romantic relationship offers at least the possibility of the mutual fulfillment of both partners' needs, the former client will now face the pressure of meeting the former therapist's own needs. Sociopaths will only be equipped to respond to this demand with the offer of a mutual-use pact—or, if their feelings of rage and betrayal become predominant, they will take terrible advantage of this person who had once held out a hope that things could be different.

If the therapist takes an opposite approach and responds in a defensive and curt way, then clients will not only get the message that this individual does not share their feelings, but will also conclude that they are essentially unlovable. After all, if the person who knows them best in the world does not love them, then no one ever will.

The best approach is for the therapist to set aside his or her own feelings and think through the most helpful response for the client. Sometimes, I have found it best to say that a romantic relationship is something that I simply cannot discuss. This approach works well with clients who would become disorganized by any further discussion; generally, these are clients who have an active fantasy life about an intimate relationship with the therapist and who could not tolerate too much interference from reality.

With clients who genuinely want to know and can tolerate hearing it, I tell them the truth. I tell them that the therapy process brings people very close and gives them very positive feelings about each other. I admit that a good therapy relationship does contain aspects of a romantic love relationship—trust, warmth, and concern for the other person. But, I add, the boundaries between client and therapist need to stay where they are. I explain that even though I have a lot of strong feelings for people, the nature of my work means that I can only explore these feelings up to a point, and I cannot go beyond that point. So the honest truth is that I really don't know whether the feelings are mutual, and I will not do anything to find out.

This response accomplishes three functions. First, it derails the resistance inherent in the client's declaration (which, in this sense, is actually a request to stop the treatment process). Second, it forces the client to struggle with accepting the limited nature of external nurturing. Clients typically experience this struggle as a feeling of grief; it is a grief that comes from the realization that even this person, who has become so important to them, cannot create an environment that meets all of their needs. Third, this response establishes an interpersonal boundary between client and therapist (for the first time since they merged). If this boundary is not in place, the client will lose the ability to internalize changes and will forever remain dependent on the therapist.

Modell (1991) described the complexity of balancing between relating to clients as individuals in ordinary life and relating to them as individuals within the therapeutic frame in the following manner:

> Gratification at any one level of reality leads to paradoxical
> frustration at another. If a female patient demands love from a male

therapist and if this love is gratified as if the participants are two ordinary people, the treatment, as we well know, will be destroyed. If, on the other hand, the therapist interprets that her wish to be loved is only a displacement of her wish to be loved by her father, she might feel that such an observation is patronizing and rejecting, as if the therapist is saying that this wish is only a transference reaction. Further, if she experiences within the therapeutic relationship a father love that she had lost or never had and experiences the love in relation to the therapist as if he were a father, the gratification might lead to an acute sense of loss. Gratification of a father transference in current time may induce a mourning for what had been lost. (26)

With an interpersonal boundary in place between the therapist and client, the client can progress from the second to the third phase of the middle stage of treatment. Since this is the first time that the client genuinely experiences an intimate other as a separate being, it is also the first step in the development of the client's sexual identity. With this boundary in place, sex no longer involves the destruction of interpersonal boundaries. Instead, it becomes a form of communication that takes place between two distinct individuals. If client and therapist become sexually involved rather than establish this boundary, then the therapist will destroy the client's ability to develop a sexual identity (unless the client gets a lot more help in the future).

> **Case note.** Thomas, an incarcerated 28-year-old African American, requested treatment because he no longer wanted to use and sell drugs, but knew no other life. He was cooperative and articulate during the beginning stage of treatment, so much so that I could not get much of a diagnostic picture. In the middle stage, Thomas was more open about his activities in the prison. He continued to deal drugs and used them sporadically. He felt that doing so was okay so long as he did not develop a habit. He discussed his violent relationships with women. When women "dissed" him, he would beat them so that they "knew their place." His family history established a picture of emotional neglect compensated for by some limited material items and money. He considered it a perfect upbringing, although he couldn't understand why such a perfect upbringing had resulted in his being a career criminal.
>
> Thomas explained how drug dealing made him feel in control of things. He had money, and people came to him when they needed things. He enjoyed making deals. Thomas talked about money as a source of self-esteem: he was desirable and attractive with it, and not so without it. He had no qualms about selling drugs; after all, he did not sell drugs to children and was not addicting anyone himself. Those he sold to were seeking drugs of their own accord; he was only providing something they were requesting.

We discussed institutionalized racism a great deal, particularly as it had affected Thomas throughout the course of his life. When I brought up Thomas's role in the destruction of his own people, it gave him pause to think. He began to look more closely at the needs that he was getting met by dealing. We worked out ways for him to continue to make "deals" with people and to have them come to him when they needed things—but now these things were either legal items or emotional support or advice. Thomas began to feel ashamed of the way he had treated people, and he attempted to make some amends, particularly with women he had beaten.

There was no struggling and no difficulty in working with Thomas; in other words, we had been working at a cognitive level thus far. Thomas was quite skilled at maintaining a barrier around his affect. That changed when he told me his feelings for me. He said that he had changed and that we could make a life together. I went through my set response to this, but he did not understand the whole concept of "boundaries." As we discussed different types of interpersonal boundaries, it became clear that Thomas did not have people in his life who maintained boundaries with him, and it became equally clear why: no one had ever said no to Thomas without him eventually winning them over or threatening them into compliance.

So Thomas set about to win me over. He was charming and warm and funny and intelligent. He was concerned about me and interested in my thought processes and opinions. He appeared to love my sense of humor. He tried every argument he could think of to persuade me that it would be fine for us to begin a romantic relationship.

He would have stopped pursuing if I had told him that I was married or otherwise "taken," but I would not discuss my marital status. Doing so would have circumvented the process and validated his attitude that I was unavailable only because I was someone else's property. He also would have stopped pursuing if I'd told him that I did not find him attractive. Again, that was not the issue. And it also would have been a lie.

As Thomas ran out of arguments, he realized that he had never failed in this type of endeavor before. We talked about how vital it is to be able to hear people say no and accept it when they do in order to survive and succeed in the "straight" world. While Thomas did accept my refusal, his idealization of me grew. He also began to say no to himself and was able to experience the internal conflict of managing his impulses. Often he would succeed at containing them. Sometimes he would not. I had the sense that he was no longer being as honest with me about the extent of his illegal activities.

At this point in the treatment process, Thomas was transferred to another facility. He wanted to remain in contact with me, but chose not to when I explained that it would only be for the purpose of maintaining a counseling relationship. Several years later, I noticed Thomas's name on the daily inmate list (which indicated that he had been reincarcerated). He did not attempt to contact me, and since I changed jobs shortly thereafter he did not have the choice to contact me later in his sentence.

Coming to Terms with the Past

As clients feel adequately held and contained by the therapeutic relationship, they begin to explore their past. They disclose what has happened to them as well as what they have done. They also begin to explore the nature of their intimate relationships—those with family members, close friends, and girlfriends and boyfriends. It is a time characterized by feelings of grief, sadness, rage, and loss. These feelings are genuine and should feel as such to the therapist. Acting out should be at a minimum.

Balint (1968, 183) describes this process as one of mourning the original defect and loss that led to the establishment of the fault or scar in the client's mental structure. He notes that although the fault may heal over, its scar will remain forever; that is, some of its effects will always be demonstrable. Again, reliance on Twelve Step and recovery literature on dysfunctional families can be very helpful as a cognitive frame for clients.

As superego function work continues, clients will be able to increase the integration of their "good" and "bad" parts. Personality traits should show some flexibility at this point; good traits have bad to them and vice versa. The "bad" should be explicitly labeled as "taking advantage of other people" and all of the wrong associated with doing so. This aspect of their personality will not go away, and clients need to learn to observe and monitor it continuously so that it does not become active.

Clients will perceive themselves and their families differently with their new knowledge. At first, it will become clear to them that they were not the villains that their role in the family made them out to be. (In other words, a good deal of pathology must have been present in their family structure in order to create such a role for a child.) Clients who are "doing life on the installment plan" (serving multiple short sentences) often discover their role as family scapegoat. They realize that they have sacrificed their own potential so that family members can project their blame and responsibility. Clients tend to become very angry at family members at this point. Clients also compare the nurturance they receive from the therapist with how their parents treated them. They begin to realize the role that material items and other external factors have played and how these things substituted for missing elements in their relationships with parents and other family members.

As clients perceive themselves and their behavior from the context of the family, they understand and can forgive themselves for what they did. They also come to understand that family members did the best they could, usually in very trying circumstances. Clients begin to behave differently toward family. If a reconciliation is possible, it is sometimes attempted. Short-term family work can sometimes aid the process, but it is not always necessary; often, clients can manage this part of the process on their own.

New Relationships

At this stage in the process, clients will begin to look and act like very different people than they were when they began therapy. They will seem more mature, calmer, wiser, more giving, more settled. Often, they will begin to serve as peer counselors and role models for others. Some regression into narcissism can occur here, so it is important to work with clients to make sure that they do not present themselves to others as "cured." After all, role models need to show how to struggle with things, too. It is also important for the client to learn that relationships outside of therapy ought to be reciprocal; when they are, true friendships are possible.

As clients expand their relational world, they rely less on the therapist. They also begin to notice differences between the therapist's personality and their own. Often clients discover things about the therapist that they don't like or find things that they can do better than the therapist. This development indicates that clients are beginning to differentiate and separate themselves from the therapist. It also indicates that the middle stage of treatment has begun to evolve toward its third and final phase.

> **Case note.** John, a 37-year-old African American inmate, requested treatment because he wanted to stop being a gang member. He had lived a very violent and dangerous life. He was unsure if the gang would let him leave, and he knew that he could not continue to react to everything violently if he wanted to settle down and participate in raising his family. He had never requested any kind of treatment before and was unsure if a white, middle-class female could be of any help to him with this situation. However, he had been referred by a friend who told him that I could be trusted.
>
> John did not do much testing of me. He stated that he'd know very quickly whether I could be trusted and that he needed to work quickly to resolve his problems. So we began by spending a great deal of time on problem-solving techniques that did not include violence, threatening, or intimidation. John was perplexed. His definition of manhood involved being able to put on a show of force. He reported feeling like "a wimp" when he had to resort to nonviolent means of conflict resolution, particularly when he was dealing with his gang. We did work out a way for him to extricate himself from the gang without his getting hurt or hurting anyone else, but the process was frightening for him as well as for me. He finally decided that he had to stop restricting his behavior and go

about his business as he had before. He also contacted the head of the gang and was able to convince this person to "grant him leave," so to speak.

Once the acute threat to his life had passed, we worked on how to contain and express angry feelings in a nonthreatening way. John discovered that his rage masked many feelings, and that, in fact, he was quite emotionally sensitive. At first, he was concerned, thinking that this sensitivity meant that he was less manly. However, when I suggested that these are necessary traits for being a good parent, he accepted them. We also discussed the notion of boundaries; choosing not to be violent did not mean that he could not appear menacing to people if he needed to defend himself. His sensitivity was something to be shared only with people who were trustworthy and with whom he was intimate.

That was all that John wanted, and we ended at that point. I would see him from time to time in the corridors. He would always drop his prison face and give me a quick, warm smile.

The Third Phase of the Middle Stage

As therapy progresses, the course of treatment for sociopaths begins to resemble the course of treatment for clients in general. Issues for recovering sociopaths are much the same as issues for clients with other types of personality disorders, and so the description of what occurs in these last phases and stages of treatment are not specific to sociopaths.

The third phase of the middle stage of treatment is the beginning of the end and the prelude to termination. The shift to this phase occurs when clients actually begin to internalize and integrate the changes to their personality. They begin to behave differently and rely very little on splitting, projection, or denial as defenses. And they begin the process of separating from the therapist.

The Negative Impact of Incarceration

It is here that incarceration really begins to interfere with the treatment process. Up to this point, incarceration has served as a life-saving external mechanism of containment. There is (usually) no escape. There are rules and a gargantuan, inflexible structure. Opportunities for access to drugs, alcohol, and weapons are much more limited than in the community outside. Although nutrition and health care are often inadequate, they are still better than the diet and services that many people are accustomed to receiving when they are not incarcerated.

Prison supports and enhances sociopathic pathology. In addition to preventing people from structuring themselves, it also encourages and rewards game playing and manipulation. Prison is an environment of extremely limited supplies for day-to-day life. Many niceties of daily life are contraband inside. Food is limited. Clothing is limited. Work is limited. Pay is limited. Healthy, intimate relationships are extremely limited. Many facilities are now nonsmoking. Overcrowding increases clients' violent impulses (Roth 1987, 212). (For an eloquent discussion of the impact of incarceration on the human spirit, see Toch 1992.)

Just as rules multiply in prison, so do the ways to get around them. Custodial staff are subject to little if any accountability, and so they are free to bend the rules for favored inmates. The inmates who are most successful at getting around the rules are those who enter into mutual-use pacts with correctional staff. Inmates know that if they say the right things, they will most likely succeed at getting whatever it is that they want. If inmates are honest and direct and want to take responsibility for their own behavior, they usually get punished.

The more sociopathic inmates will generally be the most successful at getting access to things that will make incarceration more tolerable. So when sociopathic clients reach the end of the middle stage of treatment, they will suddenly appear to custodial staff as if they have lost their minds. Clients lose access to some of their most treasured items. They forfeit relationships with the more sociopathic members of the custodial staff. Clients want to put what they are learning into practice, and often their efforts are not well received. For example, if an inmate approaches a guard and asks for an apology for a hurtfully disparaging remark that the guard made about him in front of other inmates, the response is seldom positive or productive.

Custodial staff tend to be quite negative toward treatment, believing that it is ineffective and a waste of time and money. Inmates who consistently attend programs are viewed with suspicion, especially when they speak highly of treatment. Work supervisors do not want to let their workers go to attend programs or therapy. Sometimes inmates are given an ultimatum: work or treatment.

If clients want to proceed with treatment, they are forced to do their time quite differently. In many ways, this is a benefit. Incarceration must become alien and uncomfortable in order to help clients push themselves to tolerate the even more unfamiliar and painful experience of attempting to live in the community sober and crime-free.

Integration: Beginning to "Walk the Walk"

Clients in this phase will make new friends and associates among the inmates and find themselves relating with different officers—those who are healthier and less sociopathic. Clients may seek out jobs that give them contact with civilian staff so that they can practice appropriate social behavior. Sometimes they decide that they are not going to swear anymore. (This is actually a rather substantial undertaking in an environment where virtually every other word out of most people's mouths is "motherfucker.") Often clients stop smoking. In other words, clients at this stage will seek out a variety of ways to practice their new-found self-control.

In doing so, clients also begin making increasingly sophisticated decisions and judgments for themselves. They will often disagree with the therapist about a direction to take, but their decision will be well thought out and appropriate.

Clients' insight into their own behavior as well as that of others should be accurate and deep. They can almost work a session by themselves at this point; they know what the therapist will say and what they need to work on. Clients can monitor their own affective states and intervene when they detect something that is heading toward becoming overwhelming.

The connection between client and therapist feels more like a peer relationship. There is less of a power imbalance. Client and therapist know each other quite well at this point, and there is little interpersonal struggling between them. Communication difficulties and misunderstandings are rare. The client needs less and less of the therapist's help to work on things. He or she can do the vast majority of it alone. It is time to end.

13

The End Stage

Termination of treatment at the point when treatment is actually finished is a relatively rare occurrence in work with sociopaths, as it is with most other types of clients. Given the external structures usually in place in a sociopath's life, treatment often ends due to circumstances that have no bearing on how well the client is doing. Unfortunately, terminations of this kind are becoming more and more the case with nonsociopathic clients as well, due to the constraints of "managed care."

Premature Terminations

If a sociopathic client is in an inpatient setting (where most treatment of sociopaths takes place), therapy with a particular therapist is over when the client's preset length of stay is over. In a hospital setting, this end date is generally known when the treatment begins. With an incarceration, things get more complicated. Inmates do not stay in one facility for their entire sentence. They are moved about among prisons and jails depending on their legal status (pretrial versus convicted), how far along in their sentence they are, how much trouble they get into, and the nature of their crimes. All of these factors pale beside the one force most likely to decide where an inmate is housed: overcrowding. Since it is generally very difficult to determine how long any given inmate will be housed in any one facility, inmates enter into long-term treatment at their own peril.

Clients in inpatient settings tend to drop out if they discover that they are not getting the specific results that motivated them to sign up in the first place. For example, if a drug-addicted client who enters a detox program in order to make her habit smaller feels that the medication given her is inadequate, she will probably leave. When clients mistakenly believe that the termination of a parole or probation or the removal of a stipulation depends on program attendance, they may drop out if they discover that these expectations are not accurate.

If treatment is taking place in an outpatient setting, the client's own behavior often ends treatment. The client may be arrested for new crimes or drop out due to continued criminal activity.

An abrupt termination in the beginning stage of treatment is generally much easier for the therapist to deal with than one that occurs during the middle stage. At a stage when the therapist feels deeply committed to a client, it can be extremely distressing to find out that the client was not being entirely honest about his or her activities. A client who is actually doing well can still have incidents of acting-out behavior when circumstances become overwhelming, and therapists often feel very guilty when treatment ends for a reason of this kind.

Such an ending is not so much a termination as an abortion of the treatment process—and an indication that real termination is still some ways away. Yet, as people in Twelve Step recovery programs are told over and over again, it took clients a long time to become as ill as they were when they began treatment, and it will take them a long time to become healthy.

The middle stage of treatment takes years and years to work through, and progress does not occur in a linear fashion. People generally take five steps forward and four steps back, and sociopaths are as prone to slip as anyone else. And sociopaths remain sociopaths—when they slip, slipping means lying and engaging in criminal behavior. Often, the course of treatment occurs with multiple therapists in multiple programs over time.

I do not consider setbacks of this kind to be treatment failures. In my view, a treatment failure only occurs if the client decides not to continue to pursue getting healthy.

What the Therapist Can Do

When a client's acting-out behavior brings treatment to a close, if it is possible to learn what happened to the client, I recommend writing to the client to put some closure on the treatment. Such a letter can encourage a client to continue treatment by offering the reassurance that although the therapist is sorry that treatment ended in this way, he or she does not consider the client to be hopeless.

When clients stay in treatment long enough to get to the middle stage, then they can often teach the next therapist how to proceed. In the best scenario, clients sign a release to permit the new therapist to contact the previous one so that continuity of care will be at a maximum.

On occasion, clients end up back in the same facility, and the therapist is still there. In this instance, it is vital to let clients know that the therapist is not going to reject them because of the slip. Much work on superego functioning can be accomplished as the result of this situation. Clients learn how to accept and understand what happened in a way that does not cause more acting-out behavior, and treatment can then proceed from there.

Sometimes it is the therapist who is leaving. In this case, advocacy becomes vital. Most therapists will not want to add a sociopath to their caseload, and the treating therapist may have to convince the other clinician that this client is quite workable. The therapist will then have to convince the client that he or she should continue in treatment. It is important to reassure clients that it is not their behavior that is causing the therapist to leave. If it is at all possible, the therapist's departure should be planned to allow time to work through termination issues with clients.

Treatment Failures

There are, of course, treatment failures. A client might behave in such a way that the therapist is no longer able to maintain proper emotional distance—for example, by attempting to act out violently toward the therapist or by placing the therapist in jeopardy by engaging him or her in some sort of scam without his or her knowledge. (Actual events of physical harm of the therapist will be discussed in chapter 14.)

If the therapist cannot tolerate his or her own countertransference reactions (or should not tolerate them, as in the case of being placed in physical danger), then the client will need to be transferred to another therapist. If possible, a three-way meeting should take place, and the therapist should be honest with the client about why the transfer is occurring. The next therapist should be warned about the behavior in the client's presence. In the case of threatened physical danger, safety mechanisms should be put into place. The client should be required to verbalize a commitment to treatment and to state a reason why this is not going to happen again. This is not to say that any of the client's statements should be believed, but it is important to confront the person about his or her behavior and communicate that continued instances such as this will not be tolerated.

Successful Terminations

It is a relatively rare instance when termination occurs in response to the success of the treatment and there is adequate time to cover what is needed for a proper ending. In this case, the phases of termination and its goals are similar to those for most character-disordered or neurotic clients. The major difference is the type of behavior that sociopathic clients engage in during periods of regression.

The goals of the termination process are as follows:

1. To ensure that the client fully internalizes the changes made

2. To teach the client a healthy way to say goodbye

3. To help the client experience loss in a nondestructive way

4. To end the relationship

Many people who work in the mental health field believe that a lack of capacity to cope with the loss of significant relationships is the main cause of most mental illness. If this is true, then the work of the termination phase is the most important work of all.

Clients generally know when it is time to terminate. Often, they will say so. It is important to work out a schedule for termination together which suits the client's needs. For example, some clients want to continue weekly meetings and then end at a specified time. Others, particularly those serving long sentences, prefer to decrease the frequency of the meetings slowly in order to get used to the change in routine. A time limit for the whole process should be determined at this point, and this schedule should be maintained even if there are late-breaking crises.

Approaching the End of Treatment

Termination can be approached in much the same way as the middle stage of treatment was. Clients need to have a cognitive frame in place with which to understand the process and to tolerate the affects. I explain to clients how termination typically proceeds, what needs to be discussed, and what they can expect to happen.

The first way I engage a client in the termination process is to begin to reminisce with him or her about the whole course of the therapy. Memories can be exchanged about each person's perception of the first meeting and of each of the stages. Each person's "highlights" can be shared, events that were markers or particularly high or low points. At this point, client and therapist are talking with each other in a different way than they ever have before; they are both "on the same side of the desk" looking back over what has happened. This boundary change is one that needs to occur as part of the separation process.

Reminiscing may take up several weeks and occur while clients are still using the sessions for other purposes. As the memories get closer to the present, clients' anxiety tends to increase. As they struggle to contain it, they experience a great deal of ambivalence about giving up the therapy relationship. The therapist has served as a soothing mechanism for a long time, and it is frightening for clients to think about facing their panic alone.

Some acting out may occur at this point. Sometimes clients regress all the way back to beginning stage behavior and defenses. And some clients can verbalize what this behavior means—that they are trying to prove that they are not ready to end. It is important to help the client articulate the feelings associated with this regression. Feelings of sadness, fear, rage, hatred, abandonment, rejection, and anger are all present and need to be verbalized.

Therapists can find it difficult to maintain the optimal emotional distance here. It is easy to take it all personally, feel terribly guilty, and want to race in and protect the client from these hurtful feelings, or to back away from all of this emotional turmoil and become too distant. And since termination is a struggle for therapists as well, they are likely to do all of these things at one point or another. Therapists need to rely a great deal on their supervisors during this time for the support and guidance that they need.

Once the memories are caught up to the present, then client and therapist need to discuss how the client is doing at present. Both strengths and weaknesses should be articulated. Clients should be able to describe their own functioning, and do so accurately enough to quickly and easily provide a new therapist with an understanding of their needs if a readmission to treatment is needed in the future. The discussion should include spelling out for the client what issues are left to work on and how the client could access treatment services for these issues.

Evaluating Treatment

With this groundwork in place, client and therapist should then share what they thought was both good and bad about the therapy. (If this discussion occurs earlier, clients will be reluctant to say what was bad or to voice any criticisms.) Good aspects can be described first as a way to ease into discussing the bad or disappointing aspects.

It is important for clients to voice criticisms or negative feelings for a number of reasons. First, it is good practice for clients to be able to say these sorts of things to people with whom they are in close relationships. Second, inviting criticism is an important way to reinforce the fact that negative feelings are not causing the end of the relationship. Third, this discussion continues to reinforce the new level of separation between client and therapist. And finally, acknowledging criticisms reduces idealization. The therapist can be seen as more human and less of a perfect being.

I think that it is also extremely helpful for therapists to share mistakes that they think they have made with clients. It is fascinating to hear how clients have experienced these events. Often, interventions that the therapist considers treatment errors have had little impact on clients, while other events that the therapist failed to notice may have seemed disastrous to clients.

> **Case note.** A client who was nearing the end of his prison sentence grew very depressed and withdrawn after I told him that we needed to start working on termination issues. I assumed that his depression had to do with the termination itself. During our discussion of mistakes I had made, the client made it clear that termination itself had not caused his depression; after all, he knew when his prison sentence was going to be over. The real cause was that I had chosen to introduce the subject of termination at a time when he was utterly unprepared to think about it. I realized that I had chosen to bring it

up when I did in response to my own anxiety about it, and not in relation to his own situation and needs.

During this same discussion, we also talked about my tendency to permit him to change the subject. Most of the time, I had made a conscious decision to do so because the new subject seemed more germane to our topic. He told me that doing so was an error, since the subject that we had passed over was invariably more painful than the material he had offered as a replacement. I have not made that mistake since.

In the termination process, each person needs to be able to internalize both memories of what has occurred and the image of the other person. I ask clients whether they can elicit my presence through thought on demand. I assure clients that I will not forget them. (And I don't. A number of the case examples in this book are drawn from work that occurred ten to fifteen years ago.)

When clients feel that they have been given a great deal by the therapist, they are often led to wonder what the therapist has gained from their work together. What has the therapist learned from the client? It is important to prepare for this question and to give it some thought. Clients have usually been pleased when I have told them that hearing their experiences has helped me to understand others; for sociopaths in particular, this is a way for them to feel that their past crimes are being used for a positive purpose. The therapist's response to this question is also a way for clients to know that they will live on for the therapist.

Boundary Issues

The discussions of how much the client has gained from the therapist and the internalizing process usually bring up the issue of gifts. Although I was trained never to accept gifts from clients (doing so was considered a boundary violation), I have never turned down a gift from a sociopath who was terminating treatment. I am delighted to accept a token of gratitude from someone who has so little experience in life giving to others. I am particularly pleased with hand-made items, things that are original and took time and effort to make.

I will also sometimes give gifts. (This reversal of the gift taboo was never even talked about in school!) I want lower functioning clients who do not have good abstract and symbolic thinking skills to have a physical representation of me, something they can see that will elicit a memory. Sometimes, I write a card so that my words are there and can be looked to for support or for soothing. I see the need for a transitional object as outweighing any concern about boundaries during a termination. After all, the client-therapist boundary is about to become quite inflexible.

Another issue that causes a great deal of disagreement and tension among therapists (particularly those in prison) is hugs. Should a therapist hug a client goodbye? My answer is yes, if a hug is something that the client wants to do and can handle appropriately. In prison, this gesture needs to occur in the privacy of one's office, because inmates and staff are not allowed to touch one another except for restraint or security purposes. Any other type of physical contact is considered to be an assault.

I have found it useful to raise the issue with incarcerated clients who might want a hug goodbye but who would not risk doing so without permission. Sometimes we need to plan them. This is a particularly useful endeavor with clients with a history of sexual offending. They take pride in being able to touch someone close to them in an intimate fashion with complete consent and reciprocity.

Sometimes, one does not have a choice in the matter, and I have received some intense, genuine, and spontaneous hugs at the end of treatment. These I have never experienced as a problem. Most incarcerated men who do this only hug with the upper half of their bodies so that the contact does not become sexualized or intimidating in any way.

It is helpful to have both the client and the therapist articulate their feelings of loss. Many clinicians avoid doing so—sometimes because the subject is painful, and sometimes because they are afraid that they will cry. My opinion is that worse things have happened, and that it can be quite reassuring to clients to know how important they have been to the therapist.

Although I well up fairly often when clients are talking about overcoming something that has been debilitating for them in the past, I tend not to cry at the very end, when I am focusing my attention on the client's loss. However, when an appointment is going to be my last with someone with whom I've worked very hard, I do not schedule the following hour. I need the time for myself. Sometimes, I will not fill the client's hour with another client right away. In this case, for me, the former client needs to own that hour for a little longer.

Should Therapy End?

The last question that needs to be addressed concerning successful terminations is whether they should happen at all. Clients such as these generally need contact with social service personnel throughout the course of their lives. Sometimes it works out that although the formal weekly hour no longer occurs, clients can get in touch for a meeting or two now and then to address crises or for short-term work about a particular issue. I welcome this type of arrangement with clients as long as they are responsible about maintaining the appointments properly. Madden (1987, 68) states that it is essential for this type of client to know that the therapist will continue to be available to them after therapy has been formally terminated.

In some cases, clients have continued treatment with me on an outpatient basis in my private practice immediately after they are discharged from prison, and this arrangement has worked out well in several instances. After all, there is no other time that the issue of continuity of care is more critical. If clients do indicate an interest in continuing therapy, I make time and space available and make it clear that I expect them to pay an affordable fee and to be responsible about showing up. Sometimes with incarcerated clients, the work that can be accomplished in prison is done, but clients are not going to be released for an additional period of time. In this case, I may remain in contact with former clients by mail if it seems useful for them to maintain a connection. Contact with people on the outside is very important to people who have long sentences to serve, and as long as the person can maintain appropriate boundaries with me (and I spell out what they are), I consider this to be an appropriate form of volunteer work. Such an arrangement can at times be confusing for former clients; while the correspondence is a product of the therapeutic relationship, it is a different form of communication. It isn't therapy, and there is no other name for what we are doing. Sometimes, former clients cannot adjust to the change in boundaries and interpret the correspondence as a desire on my part to become romantically involved with them. If this development occurs, I explain my motives and boundaries and give them the opportunity to adjust. This approach is successful in some cases; in others, I have had to terminate written contact when former clients remained demanding and inappropriate.

When, how, and if to end are questions that demand as careful an assessment process as do the diagnostic issues of the beginning stage. And as in the beginning of treatment with a sociopath, in the end, the therapist is flooded with countertransference responses. If acted upon impulsively, these responses will impede and damage the assessment and decision-making process. If they are contained and explored by the therapist and his or her supervisor, they can generally provide the path for the most productive and beneficial termination.

> **Case note.** Joe, a 37-year-old Puerto Rican male serving a sentence for manslaughter, requested treatment. He was a Vietnam veteran and a gang member with a long history of drug addiction and criminal behavior. He said that he desperately wanted to stop using drugs, but that he could not face the flood of self-hatred and suicidal and homicidal impulses that overwhelmed him when he tried to quit. He was very isolated, feeling that everyone wanted to take advantage of him. He used people, but did not seem to enjoy doing so in the way sociopaths typically do. Rather, it seemed that he became overwhelmed and stopped being able to see the people he took advantage of as human beings.
>
> In this case, although psychopathic traits were evident during the beginning stage, Joe did not attempt to anger me to arouse himself. Accordingly, I made the diagnostic assessment of a borderline personality organization combined with psychopathic traits and sociopathic behavior.
>
> It was very painful for Joe to attach to me. The closer he got to me, the more pain he experienced from memories of other past relationships and the greater his need became for emotional connection with people. He continued to use drugs and sometimes would develop habits. However, he did manage to work through some of this, learned to tolerate some affect, manage some impulse control, and cut down on his drug abuse and his violent behavior.
>
> Unfortunately, Joe's gang activity caused him to be transferred

to another maximum security facility. I offered to remain in touch with him, and he wrote and asked me out on a date. Some time after that, he was transferred back to the original institution.

It was shocking to see him upon his return. He was on a hunger strike. His life was in complete chaos. However, one of the reasons for the chaos was that he had fallen in love for the first time in his life. He was maintaining enough emotional connection with this woman that she was deeply attached to him as well. He was transferred after several months so that we could not continue our work. But during our short number of visits, he was able to articulate that it was our meetings that had enabled him to be vulnerable and trusting with another person. He was now paranoid and dependent and terrified—in other words, more borderline and less psychopathic. That was the work that we were able to accomplish. And although this man has many years of treatment ahead of him in order for him to become well enough to live peacefully outside of prison, I feel hopeful that he is capable of it. The capacity to relate was internalized, and our termination work was what made that clear to both of us.

Case note. Sam, a 31-year-old African American inmate, was transferred to my caseload after receiving psychotropic medication for a year without any case management. Sam suffered from delusions of religious grandiosity, alcoholism, a gambling addiction, chronic depression, and a long history of committing nonviolent offenses. Sam was much more comfortable in prison than he was anywhere else, and although he had received a sentence that seemed to me inappropriately long, he was unconcerned about it.

In the beginning, we met monthly because Sam did not have much to say. As treatment progressed, we met more often. Sam began to talk about his family and about his relationships with other inmates. He learned to assert himself a little more and began to entertain thoughts about what kind of life he would like to have in the community. Sam had never remained on his medication after he was released from prison in the past; although he recognized its importance, he had never had any motivation before to follow through with anything. After some progress, our sessions began to focus on his depression.

Eventually, Sam took his case back into court and won a reduction of his sentence. Although this meant that we no longer knew exactly when he would be released, we did manage to spend a great deal of time in the last few months talking about decision-making skills for life in the community.

Upon release, Sam was motivated to pursue treatment—for the first time in his life. Unfortunately, the local community mental health agency had had experience with him in the past and was not in a rush to help him, and he could not find another agency willing to provide his medication and continue treatement. He called me, and we were able to find a place that Sam could go for his medication. He remained in contact by phone until his new treatment was in place, and he continued to sound motivated and optimistic. I wish him well.

Section IV

Special Considerations in Work with Sociopaths

14

Safety Considerations

Safety is not a concern unique to work with sociopaths, nor to work with clients with sociopathic traits; similar concerns apply to lower functioning clients in general. But given the primary function that aggression plays in the personality structure of sociopaths and their lack of impulse control, management of the sociopath's aggressive impulses toward others must be an integral part of treatment.

This chapter will address the dynamics of aggression and introduce techniques for handling aggression directed toward the sociopath's therapist or toward other staff. Specific techniques to deal with aggressive behavior toward other clients or residents will be addressed as well.

The Dynamics of Aggression

Aggression in this context includes either violent or sexual acting out or both. It can be communicated physically, verbally, or through body language.

Acts of aggression are labeled as such by the receiver, not the sender. Sociopaths will often deny that their words or behavior are threatening or damaging, and sometimes they genuinely will not know that what they are doing is aggressive in nature. In the beginning stage of treatment, sociopaths do not have the capacity to identify with other people and accordingly cannot gauge the impact of their words or behavior on someone else. However, the aggressive nature of an act is not their determination to make. It is the person to whom the sociopath's words or actions are addressed who determines whether or not the behavior is intimidating or hurtful.

As discussed in the section on diagnostics, aggression is used in a sociopathic system to discharge affect (usually anxiety, fear, or rage), establish control, and modulate interpersonal distance. If the client has a preponderance of paranoid traits, aggression is most often an attempt at self-protection. If the client has more borderline traits, aggression is most likely to be an attempt to set an interpersonal boundary. If the client has psychopathic traits, aggression is also an attempt to form a relationship. With lower functioning sociopaths where the boundaries between different types of mental illness and personality disorders are less clear, aggression may serve all of these functions.

The greatest risk for violent acting out on the part of a sociopathic client is during the beginning stage of therapy, when the client does not consider the therapist to be a person. The exception to this rule are clients with a preponderance of psychopathic traits. For these clients, the risk of violence is greater in the beginning and middle stages of treatment.

While clients with psychopathic traits may take advantage of opportunities for violence or aggression during the beginning stage, violence during the middle stage is an attempt to contain the increasing amounts of distress they experience due to the emotional demands of the work. Violence is also an attempt on the part of the psychopath to become more intimate with the therapist.

Since sociopaths tend to be more violent in the beginning stage of treatment, and since a full diagnostic assessment cannot be made until the end of the beginning stage, how can a therapist know whether a client is a sociopath in this early stage? The answer is that he or she can't. The precautions described here should be taken whenever a clinician is working in a correctional setting or in an agency that specializes in treating sociopaths. In fact, I think that these precautions should be kept in mind even in work in private outpatient settings. I relax when I know clients, and I may then choose to see them when I am alone or without immediate access to a telephone. But I believe that it is ill advised for a therapist to be this nonchalant with any new client, no matter what the setting.

In any treatment setting, the most important factor in reducing the risk that a sociopathic client will act out violently is the therapist's ability to contain and make safe the interactions between them. This is accomplished at several levels: the individual level, the interpersonal level, and the physical level.

The individual level is made up of the therapist's internal response and what he or she can do to best cope with these feelings to reduce the client's fears and anger. The interpersonal level involves what is said to the client. The physical level consists of adaptations to the physical environment to enhance safety and includes the option of last resort: using physical means to establish or maintain safety.

How to Reduce or Prevent Acts of Aggression

The Individual Level

The most important preparation a therapist can make to prevent clients' aggressive behavior is to keep in mind that acting out in this way is almost always a possibility. In other words, I suspect that most therapists who end up with an out-of-control client on their hands are in such a situation because they had never considered the possibility that an outburst might occur. When an outburst does happen, they are unprepared for it, and they panic.

Some therapists who work with dangerous clients maintain a sense of denial. They feel that since they are nice, well-meaning people, they will not be hurt. And chances are good that they will not be. However, sociopaths see a person such as this and may think: "Victim!"

The other extreme is to become so paranoid that all clients are viewed as adversaries. Obviously, this stance is not going to work; in fact, it may very well set up the conditions it is intended to avoid, as clients can become quite angry in response to an adversarial or unremittingly suspicious attitude.

A middle ground is the best approach. The therapist should remember that sociopaths are angry people who have little impulse control and they should stay out of vulnerable situations with clients who are not well known to them.

The second most important thing therapists can do to prevent aggressive incidents is to learn to remain visibly calm in the face of clients' rage. Therapists must project the image that they are in control and sympathetic, but unwilling to tolerate out-of-control behavior. Any demonstration of anger, anxiety, or fear on the therapist's part will simply exacerbate the situation.

The Interpersonal Level

Preventive techniques. The single most effective way of reducing the risk of violence is a very simple technique. It is to treat clients with respect. Say "please" and "thank you." Refer to clients as "Mr." or "Ms." or ask for permission to call them by their first names before doing so. Refrain from using a sarcastic or irritated tone of voice or acting in a condescending manner. While these may seem like obvious courtesies, I have seen workers in this field who radiate such noxious levels of hostility that it is truly surprising that clients are able to maintain control of themselves in their presence.

Another extremely effective technique in reducing the risk for violence is to help clients articulate feeling states in words. If a client seems upset or angry, don't simply ignore these feelings; ask the client to tell you what is going on. While these may sound like pretty basic suggestions, I am continually surprised to find therapists and counselors who become uncomfortable with clients' affect. Some simply ignore feelings, as if not talking about them will somehow make them go away; others find more subtle ways to avoid hearing about their clients' feelings. They focus on trying to fix whatever the therapist feels is the problem (so that the affect will then disappear), or they reassure the client that everything will be okay. These common errors that beginning therapists and counselors make engender anger and frustration on the part of clients (or anyone who is spoken to in such a way). These interventions also often come across as patronizing and as a message that further communication about that subject is unwanted.

The most difficult type of client affect for some therapists to accept is affect that is directed at the therapist. Clients who do not handle anger well usually do not have a lot of experience in calmly verbalizing negative feelings to the person who is causing them. Such clients will show physiological symptoms instead, or become withdrawn. Male clients who appear angry may actually be experiencing any number of strong feelings.

If the therapist cannot help clients to talk about their feelings, then they will remain bottled up, and eventually the client will explode. While the explosion usually occurs outside of the office, if there is enough pressure and too little impulse control, the outburst may occur in the therapist's presence.

Responses to intimidation. Sometimes, the client acts in an intimidating way toward the therapist. The therapist needs to trust his or her own level of discomfort concerning the level of aggression. Even if there is no overt threat, if the therapist senses that something is wrong, it is vital to stop the process there.

The therapist should assess what the client is doing to cause the feeling of danger. Maybe it is a stare. Maybe it is a body posture. Maybe it is the use of graphic detail in discussing sexual or violent activities. Maybe the client is getting up and walking around the room or intruding on the clinician's personal space. (See the case note and discussion in the section on clients' use of intimidation to attempt to control the session or break the rules in chapter 11.)

It is important for the therapist to make it clear to the client that the behavior is making him or her uncomfortable. It is equally important for the therapist not to sound afraid while doing so. If the behavior continues or escalates, then the therapist should decide whether the session should be ended early. (If a session is ended early due to the client's lack of control, the therapist should discuss the incident with his or her supervisor. A determination can be made at that point how to address the issue further with the client.)

Deescalation techniques. If the therapist feels that the client is beginning to lose control, it is important for him or her to remain calm toward the client. The client is angry, but also afraid. He or she is counting on the therapist to remain in control. In response to clients' rage and their own fear, some therapists become paralyzed, and others bait and harass the client. Either of these extreme responses will only exacerbate the situation.

Deescalation techniques should be relied upon here. (See appendix B.) The therapist should speak in a calm and soothing tone. Statements should be kept simple and short and should generally be of one of two types: directions to control behavior (for example, "Please lower your voice" or "Please sit down") and questions asking for neutral, factual information (for example, "What day did this happen?" or "Was that after you had finished shopping?").

Why ask questions like these? First of all, people in a rage are on sensory overload. They cannot hear or process much. Any thinking that they can do will help them to calm down. Stopping for a second to think what time the event occurred gives the client a chance to take a breath and recover.

Clients will sometimes answer with annoyance: "Who cares what time the damned thing happened?" When this happens, I respond by smiling sheepishly and saying, "Sorry. I was just wondering, and it occurred to me to ask." Clients will then generally calm down, as a low-key response of this type helps them to see their level of anger from someone else's perspective.

If the client is able to use these different interventions to calm down, it is then important to validate his or her anger. I usually say something like "I can certainly understand why you are so angry about that" or "You have every right to be that angry."

Sometimes these episodes repeat themselves. If another outburst occurs, I ask the client if he or she is mad at me. Generally the answer is no, and I then go on to explain that the client's yelling or physical agitation had made me wonder if that was the case. Clients usually respond by trying to present their anger more calmly in the future. An exchange like this can greatly improve clients' impulse control and ability to tolerate feelings.

If none of these approaches work and the client continues to escalate, then the therapist needs to start setting limits: "If you can't lower your voice and sit back down, then I will have to ask you to leave until you can calm down." The therapist should then be quiet, and let the client think about that announcement for a minute. Those clients who conclude that they should leave are usually embarrassed by their behavior and uncertain whether the therapist will want to see them again. I reassure clients that I am not trying to get rid of them; they can leave without notice if they need to, but I want them to return if they are able to calm down. If they cannot, they should still plan on returning for the next scheduled appointment.

I have never had a client continue to escalate past this point, to a stage where intervention by other staff is the next resort. If other staff are nearby, they will usually be able to hear all the ruckus, and one of them will be alerted to knock, come in, and ask if everything is all right. If no one does interrupt, or if the therapist is alone on the floor, then the therapist needs to pick up the phone and, while dialing, tell the client that he or she needs some assistance to help the client to calm down.

Physical Considerations

The physical environment. Since there is always a potential for violence in work with sociopathic clients, the therapist needs to ensure that the physical surroundings do not aggravate individuals who are already struggling to maintain control of themselves. Before the first meeting with a sociopathic client occurs, the therapist should know what he or she can do in the case of a violent reaction on the client's part.

The room where the meeting will occur should contain a working telephone. It should also contain things that could be easily and noisily broken to draw attention. Staff should be nearby and preferably should include physically strong or large individuals. As will be discussed later, these staff people do not need to be strong or large in order to do battle with clients. But the sight of a physically large staff person helps to soothe a sociopath's impulse to intimidate others.

There was a lot of debate in the correctional facility where I worked about whether the client or the therapist should sit closer to the door and whether or not the therapist should be behind a desk. Many staff felt strongly that a desk should be between the client and therapist; if the client were to lunge unexpectedly, the desk would give the therapist time to get out of the way. These staff also felt that the therapist should be the one closest to the door; that way, the client would not be able to prevent the therapist from escaping.

I suppose that this is a logical train of thought if the therapist went into a session actually expecting to be able to physically outmaneuver a sociopathic client. My personal assessment is that if a young, strong, physically fit male wants to attack or restrain me, there is not a great deal I can do to combat him at a physical level. I also recognize that physical violence is an area where sociopaths tend to have a certain amount of expertise. For example, inmates incarcerated at the prison where I worked knew all of the security procedures to be used in case of emergency. They all knew that if they wanted to restrain someone, the first thing they would need to do was to ensure that the staff person did not have access to a telephone. Since I am not about to invite a client who I know is planning to attack me into my office, it is obvious that any attack that does occur is going to be unexpected, and that I am going to be unprepared for it. In this situation, I know that if there is a race for who gets to the phone first, I'll lose.

Once we discard the notion of attempting to arrange the office for the purpose of maintaining physical control of the client, other considerations arise. Since I know that humiliation increases sociopaths' aggressive impulses, I arrange the office in a way that reduces those feelings. This means that I do not sit behind a desk, because I think most people find it humiliating or intimidating to be on the other side of one. I prefer to have the client sit to one side of the desk; that way there is still a piece of furniture between us (more as a symbolic boundary than anything else), but it does not increase negative feelings. (Obviously, when the telephone is a security device, it should be kept on the other side of the desk from where the client sits.) I always give the client the door. Always: the last thing I want is for an angry, out-of-control client to have to think about how to get around me in order to be able to exit from the office.

Although these are my personal preferences, I recognize that the individual therapist's feeling of safety and comfort is more important than any theoretical discussion about the ideal physical layout of the office. If a therapist feels safer and more in control with the client away from the door, then that is the way that his or her office should be arranged.

In agencies where many sociopaths are treated, the physical layout of the waiting room should also be considered. In my former workplace, the mental health unit was the only area in the prison where inmates from all housing areas were able to congregate, and although there was an unspoken sense that the unit was neutral territory, no one was quite sure if that actually was the case. Members of rival gangs would often have to sit near each other while they waited to meet with staff. One client told me that he had found the brother of a man he had killed alone in the waiting room when my client entered. The client had no idea how the man would respond to seeing him.

Some situations of this type are unavoidable. Prudent measures to take are to form an idea of clients' gang affiliations and to talk with individual clients about how they will manage to relate with other gangs' members if they meet in the mental health agency.

Responses to acts of physical aggression. If an incident of aggression cannot be avoided, it must be dealt with swiftly. Since there will not be time during the incident itself to observe and choose the most appropriate means of intervention, staff must be prepared to do three things. First, the immediate threat must be contained and safety must be reestablished. Second, victim and aggressor must come to an interpersonal resolution. And third, the therapist can then attempt to place the behavior in a context and to formulate (or reformulate) the client's treatment plan. Although a therapist would normally prefer to do the evaluation first, since aggressive behavior is a main mode of communication for sociopaths, the assessment will most likely occur after the fact.

Sometimes other staff will witness the behavior. In this case, the appropriate staff needs to intervene in whichever way they are trained to do so. When staff members observe tension building before an outburst, they can use a variety of deescalation techniques to attempt to calm and divert the client. These techniques include not behaving in a threatening way toward the client, keeping one's voice low and calm, keeping one's hands at one's sides, making eye contact, and not showing any fear. If these techniques do not work and the client will not back away from the situation, then police (or custodial staff) should be called.

Physical restraint. Mental health staff should not attempt to restrain clients, nor should they intervene physically in any other way unless they feel that someone's life is at risk. Not only do they risk physical injury themselves, they also risk increasing the damage to others. (For example, the client might have a concealed weapon.) In addition, if staff are hurt, then they will no longer be able to supervise other clients.

I also consider physical restraint by mental health staff a violation of clinical boundaries. Very disturbed people experience therapy as extremely intrusive; in order to create an interpersonal field that is safe and growth enhancing, the very intimate aspects of therapeutic relationships must be balanced by limits and controls (for example, rigid rules about things such as appointments and confidentiality). Sociopaths also experience external control as humiliating, and in addition to breaching an interpersonal boundary, any attempt at physical intervention by a therapist will simply increase these feelings. Physical restraint should be carried out by people whose job it is to physically restrain. The mental health staff who are present can attempt to distract the client or dissuade him or her from continued aggressive behavior.

Aggression against Other Clients or Residents

When aggressive incidents occur in a hospital or group home setting, it is often difficult to prove that abuse occurred because the behavior is usually not observed by staff. A common situation is that a chronically mentally ill person who is quite passive (and perhaps actively delusional) is taken advantage of by a higher functioning mentally ill client with sociopathic traits. In such a case, the sociopathic client will deny the behavior, and an accurate report cannot be obtained from the victim. Another common situation is one in which male clients offer female clients cigarettes or small amounts of money to perform sex. Neither will admit to the behavior because each feels that the mutual-use arrangement is acceptable.

Staff need to approach situations like these at the same three levels: containing the behavior, facilitating a resolution between the victim and the aggressor, and adjusting the sociopath's treatment plan if the assessment of the behavior indicates it.

First of all, sociopathic clients need a structure that will at least limit what they are doing. Staff should actively monitor the house. They should make rounds on a regular basis, particularly at night. They should attempt to observe residents when the residents are unaware of the staffs' presence in order to witness the behaviors in question.

Yet group homes are not prisons, and they should not have to be turned into prisons in order to respond to a sociopathic resident. Although consistent good-faith efforts need to be made to monitor the house, staff should bear in mind that an alert sociopath will find a way around even the most vigilant surveillance. What this means is simply that staff needs to talk with the residents about what is going on. Victims need to hear that they can and should assert themselves. They should be told clearly and often that they can approach staff and that staff will help them assert themselves.

Staff need to be especially careful to avoid the typical correctional response to aggressive behavior. In prison, the victim gets locked up in protective custody, not the aggressor. In a group home, victims should never be restricted or have privileges removed for their safety. It is the aggressor who needs to be contained, because otherwise victims learn that they will lose out as a result of any attempt to engage staff and deal with the situation directly and appropriately.

The aggressor needs to be confronted. Limits need to be communicated as clearly, consistently, and neutrally as possible. Sociopathic residents will generally become indignant and quite angry when they are accused. Staff need to remain calm and repeat why these behaviors are not acceptable. They also need to avoid getting into a power struggle with residents over whether the staff can "prove" their guilt. An effective approach is simply to state that the rules apply to everyone. ("Then why are you singling me out?" "I'm going over the rules with everyone.")

At the same time, sociopathic clients must have an appropriate and legitimate way to express anger and frustration; otherwise, they will have no choice but to act these emotions out. It is also imperative that sociopaths who act out in this manner are not ostracized or inappropriately punished by the staff, particularly by the staff assigned to them. Staff must set the rules and limits, but also remain supportive of the client, just as they do when a chronically mentally ill client acts out toward other residents.

After the dust has settled and an understanding of the behavior has been gained, an assessment of the event can be formulated by the treatment team. The team can then determine if the sociopath's treatment plan should be adjusted in response to the new information.

If the abuse constitutes a violation of the law, staff should help the victim consider whether criminal charges should be filed. Here, the final decision needs to be made by the victim, not by the staff; otherwise, the victim's passivity is reinforced. Personally, I believe that everyone ought to be held responsible for his or her behavior, particularly when it damages someone else. It is also an excellent reality test for a mentally ill client to have the police show up and question him or her about an incident.

Ultimately, however, it is ideal for residents to confront each other (appropriately, of course) about these types of behaviors. Sociopaths will stop abusing others in the house if they know that such behavior will not be tolerated. Staff should be prepared to facilitate these discussions whenever they need to do so.

Aggression against the Therapist

On occasion, the client's aggression is directed toward the therapist, and it occurs when the client and therapist are alone together. In some instances, there is evidence of a buildup of tension or anger prior to an outburst, and all of the therapist's attempts to intervene have failed; in other cases, the explosion seems to happen spontaneously. Sometimes, if it is a very new client, the therapist may not see the precursors or may not realize what he or she is doing to exacerbate the situation.

If the client assaults the therapist (a common legal definition of an assault is any type of unwanted touching), the therapist's physical safety comes before all other considerations. In other words, boundaries be damned. The therapist should do whatever seems necessary to stop the assault and assure his or her self-protection. Personally, I would also file criminal charges.

If a breach as serious as this occurs, I firmly recommend that the therapist no longer work with the client. Naturally, the therapist's supervisor needs to be involved, and a determination should be made whether the agency will continue to treat the client at all. If the client is to continue with the agency, a meeting should be called with the client present to discuss treatment options. Therapy should also be offered to the therapist, and great care should be taken to ensure that the therapist feels safe in his or her workplace if the client is still being treated there.

Incidents of this kind are a frightening subject. My impulse is to want to reassure the reader that this type of event rarely happens—and when it does, the precipitating factor is often that the appropriate preventive measures were not taken. I have worked in correctional settings for fourteen years in both volunteer and paid capacities, and only one client has ever touched me in a way that frightened me. A paranoid and delusional client attempted to hug me at the end of a session. I backed away, offered my hand for him to shake, and stated that hugs were not allowed in that facility. He replied that he was confused why we couldn't hug now when we had hugged so many times before. (We had never hugged before.) I transferred him to a male case manager. I have never been physically hurt by any client or former client.

Personally, I have found the locked wards in psychiatric hospitals to be much more dangerous than any environment where I have worked with sociopaths. Patients in state hospitals are frequently miserable and unpredictable, and staff is often hostile and enjoys baiting clients. But again, in this situation, the preventive techniques detailed here should help to avoid all but the most impulsively aggressive behaviors.

15

Cross-Racial, Cross-Cultural, and Cross-Gender Work

Perhaps more so with sociopaths than with other diagnostic groups, therapeutic work occurs between clients and therapists who are from very different walks of life. Clients are predominantly male and members of minority groups; most are poor and live a criminal or drug-addicted lifestyle. Therapists (particularly nurses and social workers) are predominantly female and white and generally law abiding.

Volumes have been written about the therapeutic issues that arise when clients and therapists come from different backgrounds, and every school that offers coursework in human services has at least one required course in racism or cross-cultural work. Here, I will simply add what I consider to be the salient features in successfully establishing a therapeutic relationship when some or all of these factors are present. Since sociopaths are so often gang members, gangs will be discussed as a subculture in a separate section of this chapter.

Issues of Difference Between Therapists and Clients

The strength of the therapeutic relationship is reinforced by a power imbalance that is built into its structure. It is the therapist, not the client, who must control the establishment and maintenance of appropriate therapeutic boundaries. When therapist and client are from different racial or cultural groups or socioeconomic classes or are of different genders, these differences increase the power imbalance in the interpersonal field as well.

In these instances, the imbalance serves no clinical purpose. Because such differences are value laden, they often lead clients and therapists to have preconceived ideas about each other. When these issues are not dealt with directly, this imbalance will weaken the therapeutic bond.

Clients and therapists from the same minority background will also encounter issues related to prejudice. For example, African-American students I supervised in prison often found that their African-American clients assumed that their shared racial background meant that the students would not hold them accountable for their behavior. If students did set limits, clients would accuse them of having "sold out" and betraying "their own."

When the client is also judged to be "difficult" and has significant trouble relating with others, as is the case with many sociopaths, the imbalance increases, and an already strained therapeutic alliance can easily be shattered.

Racial, cultural, and gender differences remain among the most intractable problems in therapeutic work. For the most part, therapists want to form productive therapeutic relationships and be helpful to others. Why is it that racism and prejudice continue to get in our way? Several factors seem to be at work.

First, people have a very basic need to form groups. Human beings generally do not do well alone.

Second, people in the majority racially, culturally, or by gender do not typically perceive the amount of difference that members of a minority group do. People of European descent on average do not perceive as much racism in this society as African-American people do. Men often do not see as much sexism as women. The perception of being shut out of mainstream society that those who speak English as a second language have is generally not endorsed by native English speakers. Often these differences in perception have to do with the majority feeling threatened by demands for acknowledgment and parity from the minority.

In any case, even though a minority client may experience some of the therapist's attitudes as prejudiced, the therapist may not. And when clients describe painful experiences that they believe were racially motivated or based on prejudice, the therapist may not share their perception.

Third, it is human nature to want to avoid conflict. Perhaps this tendency relates to our need to form groups, as conflict is frequently seen as threatening to the group structure. People rarely feel comfortable bringing up the subjects of racism or sexism, and they are especially hesitant to do so if they are unsure how the other person feels. Fear of hurting the therapist's feelings or causing discomfort will make clients extremely reluctant to raise issues of difference between themselves and their therapist, especially if they like the therapist.

Avoidance

All of these factors place the responsibility for raising these issues with the therapist. Everyone is taught that principle in school and reads it in the literature on difference. So why does a discussion of differences happen so infrequently, or only after a conflict is already in progress?

Therapists who avoid the topic offer a variety of justifications. Racism or sexism is irrelevant to the subject matter of the treatment. Differences just don't seem to be an issue. Why force a discussion of a topic if the client doesn't bring it up? The therapist feels unsure when or how to start the discussion. The therapist would feel stupid if he or she raised the issue and the client denied that racism or sexism was a problem.

As an aside, these reasons sound to me very similar to what parents say when they want to avoid talking to their children about sex. Is a similar dynamic at work here too?

As human beings, therapists would also prefer to avoid conflict and discomfort. And, as we have been told over and over again, we do not want to confront our own prejudices.

Obviously, there is significant interpersonal pressure to avoid the subject. However, as with aggression, this is an issue that simply cannot be ignored if a genuine therapeutic relationship is to be established and maintained. Therapists know that the level of discomfort someone feels about a particular subject indicates its importance. Therapists who avoid talking with clients about prejudice should know that even if they do not know how to approach the subject, it still needs to be discussed.

Additional Issues of Difference for Sociopaths

Sociopathic clients also experience discomfort about issues of racism and prejudice—including their own attitudes toward the therapist and their fears about judgments that the therapist might be making about them. Since sociopaths have opted out of mainstream society, they also have that issue to cope with in addition to any other racial, ethnic, or gender differences.

The therapist represents mainstream society (no matter how "countercultural" individual therapists may actually be or perceive themselves to be) and is often an authority figure for the client as well. Since sociopaths at the beginning of treatment cannot possibly experience this other as a person like themselves, the therapist can only be a symbol—a symbol of something that sociopaths desperately want, but feel incapable of attaining. A good deal of the rage that sociopathic clients feel at the beginning of treatment is about this conflict. To avoid discussing it is ultimately to reinforce these clients' perception of the larger society as unfeeling, uncaring, and ultimately unattainable.

Mechanisms of Perception

I had a real problem with the way that ethnicity and racism courses were taught when I was in graduate school. First, at the beginning of each class, before the teachers knew us or anything about our backgrounds or life experiences, we were told unilaterally that we were all racists. That observation was a given, and it would not have been acceptable to challenge it—even though it sounded like a fairly prejudiced remark, and the point of the course was supposed to be to teach us how to respect the fact that people are different.

The teachers then went on to discuss other types of cultures. We spent about a half an hour of class time on each one, and we were assigned reading material that briefly described several cultures. (McGoldrick, Pearce, and Giordano 1982 provide an example of this type of treatment of ethnic groups.)

I know that many of my classmates walked away from these courses feeling confident that they now knew enough to do competent therapeutic work with members of these other cultures. My experience was apparently not unique. Gould (1995) states that most social work curricula in diversity is geared to provide information about specific cultures and that it is believed that this information will enable students to engage in ethnically sensitive practice.

What we were never exposed to in these courses is material about how people actually categorize each other. What do we perceive as similar in others? What do we perceive as different? What meaning do we give to the similarities and the differences? This is the kind of material that I would have appreciated learning. Instead, I learned how to deal with these issues by struggling over them with clients.

Over time, I learned to operate from several principles. The first is that people make dangerous assumptions about both similarity and difference. The second is that we do so because it is human nature both to fear change and to perceive other groups as threats to our own group's power and control.

The dangerous assumption that we often make about similarity is to equate it with being identical. In this way, we avoid facing the differences inherent in those with whom we share some traits or habits, and we also reduce the amount of assessment that we have to do. If we know one factor about a client's background, we can then recall the five other things we learned about that client's culture in our last racism class and assume that those five things are also true about this individual. Relying on this kind of inductive reasoning and reaching a conclusion about many things based on information about one thing can only lead to stereotyping.

Drug users provide an example of this practice when they ask how someone who is not in recovery and has never been addicted to anything can help them with their problem. The assumption here is that all addicts share the same lifestyle, beliefs, and value system. But even if I had been an addict, how much would I have in common with a male, street drug addict? Many women are addicted to prescription medication, and the few who are tend not to live on the street or be familiar with its lifestyle. If I had been on the street, in all likelihood

I would have prostituted myself for money and drugs, and few men do this as a primary means of making money. Male street addicts rob or steal; if women steal at all, they tend to shoplift. The internal dynamics that motivate drug use do not necessarily correlate with any particular type of background, experience, or personality.

When similarities are overgeneralized, the resulting stereotypes come across as patronizing. At the other extreme, differences are so emphasized that the other person becomes alien to us. Whether in an attempt to respect difference or to reject it, we assume that because one thing is different, there are no similarities. This stance also leads to stereotyping, but since it comes from a lack of information, rather than from stray bits and pieces of data, it comes across as hostile, instead of patronizing.

The most extreme example of this stance is to consider people who look or act differently as nonhuman. Sociopaths already consider everyone else to be nonhuman; racism and prejudice just add another layer to this symptom of their illness.

Therapy can be difficult when therapists patronize clients in an attempt to understand them. It becomes dangerous when therapists perceive their clients as nonhuman. It is this stance that I observed over and over again in the prison system among staff who projected their own sociopathic impulses onto inmates. Correctional guards, medical staff, and administrators who viewed inmates as nonhuman and inmates who viewed staff and each other as nonhuman would use this perception as a justification for incredible amounts and types of cruelty and sadism.

Revisiting Similarity and Difference

Making judgments about others based on inductive reasoning about similarities and differences has never made a great deal of sense to me. Although the sociology courses I took as an undergraduate taught me a great deal about group membership and behavior, I often found myself questioning the accuracy of these studies because I could not apply the logic underlying them to myself.

I found that although I was a member of many social groups, my own value system and beliefs were more often than not different from those espoused by the group. When I began to study psychopathology and social work, I was awed by how complex each of us is. To a vast extent, the motivations and conflicts that make every person a unique individual are unclear even to ourselves. From this perspective, people appear very separate. Any attempt to argue that we share significant common ground by group membership alone seems absurd.

To me, it is not group membership that determines belonging or not belonging, but something much more basic than that. Psychodynamic theory seeks to describe human personality structure: thoughts, feelings, attachments, conflicts, motives, values, beliefs, and so on. Every living person has a personality structure and therefore fits within this theory. Every one of us shares these components of the human personality, no matter where we are from, what we look like, or how we have lived our lives.

Everyone has feelings. Everyone has some means of defense to cope with them. And everyone gets overwhelmed by them at times. Even granting a huge range of individual variation within those categories, it is still my belief that this is our common connection. I also believe that each one of us deserves to be treated with a basic level of respect and dignity simply because we are all alive here together. Treating others in this way is something that I consider to be basic to my own personality.

People have myriad ways to find themselves a niche and are members of any number of social groups: those of race, culture, gender, class, religion, sexual orientation, job, geographical location, psychiatric diagnosis, and so on. To look at these groupings from this perspective of similarity and difference makes the former assumptions about similarity and difference moot.

While we all share some traits and habits due to similarities in background or membership in certain groups, to my mind none of these things can render someone else known or necessarily understandable. I can have a client who is identical to me culturally, by gender, race, and class, and still have little or nothing in common with her in terms of values, beliefs, preferred activities, or lifestyle.

The stereotypes apply in some cases; just as often, they do not. And differences of race, ethnic group, or gender do not turn anyone into an alien being. I may know little or next to nothing about how someone else has lived, but we still have a basic human personality in common.

Applications

As a therapist, I need to learn all sorts of things about my clients before I can have an impact on their personality structure. I am there to establish a relationship with someone whom I do not know, and I will need to get to know his or her personality in a way that is probably more intimate than that of any other relationship in this person's life.

Group membership is one of the crucial things I need to know, and I try to learn about it in the same way that I would learn about any other important aspect of a client's life. I try to do so without judging or imposing my own value system. I use the information I obtain to fill in the mental image that I maintain of my client. I apply what I learn about this person's personality structure to the other components of identity: culture, race, gender, and so on. In this way, I hope to learn what those influences mean to this particular person.

From working with clients over time, I have learned some generalizations about individual groups, cultures, and subcultures. But when working with a new client, I always operate from the stance that I do not know if this particular individual shares any of these traits or habits. My experience has given me a great deal of knowledge about the male inmate subculture (or, more accurately, subcultures). If I am conducting a first meeting with a man who has done a lot of time, I keep all of the information I have about male inmates in mind. But I never assume that it applies to him. If I think that something might apply, I ask.

For example, I know that long-term inmates often have very ambivalent feelings about maintaining contact with their families. On the one hand, a connection to the outside is life affirming. On the other, while inmates do not want to bore or upset their families by detailing the daily events of prison life, they have little else to talk about. They also have trouble coping with the frustration and anxiety that limited and controlled contact brings. As a result, those inmates who do not tolerate ambivalence well tend to shut off their families.

Even though I know these things, it would be stupid for me to assume that the next ex-inmate who comes in for counseling is someone who shut off his family when he was incarcerated. If he talks to me about difficulty in his relationships with his family, I can certainly ask if it was hard for him to maintain touch with them when he was inside. By using my knowledge this way, I come across as understanding instead of as judgmental, as I would have if had I assumed without asking.

How does this apply to work with sociopaths? I know a great deal about the sociopathic subculture, but I do not how much of it will be meaningful to my next sociopathic client. I know that this next client will in all likelihood have all sorts of immediate responses to me, based on my gender, age, general presentation, line of work, and so on. In addition, he or she will have lots of fears and concerns about my prejudices about him or her.

As I have mentioned in chapter 11, I bring up our differences early on in the treatment when it seems appropriate to the topic to do so. Regardless of their race or ethnic group, inmates always complain about racism in the prison system, and I take the opportunity to talk about racism between us. Comments such as "Women are just like that" will trigger a discussion of gender. We are free to discuss inmates as a subculture and stereotypical notions about them, as well as issues concerning drug addiction, AIDS, gang affiliations, religious or sexual orientation, or any other factor meaningful to the client that involves membership in a group.

If clients are members of ethnic groups with which I am unfamiliar, I say so. I ask permission to ask questions about their culture, and I thank them for being helpful by teaching me about it. Clients will then usually respond by telling me some of their thoughts about me and the stereotypes that those thoughts involve. (For a clear and detailed framework on how to approach issues of race in a clinical setting, see Davis, Galinsky, and Schopler 1995.)

Some clients are extremely racist or sexist or both. I have had many clients tell me that my place is in the home, not in a prison, or tell me that if we were married, they would not allow me to do this kind of work. Other clients have insisted that I must have negative thoughts or beliefs about them based on their race. To me, these are issues that will evolve over the course of the treatment. As our relationship changes, so do these beliefs and feelings.

I know that I am not a person to my sociopathic clients at the beginning of therapy. And I know that in order for them to be able to find a way out of sociopathy, I must become a person to them. In order for me to become a person, I must first experience each individual client as a human being. How can I do this when sociopaths are so distancing? I do it by connecting with our common bond. I know what it is like to feel abandoned, humiliated, full of rage, ignored, alienated, treated with disrespect, used, and afraid. I know what it is like to feel that no one, including myself, understands me. For me, those connections are the glue. Everything else, including all the differences, is material for an exercise in exploration.

I do not know what to suggest to clinicians who are prejudiced and wish to remain so. It may be that these therapists do not want certain groups in society to have more power or control. It may be that they would not want members of certain subcultures to be accepted into the mainstream.

If that is the case, I would certainly recommend that these workers refrain from taking clients from any of the groups they regard in such a way. While those feelings and beliefs may be acceptable at a personal level, in professional terms they must be treated as countertransference material. As such, they should only be brought into the therapeutic relationship to the extent that they promote the health of the client. And I suspect that doing so is something far easier said than done.

Gangs

Turn on the news lately, and you are sure to find a talking head bemoaning the existence of gangs. Commentator after commentator tells us that gangs are ruining neighborhoods, families, and lives. Gangs cause death and destruction. They traffic in drugs and crime. The solution? More patrol cars, more heavily armed officers, longer and harsher prison sentences. Or maybe we should try public whippings for gang members who spray-paint graffiti in our crumbling public spaces.

Much of the bad news is true. But the one question that the sound bites never seem to address is why people join gangs at all. Why are gangs so popular?

Some Redefinitions

First, what is a gang? A gang is a essentially a group of people who have chosen to associate with each other by following a prescribed set of rules. There is usually a set of activities that the gang does together such as protecting turf and making money from criminal endeavors. Membership in gangs is generally ethnically or racially based. For the most part, females are not allowed in as full members of male gangs. There are some female gangs as well.

The rules that gang members follow are usually very strict, and punishment can be severe when members break the rules. A kind of level system is often in place, with increasing amounts of power as members travel up through the ranks. The gang usually has a single leader who has literally had to fight his way to the top. Many gangs' organizations resemble that of the military, and gang officers are sometimes referred to as lieutenants or by other military terms. Gangs can range in size from a small local group to a nationwide organization with a complicated regionalized bureaucracy to run it.

Gangs have been around for a long time in this country. They usually crop up in poor neighborhoods and are comprised of an ethnic or racial minority. When gang members are asked what their organization is about, they typically say that it is has to do with pride in one's background and history, obtaining respect from others, and showing loyalty to one's own.

When sociopaths refer to "pride," "respect," and "loyalty," they are talking about concepts that nonsociopaths would be more likely to think of as power, fear, and protection. The standard definitions of pride, respect, and loyalty all involve interpersonal dynamics that are simply beyond the capacity of most sociopaths.

What does a sociopath see when he or she watches someone showing respect for someone else? To the sociopath, it looks as though one person is doing what he or she is told to do by the other person. Why would someone do this? The only reason that makes sense to a sociopath is that one person is afraid of the other. From this point of view, "earning respect" means making someone afraid.

Pride is another alien concept. What do proud people look like? To the sociopath, they look like people who are in charge of things. "Pride" equals power.

What does "loyalty" mean? It means watching someone else's back and believing that he will watch yours. It means that people who band together are a lot less powerless than they are as separate individuals.

Given these redefinitions, the gang member who talks about pride, respect, and loyalty is right: these are the reasons why people do join gangs. In one sense, a gang is simply a sociopathic version of the Lion's Club. From another point of view, try thinking what would happen if a group of sociopaths (and psychopaths) got together and attempted to form a family. A gang would be the logical result.

Clinical Work with Gang Members

Gangs are becoming more and more prevalent, and more and more sociopathic clients are gang members. What does this mean in terms of therapy?

In general, I think that the most effective approach is simply to consider the gang as an extremely dysfunctional and violent family.

Gangs also comprise a subculture. As in work with any subculture, stereotyping should be avoided. Therapists should keep in mind that there are many meanings and values operating for the client that are unknown to them, and they should be sure to ask a great many judgment-free questions.

Most gang members who are in treatment on a voluntary basis are experiencing some ambivalence about being in the gang. Or, if they do not have mixed feelings when they start treatment, they will begin to have them as they enter the middle stage. Clients will begin to be able to get their needs for pride, respect, and loyalty met in different and healthier ways as they progress through treatment.

I have heard of instances when a therapist did something in the beginning stage that an involuntary client was not happy with (for example, informing a mandating agency of a violation of stipulations), and the client threatened the therapist with retribution from the gang. (I have never had such an experience, and I have no personal knowledge of instances where such a threat was carried out.) Although I have no respect for gangs, I do fear them. If a therapist receives such a threat, increased safety precautions of the type described in chapter 14 should definitely be undertaken.

In any case, whether treatment is voluntary or not and regardless of the client's feelings about his gang membership, it is very important for the therapist to avoid placing a value judgment on the client's gang affiliation.

In this context, I learned a critical lesson in a class on couple's therapy. The teacher asked for a volunteer to help with a demonstration; the only condition was that the student had to be ambivalent about something that could be discussed in front of the class. The student who volunteered stated that she felt ambivalent about graduating, and the professor immediately took the stance that she had to graduate: it was crazy to think of quitting now when she was more than halfway through the program, etc., etc. The student responded by becoming quite defensive; she argued rather forcefully that it might in fact be a very intelligent move for her to take a leave of absence or to drop out.

The point? If someone is ambivalent about something and the therapist takes a position on one side or the other, then the client has no choice but to take the opposing stance. If a therapist pressures a client to give up a gang, in all likelihood the client will cling to the gang with greater tenacity. The client must first want to walk away and be prepared to do so, both emotionally and physically.

Emotionally, the client must be ready to face life without the gang's support. Middle-stage work should show the client that a bond with others based on ethnicity or race and shared activities alone will not produce intimacy, or the respect, pride, and loyalty that come with a genuine connection to others.

Once the client no longer needs the gang, he has to plan how to leave it. It is not easy to renounce one's membership in a gang, and part of the course of successful therapy in work with a gang member is helping him to get out. There is no set way to accomplish this goal, and it is a frightening process for both client and therapist. The client is placing himself at considerable risk and must be ready to defend himself if need be, and the therapist can do little else other than offer all the support and guidance that training and experience can provide.

> **Case note.** Carlos was a 25-year-old married Puerto Rican male with a long history of drug addiction and criminal behavior; he requested treatment for reported symptoms of hallucinations and somatic complaints. As we met, I learned that he had a very chaotic and abusive background and was a gang member. He said that he wanted to try to straighten out his life.
>
> Carlos could manage the day-to-day aspects of incarceration, but had tremendous difficulty managing his internal states. Sobriety was new to him. He was not familiar with routine feeling states. The hallucinations he described did not appear to be the result of a psychosis, and he showed no evidence of any other manifestations of a formal thought disorder. He simply seemed frightened, and when

he talked about getting out of the gang, he was clearly terrified of what the retribution might be. His discharge date was also approaching so we needed to focus on discharge plans as well.

We worked simultaneously on symptom management, tolerating affective states, leaving the gang, and his discharge plans. Although I did not believe that the prognosis was good, about a year after Carlos left I received a call from a counselor who was working with him in the community. He was emotionally shaky, but he was sober and out of the gang.

Case note. Jerry was a 22-year-old single African American incarcerated male who requested treatment for sleep difficulties. He was prescribed an antidepressant because he showed some symptoms of depression: lack of ability to concentrate, lack of energy, feelings of hopelessness. Jerry was illiterate, had no work history, and was a gang member. It was quite difficult for him to articulate his ideas in words. He enjoyed the violence in the gang and felt important as a gang member in a way that he did not feel anywhere else. He understood the consequences of his behavior and accepted the fact that he would probably spend his life in and out of prison.

Jerry did not want to change his lifestyle in the prison. He did not work. He lived in one of the worst housing areas. He got disciplinary reports regularly. He did not want to talk about his life outside of the prison, nor would he discuss his past. He told me a little about the gang once he was convinced that what he said was confidential. He attended our meetings inconsistently. I wondered why he was coming at all.

What Jerry did want to do was to engage me in philosophical discussions about all sorts of subjects, from racism to the role of men and women in society. Since Jerry did not want to change anything in terms of his internal or external world and the medication helped his sleep, I was willing to discuss whatever topics he chose. I found him to be quite intelligent once he gained some practice at putting his ideas into words.

I worked with Jerry on consistent attendance. I described it as a matter of his self-respect: we had made a verbal agreement, and I trusted him to keep his end of the bargain. That approach worked to some degree, but his lifestyle was so at odds with scheduled appointments that I did not expect complete compliance.

We worked together for seven or eight months, after which Jerry was transferred to another facility. He was not sure whether he would continue counseling.

See the case note on John in chapter 12 for an example of another gang-involved client.

16

Treatment Environments and Modalities

Treatment Environments

Although most long-term treatment of sociopaths takes place either in prison or in halfway houses or other types of residential settings, sociopaths are increasingly being treated in other environments. Sociopathic clients who are substance abusers are frequently treated in short-term detoxification programs. Sometimes sociopaths are admitted to general acute-care psychiatric facilities or to partial hospitalization programs. They are certainly seen in forensic hospital settings. And they are treated at outpatient clinics as well.

The one major difficulty in applying the principles and strategies detailed in this book to different types of clinical environments and modalities is that the vast majority of treatment staff who have the most contact with sociopathic clients in those settings are not adequately trained to provide appropriate care. Although case managers or aides who do not provide counseling services should have at least a bachelor's degree in a human service field, many currently do not. Staff who provide any type of counseling need to have a master's or doctoral degree in human services or to be enrolled in a graduate-level program and working in a field placement with adequate clinical supervision. Again, this is often not the case.

It is an effort for well-trained therapists to contain and monitor countertransference reactions with this population while simultaneously choosing appropriate clinical interventions. Any program that expects an untrained counselor, however well meaning, to be able to apply these principles and interventions is a potentially dangerous trap for the client as well as for the counselor.

Even with an adequately trained staff, each of these settings presents different challenges when these treatment strategies are applied. Obviously, it is difficult to apply a long-term treatment model to a short-term program or setting. Sociopaths can wreak havoc on less structured programs that rely on participants' honesty and initiative, even though programs of this type can be effective with other types of clients. Nonetheless, some of the basic components and interventions described here can be included, and others can be altered so that they can be applied as well.

Halfway Houses and Other Residential Settings

There are several types of halfway houses. Correctional halfway houses are funded and managed by a state's department of correction or operate under a contract with the department. These facilities are designed to provide a transition for inmates from incarceration to the community. Offenders in these settings are usually either serving a very short sentence or in the last phase of a longer sentence. Some correctional halfway houses are treatment oriented, and some are not. Stays in these halfway houses do not usually extend beyond 18 months.

Other privately funded or nonprofit halfway houses specialize in specific types of treatment. Most are either residential programs for substance abusers or group homes for the mentally ill. Stays in these programs tend to be longer, up to 36 months (or longer for group homes).

Correctional halfway houses. Although the typical circumstances that result in an individual's admittance to a correctional halfway house usually indicate an obvious need for treatment, treatment is often not a component of these programs. Clinicians are rarely on staff, and the entry-level case managers who are hired at very low wages must play a primary role of guard. If offenders exhibit any symptoms of mental illness or act out in any serious way, they are usually returned to the prison system.

The simplest remedy for situations like these is to make counseling a mandated part of the halfway house's program. Where qualified counselors cannot be retained on staff, an outside counseling or mental health agency could provide the service on an outpatient basis. Or, if this were impossible, an offender showing such symptoms could be transferred to a correctional halfway house that did provide counseling, or the department of correction could contract with private non-profit programs to access some of their beds for correctional clients.

Treatment-oriented halfway houses. These facilities are probably the most beneficial type of program for sociopaths. In addition to group and individual counseling, most halfway houses of this type have a rather rigid structure with a graduated level system in place. Residents are slowly exposed to working and to other aspects of daily living that they may never have experienced before. Weekend furloughs give residents time to acclimate to the community, and residents at the advanced levels are expected to act as role models and supervisors for those on the lower levels.

Strategies detailed in this book are most easily implemented in an environment such as this. While program structure and observance of the rules will normally provide the focus of the beginning stage of care, it is vital that the program not deteriorate into tyranny or abuse (as in the very rigid drug-treatment programs developed in the late 1960s and early 1970s, where clients' heads are shaved and they are made to wash the walls with toothbrushes). Coercion engenders only submission or acting out, not internalization.

Residents reach the middle stage of treatment when they begin to display the capacity to engage with other residents and to follow the most important rules. Residents who cannot manage these steps are not yet ready for the program and should be encouraged to try again in the future.

The diagnostic and treatment principles covered here are easily applicable to group and individual counseling provided in such a setting. Direct confrontation will usually be most effective after residents have reached a certain level of comfort and safety in the program—and it can be extremely effective when it comes from more advanced residents who are demonstrating success in the program.

The key to helping residents progress to the middle and end stages of treatment is to make the program less and less rigid as residents demonstrate competence. Residents must have the opportunity to test out their own judgment and decision-making skills while they are being monitored and it is still relatively safe for them to make mistakes. Plans for follow-up counseling should be put in place before the resident's discharge from the program. An optimal outcome occurs when residents are able to return and participate as successful "graduates."

Group homes. If treatment-oriented halfway houses for substance abusers or offenders are the ideal place for sociopaths to receive treatment, group homes for the chronically mentally ill are most likely one of the worst. Since group homes' structure focuses on meeting the needs of people with major mental illnesses, not personality disorders, staff at these facilities tend to intervene with clients from an opposite but equally unhelpful stance from the approach taken by correctional halfway house workers. While correctional case managers are often overly suspicious of residents, case managers in group homes tend to enable their clients and to avoid holding them responsible for their behavior. For the most part, group home workers see their clients as helpless and hapless, and the vast majority of chronically mentally ill clients are in fact usually quite submissive. (Generally speaking, residents who do any significant amount of limit testing are likely to have a greater number of personality disorder traits.) While correctional staff are accustomed to clients constantly testing limits, group home staff expect clients to do what they are told and often become anxious and angry when their directions are disobeyed.

In the long run, group homes and other long-term residential facilities that treat clients with sociopathic traits will find it helpful to implement a level system. Such a system would provide some structure for the sociopath and offer staff some guidelines for evaluating the client's progress. (The suggestions given in appendix A for implementing a level system in an inpatient setting also apply to residential programs.)

Staff should bear in mind that any level system can only serve as a general guide. The individual treatment plan for each resident should dictate how much structure that particular client may need. The more sociopathy or character pathology that the client manifests, the more structure the level system should provide. Clients with major mental illness and very little character pathology would become too dependent on a system constructed for sociopaths and consequently would not develop their own decision-making skills.

In addition, strict limits must be in place for residents who abuse other residents. (See chapter 14 for a detailed discussion of this subject.)

Outpatient Programs

Sociopathic clients present themselves for treatment at outpatient clinics for a variety of reasons. Most often, they are mandated to get treatment by a court or a probation, parole, or child welfare department. Some agencies specialize in treating mandated clients, often receiving funding from the given state agency to do so.

Outpatient agencies that specialize in treating sociopaths—for example, drug treatment programs, ex-offender programs, and programs that treat domestic violence and child sexual abuse—are generally structured quite differently from traditional mental health agencies. Clients must sign contracts and releases that permit the outpatient clinic workers to communicate with the mandating agency. Clients' attendance is reported to the mandating agency, as is any type of acting-out behavior. Drug treatment agencies are often contracted to do urine testing as well.

Here, therapists are placed in the position of acting as agents of authority over their clients. Since the therapist's reports will help determine whether clients remain in the community, the therapist's basic role of acting as an advocate for clients and behaving toward them in a nonjudgmental and supportive fashion is compromised by an obligation to make judgments concerning their freedom. Clients often feel angry and resentful about this conflict, as do therapists.

Client-centered therapists often tend to be suspicious and wary of authority, and it may feel like quite an imposition for them to play this role. Clients will sense this ambivalence immediately and attempt to use it to gain some control over the rules. At the extreme, therapists who are unable to manage this conflict may collude with clients and enable their acting-out behavior by not reporting it.

Fortunately, therapists with these personality traits tend to avoid working in the kind of rigidly controlled settings where sociopaths are treated. Generally, the therapists who are drawn to this work are those described in chapter 8: individuals who identify with the social-control aspects of the job and feel that is their job to protect society from the client.

From this perspective, the counselor's role is quite similar to the work that probation or parole officers did years ago, before the criminal justice system became so massively overpopulated. Combining the functions of an agent of social control and a case manager, probation and parole officers in those days would help clients find jobs and refer them for counseling or for other types of treatment. They had the time to establish relationships with their parolees or probationers so that the social control aspects were balanced with helping their clients establish themselves in the community.

The balancing act. Working with sociopaths in an outpatient setting requires some adaptation from therapists. They have to contain their own resentment or discomfort and recognize that the extra structure is necessary. The mandating agency must know if the client is attending appointments, or if the client is continuing to behave in ways that forced the mandating situation in the first place. On the other hand, the therapist's client is not society at large; the client is the mandated person. The aspects of social control that the work requires must be viewed from a client-centered perspective.

This point of view is fairly easy to maintain if one retains a clinical perspective. The therapist's job is to promote clients' health and well-being. Since any acting-out behavior that endangers clients or others is not healthy, the therapist cannot support, enable, or condone such behavior. It is also the therapist's job to help clients develop the strengths and skills they need to live in the least restrictive environment with as much responsibility for themselves as possible. If clients indicate through words or behavior that their current level of autonomy is overwhelming, then the therapist must step in and provide the ego functions of judgment and reality testing by setting limits. Such an intervention protects clients when they are unable to protect themselves and protects the community as well.

Unfortunately, many of the agencies that treat sociopathic clients structure their policies and procedures in ways that needlessly blur the boundary between social control and therapy. For example, supervision of urine testing is listed as a required duty in counselors' job descriptions in many drug treatment agencies. This policy means that clients may find their therapists with them in the bathroom watching them urinate. Although I am unequivocally convinced that such a situation involves a serious boundary violation, I was once ordered to do so even after I had registered my strong objections to the procedure. Since I had no choice, I apologized to my client, kept my back to her, and stared out the stall window while she urinated. I was not willing to mangle therapeutic boundaries further over one potentially "dirty" urine. Middle stage work cannot be properly accomplished if clients are placed in such a sexually intrusive, humiliating, and submissive position with their therapist.

The mandated, ambivalent, or unmotivated client. A common complaint about mandated clients is that they are not motivated for treatment; they are in the program simply because they have to be. Yet since sociopaths are so dependent upon externals to take care of themselves, a push from an outside force is often the only way that many of them will ever find their way into treatment.

It is also important to remember there is *always* a choice. Mandated clients agreed to the conditions of their placement. They did not have to agree; they could have chosen to remain in jail or to go to jail or to have their children removed from the home. And, in fact, many sociopaths do choose continued incarceration rather than face all of the conditions of a parole or other type of early release. (Note that those who cannot manage the conditions of a parole with stipulations are at very high risk for recidivism. These individuals' lack of flexibility and need for concrete structure indicate little ability for self-regulation.)

As long as the therapist remains where the client is, an effective relationship can still be established with these terribly ambivalent clients. The therapist must simply accept how angry the client is about the stipulation for treatment and how unfair he or she feels it is. As in the beginning stage of treatment with any client, it is vital to avoid becoming angry or defensive in response to the sociopath's feelings. In this situation, I typically say to the client that I am sorry that he or she is in such a situation and that I will do my best to be helpful.

An opportunity for negotiation presents itself here. For example, the therapist can offer clients a deal: if they are able to manage the conditions stipulated by the agency or department for a significant period of time, then the therapist will advocate for an early removal of the stipulation to counseling. Even though clients may react by labeling the therapist as an easily manipulated do-gooder, they will also begin to think of the therapist as someone who is on their side. For the therapist, such an arrangement is actually a low-risk proposition: by the time the client is stable enough for the therapist to even consider advocating for a removal of the stipulation, the client will be in the middle stage of treatment and committed to continuing therapy until the problems being treated are resolved.

There are, however, some clients whose only motivation is to avoid jail. Even though these clients may never disclose much about themselves to the therapist, if they remain within the conditions of their stipulations, I consider the treatment a huge success. As long as their behavior stays within appropriate limits, I respect their choice not to talk about themselves, and I encourage them to seek counseling again in the future when they feel more ready to talk.

If clients do not remain within their stipulated limits, then the mandating agency needs to be informed. Clients of this type have usually stopped attending appointments at this point and know that the therapist will inform the supervising agency. They have commonly returned to the prohibited behavior, and an arrest is often imminent.

The voluntary client. Sometimes sociopathic clients may apply at a community mental health agency, or, if they have insurance, approach a private therapist for care. In the best scenario, these are clients who have recently completed a program and want to continue treatment. In the worst, they are seeking a therapist whom they feel will be unfamiliar with their issues and therefore be more easily lied to and manipulated. In either case, it is especially important to spell out the conditions of the therapy at the beginning, as one would normally do with any new client.

Clients who are continuing treatment are usually amenable to signing a release of information. Clients of this type should also be fairly honest with the therapist, or perhaps even somewhat demanding in their eagerness to get right back to the issues they have been dealing with. For therapists who are new to this sort of work and willing to learn from clients, this is an ideal type of client from whom to learn.

Sociopaths who are attempting to use therapy as part of a scam will rarely attend for long, nor will they be likely to pay the fee. Chances are good that such a client will just disappear after two to three sessions. However, if clients feel that the therapist was empathetic and supportive, they may return in the future to give treatment another more motivated try.

A middle-case scenario is also quite possible. For example, a client with strong sociopathic traits who has managed to maintain a job and family life might have avoided being stipulated to treatment. If such a client shows up at a clinic or office seeking outpatient treatment, then strategies for the beginning stage of treatment can be followed. The major difficulty is that the therapist will have access to much less information than would be available if the treatment were occurring in a residential setting.

The therapist's instinct here may be to ask for a lot of historical and background information during the first few meetings. I would recommend against this approach. Clients will most likely respond to a detailed interrogation with an increase in anxiety and defend themselves by increasing their lying to the therapist. Early sessions should be used to establish a solid relationship; the questions can always come later. It is usually helpful if clients such as this attend some additional treatment programs during the middle stage of therapy (for example, a Twelve Step program or support group) for extra structure, support, and exposure to nondysfunctional relationships.

Inpatient Programs

Inpatient programs, which are generally found in hospital settings, are typically for acute-care or evaluative purposes. The vast majority of these programs are structured to accommodate clients for two-week or three-week stays.

The biggest obstacle to effective treatment with sociopaths in an inpatient program is the lack of time. Anyone with a major mental illness or a moderate to severe personality disorder cannot be successfully treated on a short-term or acute-care basis. This factor makes it crucial that inpatient program staff be clear about what aspects of the clinical work can be accomplished within a limited time frame.

When sociopaths are not simply admitted to an assessment unit for evaluation, the two inpatient settings that they enter most frequently are detoxification programs and acute-care psychiatric units.

Detoxification programs. Sociopaths most often enter inpatient programs that provide detoxification for addicts. These programs last for two to three weeks, are highly structured, and attempt to provide some discharge planning in terms of follow-up care in the community.

Since the primary function of the detoxification program is a medical one, any counseling that is provided is within the framework that detox is only the beginning of the treatment process. As a general rule, addicted sociopaths should be routed from a detox program to a halfway house. If clients return directly to the community, the risk of relapse is high.

Addicted sociopaths do not always enter detox programs in order to stop using drugs entirely. They may be going to reduce their habit, in which case they may leave after several days or a week, before the program has been completed. (An addict may repeat this tactic many times over the course of a drug-using career.) Other clients may be attending in order to avoid incarceration. Here, again, motivation to become sober is questionable.

Another reason that addicts have a difficult time following through with inpatient detox programs is the long waiting list that these programs usually have. When individuals have to wait months before beginning the program, they are often not as motivated as they were when they first requested treatment.

Acute-care psychiatric units. Sociopaths most often find themselves in mental health inpatient programs as part of a forensic evaluation. Here, the purpose is not to treat. It is to evaluate competence to stand trial.

If a sociopathic client is admitted to a traditional psychiatric inpatient unit for acute care, the difficulties are similar to those that occur in group homes for the mentally ill. Again, sociopaths can wreak havoc with a structure designed for a very different type of personality organization. When the strategy of treating the sociopath in the same manner as the unit's other patients fails, he or she is usually either unsuccessfully discharged or ignored until a full-blown crisis occurs.

Together with the lack of time, the absence of an appropriate structure is the main obstacle to effective treatment. Acute-care staff who commonly encounter sociopathic clients will find it helpful to develop a protocol for a modified level system that addresses issues specific to sociopathic personalities. (See appendix A for a description of such a protocol.) With such a system in place, some of the chronic sociopathic symptoms can be contained so that work can focus on the specific symptoms that initiated the admission in the first place.

In addition to work on reducing or managing symptoms and discharge planning, inpatient program staff can choose an aspect of the beginning stage of treatment to focus on with individual sociopathic clients. In this context, the single most important piece of work to accomplish with a sociopath (other than a successful termination) is the establishment of a solid therapeutic relationship. This is the one thing that sociopaths are least prepared to do, and if they are unable to develop such a relationship, then they will never be able to gain anything useful from therapy.

Inpatient psychiatric programs can be extremely helpful in preparing the sociopath to establish future therapeutic relationships. When sociopathic clients come away from a psychiatric program with the realization that they were not punished for the way they interacted, that someone made a genuine effort to understand, that someone could read the pain and suffering camouflaged in their rage and sense of entitlement, and that what was established between therapist and client was neither mutual use nor victimization, those clients will most likely attempt therapy again in the future. And next time, they will not give the therapist as hard a time as they might have before the hospital stay.

Treatment Modalities

Most of the material in this book has focused on sociopathic clients in individual therapy. Sociopaths are more commonly treated in groups and are also sometimes seen in family or couples therapy.

Long-Term Group Therapy

If established and managed properly, group therapy is an effective treatment option for sociopaths. It works best if it is combined with individual therapy within a residential setting. If group therapy is provided alone, it generally does not permit the depth of relationship needed for sociopaths to explore all of their interpersonal issues. It is also too easy for a sociopath to get lost in the group. Other clients can dominate the group's time, or the time can be taken up with issues that are not central to a given individual.

The one thing that does make group therapy such an important part of an overall treatment program is the amount and type of reality testing and confrontation that can occur. Sociopaths respond rather well (comparatively speaking) when confronted by another sociopath. The experience is less humiliating than confrontation by the therapist, and it simultaneously offers the client a role model that a therapist cannot provide. When a good group facilitator is present, sociopaths in treatment together will keep each other honest and focused.

If sociopaths are going to work effectively in a group, the group's therapist must avoid getting into power struggles with the group members. If the therapist feels that someone in group is lying, it is best to let another group member take on the task of confronting or questioning that individual. If the therapist does so, it is too easy for group members to ally themselves with each other against the therapist.

One major hurdle that is especially of concern when the group takes place in prison or in a residential setting is the belief that sociopaths commonly have that it is a badge of honor and manhood not to "snitch" on each other. On occasion, a whole group may collude to enable one or more of its members to continue to act out. Yet if the group members genuinely trust the therapist and are committed to changing their lifestyle, usually one or two members will eventually disclose the secret.

> **Case note**. A cotherapist and I ran a weekly group in prison for men serving long sentences (35 years plus). Some of the men were in individual therapy simultaneously, and others were not. Some were prepared to discuss issues related to mental health, and others were not.
>
> After about a year of meetings, one of the group members stole a shawl that a female staff member had left in the room earlier. I was extremely distressed by this behavior and said so often. I was more distressed, though, by the fact that the man who took it would not return it and that none of the other group members would confront him about it, inside or outside of the group.
>
> Due in part to this series of events, we concluded that although the group had been meeting for a year or so, we were still in the beginning stage of treatment. We decided to increase the structure and rules of the group as a result.
>
> Eventually, one of the group members approached me and told me who had stolen the shawl. Although I did let my cotherapist know, we could not discuss this occurrence in the group due to confidentiality and safety concerns.
>
> We did not get the opportunity to learn how the new structure would have worked, as the security level of the institution was changed and most of the long-term inmates (including almost all of our clients) were transferred out. The group remained, but its membership was almost entirely different.

It is quite another story if only one or two group members are sociopaths. In this case, it is fairly easy for sociopathic clients to intimidate other members and take control of the group. Here, the most important assessment to make is whether the sociopathic clients share the same reason for attendance as other group members.

This same factor explains why traditional sex-offender group therapy often does not work for sociopathic sex offenders. All of the group members may have a behavioral symptom in common, but the meaning of the symptom and its purpose in each individual's overall personality structure are quite different. For the most part, traditional sex-offender therapy operates on a relapse-prevention model whose core belief is that sexual offending is an addiction. This model does not work well for sociopaths, for whom sexual offenses are generally more of an opportunistic behavior. Sociopaths in these types of groups feel alienated from and superior to everyone else in the room.

In contrast, even though drug-treatment groups commonly consist of sociopaths and nonsociopaths, the reason for using drugs is basically the same. (Note that drug dealers who do not use drugs should not be included in a group of this type.) Group leaders need to gain the sociopaths' trust, make sure that they feel accepted, and then support other group members when they confront the sociopaths about their attempts to dominate or intimidate other group members.

Bear in mind, though, that group leaders should not side with any one person or collection of people in a group; rather the leaders must side with those individuals who are communicating in the most appropriate way. At times when the sociopaths are actually calm enough to hear other member's complaints, others may take the opportunity to become verbally abusive themselves. In this instance, it is important that the group leader be protective of the sociopaths.

This balance will be particularly difficult to reach and maintain if the diagnostic categories happen to divide the group along racial lines. In a racially charged environment, people tend to attribute all sorts of situations and reactions to race. If sociopathic clients happen to be the only racial minorities in the room, race and prejudice are going to need to be discussed often. While it is important to acknowledge the feelings that racism brings up for everyone, it is equally important to ensure that clinical issues do not get mislabeled or lost.

Short-Term Group Work

Groups that focus on topics such as anger management are commonly offered to sociopathic clients. These groups usually run for twelve to sixteen weeks, are cognitively based, and generally avoid discussing group dynamics or working on the interpersonal dynamics of the group members. Since the purpose of these groups is essentially to teach or to impart information, I prefer to categorize them as classes. As such, they can be a collateral resource in work with sociopaths, but should never be expected to replace therapy.

Family or Couples Therapy

There are times when the family of a sociopathic, borderline, and addicted person will request treatment to "fix" the addict. What usually becomes clear is that the addicted person has the role of family scapegoat and that family members have quite inflexible and merged boundaries with each other. In this instance, progress is slow and painful because the family is heavily invested in projecting all blame, control, and responsibility onto the identified patient. Such a role is a frightening and overwhelming one for the addict, but also one that he or she is quite reluctant to surrender.

Many of these families attempt treatment often. When they do not hear what they want from the therapist, they generally respond by dropping out until the next crisis. In order for any change to occur, the therapist first has to be accepted into the family system. Then each of the family members must be prepared to accept his or her proper share of the blame, control, and responsibility. Only after the addict is freed from some of this burden can individual therapy take place. In this case, the individual therapy will need to focus on all of the developmental catching up that the addict has to do, since he or she will not have been able to grow or mature while saddled with all of the caretaking demands of the family.

If such a sociopathic client is admitted for individual treatment, then the family can be brought in at an appropriate later time. The beginning stage is not the appropriate time; the client must be generally stable in day-to-day self-management before he or she can start to cope with delving into family matters.

Another typical scenario for family or couples therapy is that a family is mandated to treatment because a family member (usually male) has neglected or physically or sexually abused another family member or members. Here, it is important to assess the risk for continued violence. Normally, the mandating agency will have already completed an investigation and determined whether the offender is capable of continuing to reside with the rest of the family; even so, the therapist should make an assessment and communicate his or her own recommendations. The therapist should also determine whether some type of group therapy or class specific to the type of abuse would be useful for the offender.

To provide effective family therapy, it is vital that the therapist remain neutral toward the offender. How can one maintain neutrality toward a person who has just perpetrated such a horrible act against someone else? Remember that therapy has the best chance of preventing any future behavior of this sort. In order for therapy to work, the sociopath has to be invested in the process, which means that he must feel that the therapist is supportive of him and his views.

It is easy to forget that one is still treating the family system here, and that the family permitted the offender's behavior to escalate to this point in the first place. Many of these families do not express anger in a healthy fashion, and the offender is generally assigned the role of holding the family's rage. Only when the sociopath's rage and out-of-control behavior can be seen as part of the family and accepted as belonging to everyone can it be properly contained.

Family members are often angry about being mandated to treatment even though they want the specific behavior to stop. They would rather place all of the blame on the offender and avoid taking any action themselves. When the therapist confronts this stance, the family will often collude together against the therapist. In this instance, power struggles with the family need to be assessed as a symptom of their functioning. The therapist must avoid being drawn into operating from the family's own dysfunctional structure by setting realistic limits and sticking to them.

If the family is not going to stay together, then the therapist's role is to help it adapt to the change in its structure; where children are involved, the therapist can also help the family set a fair and reasonable visitation schedule. Individual therapy can be offered to either or both parents or partners so that individual issues can be explored.

Should Treatment Be Mandated?

One basic question that remains to be answered is whether treatment for sociopaths should be mandated. It should come as no surprise that my answer is both yes and no.

The discussion of outpatient settings in this chapter highlighted several situations in which mandated treatment is appropriate. Most of these occur when a court becomes involved in the sociopath's life as a response to his or her behavior. For example, if there is evidence of domestic violence, participation in counseling needs to be a condition of the client's being able to remain with his or her family. Similarly, whenever treatment is a condition of probation and is therefore being used as a means of offering an alternative to incarceration, it ought to be mandatory. In both of these instances, treatment is being used as a structuring device.

The one place where I do not believe treatment should be mandatory is in prison. Prisons are already sufficiently structured, and so treatment is not required for that purpose. In this matter, I am in accord with Robertson (1992, 115), who describes the current British system of compulsory indefinite hospitalization for inmates categorized as suffering from psychopathic disorder as a "straitjacket." When in prison, people need to be able to make choices and to bear the consequences for those choices. Rather than a mandatory treatment program, I think it is a much better idea to offer treatment with some benefits attached for successful completion.

In this case, the type of treatment offered should be limited to a short-term, cognitive, group model focused on a particular topic. This approach will serve to introduce treatment to some clients who have never been in therapy before and who otherwise would not have considered it. If the group is a neutral or positive experience, then it will increase the chances for these individuals to seek out counseling in the future.

It is equally important *not* to offer benefits along with long-term individual therapy. A client ready for this level of work needs to be self-motivated. Although the prison structure should allow this type of treatment to take place (that is, adequate staff should be in place, and inmates should not have to choose between either having a job or participating in therapy), there should be as few benefits as possible.

In one setting where I worked, I saw many inmates apply for treatment in the mistaken belief that being in treatment would guarantee them furloughs, parole, or a security reduction. While whether or not someone is in treatment should be a part of the evaluation that is performed concerning granting these privileges, the treating therapist should not be the one to make that determination, nor should attendance alone be considered a strong factor.

Applications to Other Settings

A number of other types of treatment environments and modalities were not specifically covered here. In order to develop an effective treatment program in any setting, it is important to keep in mind the basic factors affecting work with sociopaths:

- The stronger the individual's sociopathic traits are, the more structure is necessary.

- Social control aspects of care need to be placed within a client-centered context.

- Abusive behaviors need to be addressed in a consistent fashion.

- It is vital to establish a therapeutic relationship.

- In a short-term program, some aspects of beginning-stage work can be chosen as a focus while discharge plans are being formulated.

- Group and family work are important components of an overall program, but normally should not be the sole type of intervention.

Conclusions

A fellow social worker recently shared an idea with me that he heard at a conference. He put it this way: What appears simple is complicated, and what appears complicated is simple. When I thought about it, I came to the conclusion that this phrase is a good way of summarizing the distinguishing characteristics of doing therapy with sociopaths.

As a diagnosis, antisocial personality disorder appears easy enough to understand: it is simply the equivalent of the term "career criminal." Sociopathy, on the other hand, is a complicated concept. It is difficult to distinguish from its cousins, narcissistic and borderline personality disorders. How does it relate to psychopathy? What role should criminal activity play in a psychiatric diagnosis? Why does sociopathy so often appear in combination with other psychiatric diagnoses? What is the difference between a chronic drug addict and a sociopath?

Countertransference is a relatively simple concept: it is solely what the therapist feels. In work with sociopaths, however, the therapist's feelings can become a bewildering tangle, and the entire concept of therapeutic neutrality, so basic to psychotherapy, is challenged by monstrous complications. Countertransference actually encompasses everything from the traditional notions of the repetition compulsion, projective identification, and objectification, to the therapist's attitudes toward various subcultures and racial and ethnic groups, to the late-breaking crime statistics and reports of the most recent overhaul of the death penalty statutes that we hear on the nightly news.

The whole idea of treating a sociopath from a psychodynamic perspective can appear to be extraordinarily complicated, or perhaps even impossible. But it is not. Doing so is actually simple. The work is accomplished along the same lines as work with any other client population. Start and stay where the client is. Formulate goals based on the client's wishes, not on those of the therapist. Operate from the stance of maximizing the client's health.

Maintaining physical safety around sociopaths seems very complicated. It is not. Basic safety precautions and deescalation techniques work as well with sociopaths as they do with other types of clients.

Issues of difference seem insurmountable. They are not. People are people, no matter who they are or how different their lives may be.

Who is the therapist answerable to when the client is mandated to treatment? The questions that arise around this issue can seem very complicated. They become very simple when basic definitions of client health are maintained.

What do we do with sociopaths in treatment environments that are not specifically geared to them? The problem seems to be a puzzle. But aspects of the work can be applied no matter where the client may find himself, whether in a private acute-care psychiatric hospital or doing a life sentence.

The client is unlikable. The work is hard. Managing the countertransference seems like a gargantuan task. A major reason that attempts to treat sociopaths so often fail is because the work is so complex. The simple response is to ask ourselves: Why bother?

The answer sounds simple, but it is not. Why bother to work so hard with such impossible clients? The answer is because we must. Most clinicians have limited if any control over who ends up on their caseloads. More and more clients are manifesting sociopathic traits. I believe that this trend will continue. If so, most clinicians will end up treating clients with sociopathic traits whether they choose to or not.

If we want to reduce sociopathy in society, then we must not respond to sociopaths in the same way that sociopaths respond to us. We cannot simply ignore and dehumanize clients because they dehumanize us. If we do, we are increasing the level of sociopathy in the world, not decreasing it. All of the pathology in the world either exists in an unconscious and unmanageable form for both therapist and client, or it exists in a conscious and therefore potentially manageable form. If these are the choices, I prefer to act as if the latter were true.

I have a few last hints to share that I hope will make the ride easier.

Personally, I try to consider the pressure to dehumanize as a challenge. The more unlikable the client's presentation and the more that he or she attempts to dehumanize me, the more firmly I tell myself that I will not permit this individual to deprive me of my humanity. I will continue to perceive and to experience this person as a person, no matter how hard he or she is trying to get me to do otherwise.

Use the treatment team. Do not try to deal with a sociopath all alone if a team is available to help. The treating therapist needs support, reassurance, guidance, and a place to vent.

As part of a treatment team, try to provide a balance for the treating therapist's countertransference. If he or she is too angry to respond properly to the client, reinforce the client's humanity. If therapist is not angry enough, reinforce the basic precept that respect needs to go both ways.

Most important, keep a sense of humor (even though it may need to be a macabre one at times). Laughter is an extremely effective venting mechanism. It helps to keep one's thought process and personality flexible. And humor is a healthy reminder of what is uniquely human in all of us.

My goal in writing this book was not to provide the answers to "everything you always wanted to know about sociopaths but were afraid to ask." Rather, I began with a sense that many people inside and outside of this field do not know much about what it is like to be a sociopath. My hope is that the reader who has come this far with me will be able to say, "Maybe I do understand—at least, a little. And maybe being a sociopath is not so terribly different from what it is like to be one of the rest of us."

Appendix A

A Protocol for Management of Sociopathic Symptoms in an Acute-Care Inpatient Setting

Many of the ideas used here are borrowed from the level system in place at Brooklyn House, Brooklyn, Connecticut.

These are the three most effective ways to reduce a sociopath's acting-out behavior:

1. Provide adequate structure.

2. Formulate achievable goals for the patient.

3. Establish a positive therapeutic alliance.

All three of these interventions can be accomplished through the use of a modified level or step system.

The ideal arrangement is to have a step system in place for all of the patients in the unit, so that it can be administered in a consistent fashion. In those many acute-care psychiatric settings where an extended system is not possible, the next best alternative is to develop a step system as part of an individual patient's treatment plan.

First of all, the rules concerning behavior toward others must be spelled out clearly, in writing, and given to the patient upon admission. Any sort of violence or threat of violence should be grounds for immediate discharge (assuming that a court has not ordered the patient's commitment).

Second, a level system has the best chance of succeeding if enough activities are included to ensure that the patient is kept busy. Schedule enough chores, activities, and treatment appointments to keep free time at a minimum.

The level system itself should begin with the most restrictions and staff supervision and gradually progress to fewer restrictions, more choices, and less active monitoring by staff. Although the patient's schedule should remain equally busy throughout the program, less preferable chores can be assigned to the beginning steps. At the last level, patients should be allowed to choose the chores that they would like to do from among several alternatives.

Increases in steps need to be earned. Criteria for advancement should include a combination of good behavior and the acquisition of interpersonal skills. "Good behavior" means that the client participates in all scheduled activities in a responsible fashion and shows appropriate behavior toward staff and patients. Interpersonal skills can begin with basic listening skills, progress to the ability to hear feedback from others, and end with the capacity to take responsibility for one's own behavior.

Patients should be required to write a letter requesting promotion to each next step. The letter should describe how the patient has accomplished the tasks of the current level and how he or she will approach the tasks of the next level. (If the patient is illiterate, he or she can dictate the contents.)

Peer pressure can be an effective component of a level-system program. For example, the patients in the unit can be asked to vote for or against each individual's advancement from level to level. (Note that for this approach to be workable, all of the patients must be participating in the same level system.)

The therapist can play the role of coach. It must be clear to the patient that the therapist is invested in the patient's "winning." The therapist must encourage patients, provide lots of positive feedback when they accomplish goals, and advocate for them when they are accused of things they did not do.

However, coaching also involves confronting. Patients need to hear about it when they do something wrong and be told how they can correct it. If a patient's goals are not achievable, then the therapist needs to reassess the treatment plan and make its goals more manageable.

When sociopathic patients are kept busy and have a chance to feel as though they are succeeding at the program, the risk for serious acting-out behavior is vastly reduced.

Appendix B

Deescalation Techniques

Several of the items in sections 1 and 2 came from Nigrosh 1985.

Goal: To permit clients to extricate themselves from situations of humiliation and rage without resorting to violence.

1. Adopt and maintain a nonthreatening stance.

A. Avoid close physical proximity.

B. Do not touch the client.

C. Avoid authoritarian gestures (for example, standing with hands on hips or pointing at the client).

D. Keep hands at sides or hold them up, wide open, with palms facing the client (as a gesture of surrender) or facing the floor (as a gesture meaning "Calm down").

E. Do not yell. Keep your voice level and as low as possible (without frustrating the client).

F. Avoid an angry tone of voice.

G. DO NOT SHOW FEAR. (It is okay to show concern or sadness.)

2. Interpersonal responses

A. Get the client away from the group or from the person with whom he or she is having the conflict.

B. Permit the client to verbalize his or her feelings fully.

C. Support the urgency of the client's grievance.

D. Validate his or her feelings.

E. Show a nonjudgmental, accepting attitude.

F. Be respectful. Work to maintain the client's dignity.

G. Reassure the client that he or she is accepted, respected, and cared about.

3. Clinical interventions

A. Ask short, simple, fact-based questions.

B. Continue to keep your voice low and level.

C. Let the client save face. Look for ways to interpret the situation so that the client will feel that he or she has "won."

D. Offer choices that will permit the client to "win" at unrelated things.

E. See if it is possible to distract the client by using humor.

F. Support the client's internal controls. Remind the client of times when he or she did well at managing anger. Express confidence that the client can do the same now.

G. Reassure the client that external support systems are in place to provide a limit. (Do not communicate this as a threat.)

Appendix C

Clinical Workbook

Cheryl Boland's assistance in helping me formulate the ideas in this workbook is gratefully acknowledged. Several of the specific interventions come from her practical knowledge and experience.

The purpose of this workbook is to help clinicians apply the information and material in section III. The tasks are divided by stage of treatment, and since the goals and focus of the work in each stage of treatment are different, the tasks reflect these differences. Some of the specific tasks and assignments listed are for the therapist to do, and some are for the client.

Tasks are structured so that completing them will achieve the following goals:

- Increase the information available to the therapist.

- Clarify material for both the client and the therapist.

- Improve the client's ego functions.

- Increase the therapist's flexibility in conceptualizing theoretical issues.

- Increase the therapist's capacity to imagine the client's internal world.

- Increase the therapist's capacity to separate affective responses from affective perception.

The tasks can also be useful when the therapy seems stuck. (A lack of progress is often a result of a deficit in one of these areas.)

However, there are some dangers in relying on tasks. It is important to avoid assigning tasks as a substitute for proper exploration of an issue. A task is an aid to exploration, but cannot take its place. If clients are given a workbook full of assignments, they will often race through them as quickly as possible in the hope that completing the assignments will mean a quick and relatively painless resolution of the problem. The result is that clients will be sorely disappointed with the assignments (and the therapist) or that they will regress (because the tasks will raise too many issues too quickly without proper therapeutic containment).

Tasks should never be used simply because the therapist does not know how to guide the client or how to determine the general course of the work. If these situations are the case, then the clinician needs to consult with his or her supervisor.

Beginning Stage Tasks

The goals of the beginning stage are to establish a therapeutic relationship and to begin the assessment and treatment planning process. In order to establish a therapeutic relationship, clients must feel accepted and somewhat understood. They must have some faith that the therapist will be able to help.

Beginning stage tasks for the therapist are designed to help the therapist experience what life is like from the mind-set of a sociopath. This experience will be helpful both in establishing a therapeutic relationship and in formulating an assessment. The client's tasks have to do with developing the skills of observation and description.

Tasks for the Therapist

1. Focus on your own capacity for careful observation and description of the client during the first few meetings. Attempt to keep the information you gather neutral. Do not use words that are value laden or judgmental. This information can be for yourself, or it can be shared with a supervisor.

> *Example.* The client is a 25-year-old divorced white male with a history of incarceration, drug addiction, and theft. He is requesting treatment because he is mandated to do so. He does not want or feel he needs treatment. He reports feeling angry and frustrated about having to attend counseling. He questions the motives of the counselor.

2. Describe the client, preferably aloud, to a coworker or supervisor in terms of the way that the client makes you feel. Do not hold anything back. Use all of the value-laden words you can think of.

> *Example.* This asshole comes barging into my office, interrupts a meeting I'm having with a coworker, and accuses me of being lazy.

He tells me I'm incompetent because if I knew anything, I'd know that he didn't need any counseling. I can't believe this guy! Who the hell does he think he is? Does he think the world revolves around him? Well, I've got news for him. It doesn't. Not my world, anyway. He orders people around all the time and makes people so angry, and he's so self-absorbed he doesn't even know how angry people get. One of these days he's going to mouth off to the wrong person, and I tell you I'd like to be there to watch.

3. Recall that how the client is causing you to feel is how the client feels inside. Step into the description that you just gave to your coworker or supervisor. Think about how it would be to feel like this about your therapist.

Example. So this guy is asking himself, Who does the therapist think she is? She must think that the world revolves around her. Well, I've got news for her. It doesn't. She orders people around all the time and makes people so angry and is so self-absorbed she doesn't even know she is doing it. One of these days she is going to piss off the wrong person, and I tell you I'd like to be there to watch.

From this point of view, the client appears to be quite angry, frightened, and humiliated. Think about what it would be like for you to feel like this all of the time with every relationship you have.

4. Think about the following incidents:

- A time when you were disciplined by a teacher in grade school

- Your last few visits to the doctor

- Arguments or disagreements that you had with your parent, partner, or best friend that were subsequently resolved

Put yourself in the role of the other people in each of these incidents and think about how differently they would have described the event. Describe the event from their point of view.

5. Continually keep in mind the fact that, for all intents and purposes, you and your sociopathic client have been raised and have lived on different planets. Suspend all of your values and judgments when listening to the client.

Think of a situation that your client told you about that sounded like an emergency. Recall how he or she responded to it. Think about how you would have responded to it.

Think of an incident in your life that you considered a genuine crisis. Imagine how your client would have perceived and experienced the same situation.

Whenever a client shares an experience or event with you, remember that you must not ascribe the feelings that you would have felt in a similar situation to your client. The sociopath will have different feelings.

Example. The client loses his job because he was late for the fifth time in a row. The same week, he is evicted from his apartment for not paying the rent. Now he has nowhere to go and no money.

The client seems rather unconcerned about the whole thing. He laughs it off because he considers it a relief. He found all of the demands of working and keeping the apartment together very stressful and overwhelming anyway.

On the other hand, his therapist would have been quite upset in the same situation. He would have experienced a tremendous sense of loss concerning the job and housing and felt that a big part of himself was gone. He would have been very concerned about the future and how he would support himself.

Example. A genuine crisis for a therapist might be a breakup with an intimate partner. She would be very upset and depressed for quite a while. She would attempt to get support from other people in her life and try to look after her physical and emotional health in the best way she could. She would be unlikely to date until she had sufficiently dealt with her grief. She would try to figure out what her role in the breakup had been and try to identify a way to avoid the same thing in the future.

Her client, on the other hand, would probably isolate herself, neglect her health, become utterly overwhelmed by the loss, and most likely act out in several ways: by taking drugs, engaging in reckless or impulsive sexual behavior, shoplifting, or perhaps attempting suicide. She would feel certain that the breakup was entirely her partner's fault. She would immediately attempt to find a substitute for her partner and would not look for dysfunctional patterns or try to think how to avoid them.

6. Since the client's and therapist's feelings and reactions are not the same, it is logical to assume that they will also have differences when it comes to setting therapeutic goals. Therapists must avoid setting goals for their clients; clients need to set their own goals. Of course, if a client states that one of his goals in counseling is to increase his skill at stealing, his therapist is obviously not required to put him in contact with successful thieves. But therapists must remember that the sociopath's goal is probably not going to be to live a lifestyle that is a replica of the therapist's.

Misunderstandings about goals typically start at the beginning of treatment when the client says something like, "I want a normal life. I want to stop living like this. I want a life like yours." The trickiest elements of a statement like this are the words "normal" and "yours." Both therapist and client need to think what these words mean (although for very different reasons).

Start by defining "normal." Ask three other people to give you their definitions. (Make sure that two of them do not work in this field; therapists tend to have a very abnormal view of normalcy.)

Now think about your life. Does it meet your own definition of "normal"? Does it match the other definitions you collected?

Now ask yourself what your client thinks your life is like. If you have no idea, ask the client what he or she thinks. (Note: do *not* tell the client what your life is actually like.)

7. When you think of goals for your client, try to determine whose goals they are.

> *Example.* Although the therapist defines "normal" in typical middle-class terms, he does not live in a way that matches the definition. He lives in an apartment with three roommates. His weekends are spent partying, and he has little or no money in the bank.
>
> The client thinks that the therapist's life is typically middle-class: a sheltered and settled home environment, wealthy parents, access to money when it is needed, vacations out of the country, and so on.
>
> This client's goal is "to be able to keep a steady job." Whose goal is this? Did the client ever say anything about a steady job? Or does the client actually think that achieving a middle-class lifestyle means that someone else will always foot the bill?

Tasks for the Client

In order for clients to accomplish their part of the beginning stage, they must be able to articulate certain aspects of their internal world. The tasks listed here can help them develop this skill. (Note that putting words to feelings and communicating them is also a major building block of the ego function of regulation of affect, drives, and impulses.)

1. Give clients tasks in which they must observe and describe someone else's behavior and reactions. For example, ask clients if they admire anyone in their lives with whom they come in regular contact. Ask them to observe the individuals they name for a week and then come in and describe what is admirable about them.

2. Encourage clients to get "reality checks" by gathering three other people's impressions about a given subject or event.

3. Ask clients to define the following terms: *normal, sober, manipulate, control, evil, crime, power, and intimacy.* Tell them that they are free to ask others for their thoughts and definitions and encourage them to get help with defining the terms.

Middle Stage Tasks

Once a therapeutic relationship has been established and the client is invested in the treatment process, the focus of treatment shifts to shoring up weak ego functions and to helping the client develop flexible and healthy interpersonal boundaries.

Many of the instructions in this section involve using visualization to create a mental picture to symbolize a given conflict, process, or ego function. I find this approach useful in several ways.

First of all, visualization forces the therapist to view the issues in a different manner. Given all the differences between therapist and client, it is helpful to perceive and conceptualize clients' statements in as many ways as possible.

Visualization also allows the therapist to discover a client's defensive strategies that rely on reversing the experience of affect. For example, the defenses of turning passive into active, reaction formation, and projection all involve clients feeling some very different affect from the one against which they are defending.

Using visualization sometimes seems like the psychotherapeutic equivalent of those math problems that require you to imagine and manipulate a geometric figure in your mind in order to reach a solution. (By using the math problem as an example, I am actually relying on the technique of visualization to explain how visualization works.) In any case, the ability to turn something around, upside down, and inside out enables the person to view it from all angles.

Most important, I find that male clients have an easier time comprehending complex psychological processes if they are given the information in a visual form. I also find it helpful to create a mental picture when I am trying to explain something I am perceiving about him to a male client. Often, males can more easily explain their own mental processes by visual example. Sometimes, clients and I will trade images until we are clear that we understand each other.

Therapist and client tasks are much more closely shared in this section than they were during the beginning stage, reflecting the merger that occurs between client and therapist during successful middle-stage work.

Visualization Exercises

I have found it helpful to share my store of mental images about the course of therapy with clients when they have reached a stage where these images are relevant to them. Images are also particularly helpful in working through resistance. (Note that I did not say whose resistance.) Although you will want to come up with your own images, I hope that sharing some of mine will spark your imagination and suggest areas where images can be effectively used.

1. I describe a healthy personality as one that has the components of a boxing match: two fighters and a referee. One fighter represents the sober, law-abiding side of the person (the superego), and other represents the drug-addicted, crime-involved side (the id). The referee is the ego. I describe a sociopath's personality as one where one fighter (the id) beats the other (the superego) unconscious and then threatens to go after the referee (the ego) so that the referee leaves the ring. Once the referee leaves there are no rules, lots of danger, and the match is not evenly balanced.

The first step in helping the client conceptualize these aspects is to introduce this image. The second is to ask the client which player has a voice and can speak. Sometimes, the superego talks a lot, and the id does not listen. In this case, the id often has no words, only behaviors. In other cases, the id does all of the talking and threatening. Here, the superego can only whimper. (Remember that at this point in the treatment process, there is no referee. He left because the match became too dangerous.)

2. I describe affect containment in terms of a pot of water on the stove. In the beginning, there is too much water for the container and the pot has holes. However, we cannot control the amount of water we have. The only alternative we have is to repair the pot and expand its size so that it can hold all of the water that it needs to.

3. Clients with borderline traits want to race in and fix everything immediately. They usually say something like, "I have all of this stuff inside that gets totally out of control. If I can just dump it, then I'd be fine." And that is what they try to do. I describe the middle stage of therapy to a borderline in the following way:

> There is this huge chasm, an abyss, actually. (I define these words, if
> necessary.) You are on a cliff in a big truck on one side, and you
> have to get to the other side. It is too far to jump. What do you do?
> You build a bridge. But if you're in a hurry and you aren't careful
> how you build the bridge, you risk overloading it. The bridge has to
> be carefully built so that it can withstand the truck's weight.

One client countered with a bridge image of his own. The way he saw it, he was in the middle of the bridge over the abyss, and the bridge was on fire at both ends.

4. More obsessive-compulsive types of client start to panic if they cannot see concrete guideposts for how the therapy is supposed to progress. This is particularly a problem for them during the middle stage, when affect is beginning to be permitted to have a voice.

With this type of client, I describe a picture that a client drew for me to show how he perceived what was going on. It is a drawing of a bear up a tree, with another bear at the base of the tree looking up at the first bear. Behind the bear on the ground is a path cut through tall grass. The client explained that he was the bear up the tree and was afraid to come down. I was at the base of the tree telling him that he had to come down, that I had cleared the path for him, and that I would accompany him but could not walk it for him.

I say to clients with obsessive-compulsive traits that the only way to view the markers is backwards, not forwards. They can see where they have come from, but not where they are going. For that, they will have to trust their guide.

5. Clients will often describe a monster (id material) inside of them that rules their lives. They hate the monster and try to control it, disable it, and ultimately destroy it. One client described his demon as someone who had hijacked a bus with all of the passengers still on it and was driving at ninety miles an hour through crowded streets.

I respond to images like this by asking clients to imagine ways to befriend their monsters. (This suggestion generally does not go over well the first hundred or so times I offer it.) I also refer them to the image of the boxing match and remind them that you can't have a proper boxing match without two opponents.

6. When clients are feeling too vulnerable, they often regress and withdraw in an attempt to create some interpersonal distance and protect themselves. I describe such an interpersonal boundary as a brick wall. I say that brick walls are real good for certain things, like keeping everything that is in, in, and everything that is out, out. But people need a more flexible wall than that, because people want to let some things out and some things in. Besides, there are times when we want to be able to see what is out there, and with a brick wall, you can't see a thing.

The first thing we can do is to loosen some of the bricks from the inside so that the client can pull them out and see what is out there. After that change feels comfortable, we construct a door. At first, it doesn't have a doorbell or a knocker, because the client opens it only when he wants to.

When the client gets this far, I tell him that even though he can't see me I am right outside the door. I won't try to come in or even knock until he tells me its okay, but I won't leave, either.

After a while, I point out that having no doorbell means that the client doesn't really know if anyone is out there. Sometimes a protective measure actually increases danger. Still later, we work on changing the material of the wall so that it is translucent and permeable.

7. Clients and I have worked on controlled access to impulses and affect by visualizing different types of images. For example, clients visualize that the uncontrollable parts of themselves are locked up in a closet. I suggest that the client open the door just a crack, look in, and then close it. We talk about the monster's chances of getting out and explore ways to avoid that happening. We talk about the same process in terms of slipping into a swimming pool slowly, as opposed to diving in headfirst. We discuss how to move this material from the front burner of the stove to the back burner and back at will.

8. I sometimes tell clients the story of the myth of Oedipus. Freud might be disappointed, since I do not tell it to describe the son's desire to replace his father. I tell the story because it is such an accurate example of people attempting to defend themselves from something in such a way that they actually create the conditions that they are trying so hard to avoid. Whatever other significance the myth may have, it is clearly one of the earliest documented examples of the repetition compulsion at work.

Additional Tasks for the Client

Clients should also be encouraged to form their own images. One very useful way to help clients form their own images concerning affect management and interpersonal boundaries is through the use of collages, drawing, or list making.

Be sure to find out how literate the client is before assuming that writing will be therapeutic. However, do not assume that brain-damaged clients won't find writing useful. Many do. Some clients like to draw, and some don't. Work with what the client likes to do. Since these are exercises in self-expression, the mode that the client chooses should be a form of self-expression as well.

1. Clients can be helped to communicate their affective states and self-representations by collecting drawings and photographs in order to make a collage to illustrate a given idea or feeling state. One client likened himself to a car, and so his collage contained pictures of cars. Collages can be assigned to illustrate the good and bad sides of oneself, one's outside versus one's insides, the masculine and feminine sides, the past, present, and future, and so on.

2. To help clients experience ambivalence, they can be asked to list the extremes of a given situation; client and therapist can then go on to determine the middle aspects together. Or the client can come up with one extreme, and the therapist the other.

3. Clients can be asked to list feelings on index cards and then list three ways to cope with each feeling on the back of its card.

4. When clients are feeling vulnerable in terms of their own and their significant others' emotional needs, images can be used to enhance a feeling of safety and containment. For example, Twelve Step programs suggest using the image of the client in a protective bubble; no one can get any closer than the outer layer of the bubble.

Some therapists who have worked with survivors of sexual abuse suggest that clients conjure up an image of themselves as a healthy adult who will protect the vulnerable part of their self. When clients are unable to create such an image (and I find that many cannot), I sometimes suggest that they substitute my image for that of the healthy adult. If clients are feeling vulnerable toward me, I ask them to imagine how a healthy adult would respond to a child who was feeling that way. When clients get stuck, I tell them what the healthy response is and ask if they can picture their adult self acting in a similarly protective way toward the part of themselves that is hurting.

Tasks of the End Stage

When I started writing this section, I realized that I do not have a great many images for it. Although I would like to say that that is because clients are well enough at the end stage to verbalize without the use of visualizations and tasks, I am not sure if that is truly the case.

Tasks and assignments in this stage should relate to how the client will internalize the therapist as a self-object (as an aspect of his or her own self). While this process should be well advanced by the time a client is terminating, assigned tasks can be especially helpful when termination is abrupt or unexpected.

I encourage clients to "carry me with them" and to imagine what I would say in a given situation. I sometimes check to see if they can conjure up my image so that they can pretend to have a conversation with me. I give clients small gifts or cards that represent me or represent something important that we shared.

My own feeling is that clients should be encouraged to carry on an inner dialog with their therapists. When they need their therapists' support, I believe that they should just go ahead and speak to them as if they were there, because in many ways they are.

References

American Psychiatric Association (APA). 1994. *Diagnostic and Statistical Manual of Mental Disorders*. 4th ed. Washington, DC: American Psychiatric Association.

———. Task Force on DSM-IV. 1991. *DSM-IV: Work in Progress 9/1/91*. Washington, DC: American Psychiatric Association.

Balint, Michael. 1968. *The Basic Fault*. London: Tavistock. Reprint, New York: Brunner/Mazel, 1979.

Becker, Howard S. 1963. *Outsiders*. New York: The Free Press.

Bellak, Leo, Marvin Hurvich, and H. Gediman. 1973. *Ego Functions in Schizophrenics, Neurotics and Normals: A Systematic Study of Conceptual, Diagnostic and Therapeutic Aspects*. New York: John Wiley.

Blackburn, Ronald. 1992. "Criminal Behavior, Personality Disorder, and Mental Illness: The Origins of Confusion." *Criminal Behaviour and Mental Health* 2: 66-77.

Boyer, L. Bryce, and Peter Giovacchini. 1990. *Master Clinicians on Treating the Regressed Patient*. Northvale, NJ: Jason Aronson.

Brenner, Charles. 1955. *An Elementary Textbook of Psychoanalysis*. International Universities Press. Reprint, Garden City, NY: Doubleday, 1974.

Brett, Tim R. 1992. "The Woodstock Approach: One Ward in Broadmoor Hospital for the Treatment of Personality Disorder." *Criminal Behaviour and Mental Health* 2: 152-158.

Casement, Patrick, J. 1991. *Learning from the Patient*. New York: Guilford.

Davidson, Margaret. 1965. *Helen Keller's Teacher*. New York: Scholastic.

Davis, Larry E., Maeda J. Galinsky, and Janice H. Schopler. 1995. "RAP: A Framework for Leadership of Multiracial Groups." *Social Work* 40 (March): 155-165.

DSM-IV. *See* American Psychiatric Association 1994.

Frankl, Viktor E. 1959. *Man's Search for Meaning*. Boston: Beacon Press. Reprint, New York: Washington Square, 1984.

Fromm-Reichmann, Freida. 1960. *Principles of Intensive Psychotherapy*. Chicago: University of Chicago Press.

Gallwey, Peter. 1992. "The Psychotherapy of Psychopathic Disorder." *Criminal Behaviour and Mental Health* 2: 159-168.

Goffman, Erving. 1961. *Asylums*. Garden City, NY: Anchor Books.

———. 1963. *Stigma*. Englewood Cliffs, NJ: Prentice-Hall.

Gould, Ketayun H. 1995. "The Misconstruing of Multiculturalism: The Stanford Debate and Social Work." *Social Work* 40 (March): 198-205.

Hare, R. 1985. *The Psychopathy Checklist*. Vancouver: University of British Columbia.

Hedges, Lawrence. 1992. *Interpreting the Countertransference*. Northvale, NJ: Jason Aronson.

Hodge, John E. 1992. "Addiction to Violence: A New Model of Psychopathy." *Criminal Behaviour and Mental Health* 2: 212-223.

ICD-10. *See* World Health Organization 1992.

Kernberg, Otto. 1975. *Borderline Conditions and Pathological Narcissism*. New York: Jason Aronson.

Luntz, Barbara K., and Cathy Spatz Widom. 1994. "APD in Abused and Neglected Children Grown Up." *American Journal of Psychiatry* 151: 670-674.

Madden, Dennis J. 1987. "Psychotherapeutic Approaches in the Treatment of Violent Persons." In *Clinical Treatment of the Violent Person,* edited by Loren H. Roth. New York: Guilford.

McGoldrick, Monica, John K. Pearce, and Joseph Giordano, eds. 1982. *Ethnicity and Family Therapy*. New York: Guilford.

Meloy, J. Reid. 1988. *The Psychopathic Mind: Origins, Dynamics and Treatment.* Northvale, NJ: Jason Aronson.

Modell, Arnold H. 1991. "The Therapeutic Relationship as a Paradoxical Experience." *Psychoanalytic Dialogues: A Journal of Relational Perspectives* 1: 13-28.

Mullen, Paul E. 1992. "Psychopathy: A Developmental Disorder of Ethical Action." *Criminal Behaviour and Mental Health* 2: 234-244.

National Institute on Drug Abuse. 1977. *Psychodynamics of Drug Dependence.* Research Monograph 12. Washington, DC: National Institute on Drug Abuse.

Nigrosh, Barry J. 1985. "Basic Interventions for Managing Violence." Northampton State Hospital, Northampton, MA. Photocopy.

Pinderhughes, E. B. 1989. *Understanding Race, Ethnicity and Power.* New York: Macmillan.

Raine, Adrian. 1993. *The Psychopathology of Crime.* San Diego, CA: Academic Press.

Robertson, Graham. 1992. "Objections to the Current System." *Criminal Behaviour and Mental Health* 2: 114-123.

Roth, Loren H. 1987. "Treating Violent Persons in Prisons, Jails, and Security Hospitals." In *Clinical Treatment of the Violent Person,* edited by Loren H. Roth. New York: Guilford.

Russell, Paul L. 1987. "On Waiting for the Right Time: The Search for Safety in the Therapeutic Process." Unpublished manuscript.

———. 1993. "On Walking and Chewing Gum: The Psychology of Intention vs. the Psychology of Event." Unpublished manuscript.

———. N.d. "Beyond the Wish: Further Thoughts on Containment." Unpublished manuscript.

———. N.d. "Process with Involvement: The Interpretation of Affect." Unpublished manuscript.

———. N.d. "The Role of Paradox in the Growth of Affect." Unpublished manuscript.

———. N.d. "The Theory of the Crunch." Unpublished manuscript.

———. N.d. "Trauma, Repetition and Affect." Unpublished manuscript.

Schafer, Roy. 1983. *The Analytic Attitude.* New York: Basic Books.

Searles, Harold. 1965. *Collected Papers on Schizophrenia and Related Subjects.* New York: International Universities Press.

Sterba, R. 1934. "The Fate of the Ego in Analytic Therapy." *International Journal of Psychoanalysis* 15:117-126.

Stevens, Gail F. 1993. "Applying the Diagnosis Antisocial Personality to Imprisoned Offenders: Looking for Hay in a Haystack." *Journal of Offender Rehabilitation* 19: 1-26.

Toch, Hans. 1992. *Mosaic of Despair: Human Breakdowns in Prison.* Revised edition of *Men in Crisis: Human Breakdowns in Prison* (New York: Aldine, 1975). Washington, DC: American Psychological Association.

Tollefson, Ted E. 1992. "When Lies Are More Truthful Than Facts." *Utne Reader,* November/December, 58.

Tyrer, Peter. 1992. "Flamboyant, Erratic, Dramatic, Borderline, Antisocial, Sadistic, Narcissistic, Histrionic and Impulsive Personality Disorders: Who Cares Which?" *Criminal Behaviour and Mental Health* 2: 95-104.

Widiger, Thomas A., and Elizabeth M. Corbitt. 1993. "APD: Proposals for DSM-IV." *Journal of Personality Disorders* 7: 63-77.

Winnicott, D. W. 1972. *Holding and Interpretation.* New York: Grove.

World Health Organization. 1992. *International Statistical Classification of Diseases and Related Health Problems.* 10th revision. Vol. 1. Geneva: World Health Organization.

Wurmser, Leon. 1978. *The Hidden Dimension: Psychodynamics in Compulsive Drug Use.* New York: Jason Aronson.

Yochelson, Samuel, and Stanton E. Samenow. 1977. *The Criminal Personality.* Vol. 2, *The Change Process.* Northvale, NJ: Jason Aronson.

Debra H. Benveniste received her M.A. in criminal justice from Clark University and her M.S.W. from Smith College School for Social Work. Her work experience includes both direct care and clinical supervisory responsibilities in a variety of treatment-oriented settings. In addition, her experience as a clinical social worker includes nearly seven years at the former Somers Correctional Institution in Somers, Connecticut, where she established and coordinated a mental health treatment program for general population inmates. Currently, Ms. Benveniste is a clinical consultant and M.S.W. field supervisor. She is also in private practice with Canterbury Psychotherapy Associates in Canterbury, Connecticut.

Other New Harbinger Self-Help Titles